Foucault
The Art of Ethics

TIMOTHY O'LEARY

LONDON • NEW YORK

Continuum

The Tower Building, 11 York Road, London SE1 7NX

370 Lexington Avenue, New York NY 10017-6503

www.continuumbooks.com

First published in 2002

British Library Cataloguing-in-Publication Data

A catalogue record for this book is available from the British Library.

ISBN 0-8264-5626-X (HB)   0-8264-5627-8 (PB)

Library of Congress Cataloguing-in-Publication Data

O'Leary, Timothy, 1966-
    Foucault : the art of ethics / Timothy O'Leary.
    p. cm.
    Includes bibliographical references and index.
    ISBN 0-8264-5626-X -- ISBN 0-8264-5627-8 (pbk.)
    1. Foucault, Michel. I. Title.

B2430.F724 .O44 2002
170'.92--dc21   2002023447

Typeset by Acorn Bookwork, Salisbury, Wiltshire
Printed and bound in Great Britain by
Biddles Ltd, Guildford and King's Lynn

For Jennifer Rutherford

Contents

Acknowledgements   ix

Abbreviations   x

A Note on Citations and Sources   xii

Introduction   1

Part One

1. The Journey to Greece   21

2. Alcibiades Goes Wilde   39

3. The Style of Domination   58

4. The Ends of Ethics   69

5. Strange Stories and Queer Stoics   87

Part Two

6. Refusing the Self   107

7. Creating a Self Oneself   121

8. The Practice of Philosophy   139

9. The Art of Freedom   154

10. Conclusion   171

Notes   175

Bibliography   196

Index   208

Acknowledgements

I began the research which led to this book in Australia, and completed the manuscript in Hong Kong in 2001. During that time many people have given me support, encouragement and advice. I must first thank Irmline Veit-Brause and Russell Grigg for their helpful comments and advice in the crucial early stages of my work. I owe a special debt of gratitude to Barry Hindess, who gave freely of his time and expertise to read and comment upon the first complete draft. Chris Falzon answered late night telephone queries on freedom, power and subjectivity; but more importantly he provided friendship, laughter and unlimited access to his Foucault library. John Ballard read drafts of several chapters and provided me with biblio-graphical assistance. Robert Barnes generously advised on all matters relating to Classical and Hellenistic antiquity. Paul Patton responded with probing questions to an earlier draft; and I am still not sure that those questions have been answered. In Hong Kong, Dan Robins was the reader every author hopes for – appreciative, critical and demanding. His sugges-tions and many questions forced me to clarify my presentation of Foucault's project. During my last research trip to Paris, the librarians of the Bibliothèque du Saulchoir gave their usual friendly help in my efforts to listen to as many of Foucault's unpublished recordings as possible in a short time.

No book can be written without the support and love of the people we share our lives with. My children, Phoebe and Benedicte, showed remark-able patience and tolerance of their father's unending preoccupation while I was working on this project in Sydney. Finally, this work would neither have been undertaken nor completed without Jennifer Rutherford. Her continuous support, encouragement and advice, and especially her critical reading skills, made an invaluable contribution to the final work. Of more fundamental importance, however, is the fact that it was she who first intro-duced me to the art of self-transformation.

Abbreviations

The following abbreviations have been used to refer to Foucault's works. The date given is that of first publication; full details of both English and French sources can be found in the Bibliography.

AE	'An Aesthetics of Existence' (1984c)
AMV	'De l'amitié comme mode de vie' (1981a)
BHS	'About the Beginning of the Hermeneutics of the Self' (1993)
CCF, 81	Course at the Collège de France (1981c)
CCF, 82	Course at the Collège de France (1982e)
CF	'The Confession of the Flesh' (1977a)
CS	*The Care of the Self* (1984b)
CT	'The Concern for Truth' (1984d)
DE II	*Dits et écrits,* volume II (1994a)
DE III	*Dits et écrits,* volume III (1994b)
DE IV	*Dits et écrits,* volume IV (1994c)
DG	*De la gouvernementalité* (1989)
DP	*Discipline and Punish* (1975a)
DT	'Discourse and Truth: The problematization of *parrhesia*' (1983b)
ECS	'The Ethic of Care for the Self as a Practice of Freedom' (1984e)
EMF	'Entretien avec Michel Foucault' (1980b)
FE	'Foucault Examines Reason in Service of State Power' (1979)
FNC	'Foucault: non aux compromis' (1982d)
HB	'Introduction', in *Herculine Barbin* (1980c)
HL	'The Howison Lectures' (1980d)
HS	'The History of Sexuality' (1977b)
IP	'Intellectuals and Power' (1972)
MS	'The Minimalist Self' (1983c)
NGH	'Nietzsche, Genealogy, History' (1971b)
OD	'The Order of Discourse' (1971a)
OG	'Governmentality' (1978)

OGE	'On the Genealogy of Ethics' (1983a)
OT	*The Order of Things* (1966)
PE	'Politics and Ethics' (1984f)
PHS	'Preface to *The History of Sexuality,* Volume II' (1984g)
PN	'La poussière et le nuage' (1980e)
PPP	'Polemics, Politics and Problemizations' (1984l)
PS	'Power and Sex' (1977c)
PST	'Power and Strategies' (1977e)
PT	'Prison Talk' (1975b)
QC	'Qu'est-ce que la critique?' (1990)
QL	'Qu'est-ce que les lumières?' (1984h)
QM	'Questions of Method' (1980a)
RC	*Résumé des cours* (1989)
RM	'The Return of Morality' (1984i)
SCSA	'Sexual Choice, Sexual Act' (1982a)
SP	'The Subject and Power' (1982b)
SPPI	'Sex, Power and the Politics of Identity' (1984j)
SPS	'Structuralism and Post-Structuralism' (1983d)
SS	'Sexuality and Solitude' (1981b)
STSW	'The Social Triumph of the Sexual Will' (1982c)
TL	'Two Lectures' (1976b)
TP	'Truth and Power' (1977d)
TPS	'Truth, Power, Self: An Interview' (1988b)
TS	'Technologies of the Self' (1988a)
UP	*The Use of Pleasure* (1984a)
VS	*The History of Sexuality,* volume I (1976a)
WE	'What is Enlightenment?' (1984k)

A Note on Citations and Sources

In the case of citations to the works of Foucault, I refer to both French and English editions. After the abbreviation I give page numbers of the English edition I have used, followed in square brackets by the page numbers of the French edition. Hence, *The History of Sexuality*, volume II, *The Use of Pleasure*, page 11 of the English edition and page 17 of the French, is *UP* 11[17]. There are only two exceptions to this practice. First, in cases where the French edition is a *translation* from the English publication, or where the text was originally published in a language other than French, I only cite the English edition. For example, the case of 'On the Genealogy of Ethics' (OGE), an interview conducted and originally published in English; and 'What is Enlightenment?' (WE), a lecture originally published in English (although delivered in French). The second group of exceptions are texts, or more usually parts of texts, which have not been translated into English. In these cases, I refer to the French edition and provide my own translations.

My French sources have been the Gallimard editions of Foucault's books and the *Dits et écrits* (four volumes) of his lectures, interviews and occasional writings. My English sources have been the standard translations of Foucault's books and, usually, the most accessible translations of his interviews and other writings. I have decided, for two reasons, not to standardize these citations with reference to the currently appearing *The Essential Works of Michel Foucault* (Paul Rabinow ed., Allen Lane The Penguin Press, 1997–): firstly, not all volumes were available at the time of preparation of this work; secondly, since Rabinow's edition is a selection from the *Dits et écrits* volumes which I have used, and generally uses the standard English translations, it seemed that my referencing was already sufficiently definitive.

Introduction

Morality will gradually *perish* now: this is the great spectacle in a hundred acts reserved for the next two centuries in Europe – the most terrible, most questionable, and perhaps also the most hopeful of all spectacles.

Friedrich Nietzsche[1]

... the idea of a morality as obedience to a code of rules is now disappearing, has already disappeared. And to this absence of morality corresponds, must correspond, the search for an aesthetics of existence.

Michel Foucault (AE, 49[732])

THE ART OF ETHICS

According to Foucault, Nietzsche's prediction that morality would gradually 'perish' over 'the next two centuries' has already come to pass. And this spectacular demise, which is even more spectacular given its speed, is at the same time 'terrible', 'questionable' and 'hopeful'. This book focuses on the third of these characteristics; its fundamental question is, what hope is there of filling the void left by an absent morality?[2] In particular, is Foucault's idea of an ethics which is based on an 'aesthetics of existence' equal to the task of giving us – that is, anyone who experiences this crisis – the means with which we could answer the question 'How is one to live?'

In Thomas Mann's view, Friedrich Nietzsche and Oscar Wilde belong together as 'rebels in the name of beauty'.[3] Foucault seems to be well qualified to join this group: not only could we call him a 'gay Nietzschean', but his late work continuously appeals to beauty and the aesthetic as weapons which can be used to bring down the tyranny of modern morality. It is not by accident that Foucault sees his history of sexuality as 'one chapter' in the history of those arts of the self which can be traced from ancient Greece, through the Renaissance, to Baudelaire in the nineteenth century

(*UP*, 11[17]). And this is a trajectory in which not only Nietzsche and Wilde, but also Foucault himself, can be placed. In one of the most important of his late texts, Foucault refers to Baudelaire's figure of the dandy – a figure who 'makes of his body, his behaviour, his feelings and passions, his very existence, a work of art' (WE, 41–2). This 'asceticism', however, is something which Baudelaire believed could have no place in society or in the body politic – it could only be achieved in art. My claim, which I will elaborate in this work, is that Foucault believed the time had now come when such a practice could indeed have a place in society: that Baudelaire's 'art' was now ready to come out. In his attempt to realize this belief, Foucault echoes Nietzsche, for whom the artist's power of *poesis* stops prematurely: 'For with them this subtle power usually comes to an end where art ends and life begins; but we want to be the poets of our life'.[4]

For Nietzsche, only one thing was 'needful' in this work: 'To "give style" to one's character'.[5] To give style is an art which can only be practised by the strong; by those who can survey all the strengths and weaknesses of their nature and then impose *order* and *form*. A 'single taste' must inform this work and its product must be pleasing to the eye. The self is a natural scene which must be modified, improved upon and made sublime. Its creator must have an 'artistic plan' according to which the landscape will be modified, vistas will be arranged, the ugly will be concealed and the result will 'delight the eye'. Hence Nietzsche's equation of 'stylised nature' with 'conquered and serving nature' and the reluctance to give nature freedom – even in the design of gardens and palaces. In this ethics, as in gardening, 'long practice and daily work', the mastery of self and the mastery of nature, are required if we are to avoid 'the sight of what is ugly'.

For Foucault, too, style is the one thing that is needful. We can no longer allow religious systems, moral codes or scientific truths to shape our lives. We are in much the same position as those ancients for whom the question 'how is one to live?' could only be answered by the cultivation of a relation of self to self in which the self is neither given nor produced, but is continuously worked on in a labour of care (*epimeleia*) and skill (*techne*). The ancient Greek reflection on ethics drew heavily on metaphors of moulding, sculpting and creating. The arts of the self, the techniques of existence (*techne tou biou*), were conceptualized as instances of form-giving. Today, Foucault claims, 'the problem of an ethics as a *form* to be given to one's conduct and to one's life has again been raised' (CT, 263[674]).[6] The subject is not a substance, it is a form; but it is a form which is not given to us in any unalterable way. Consequently, one is – under certain conditions – free to choose whether or not to modify that form, whether or not to transform it. And what better way is there of understanding such a work of transformation than as a poetic, an artful, an aesthetic work – a *poesis*. Then one can come to see the work of ethics as the labour of giving a style to one's self or to one's life. For Foucault, intellectual work itself is related to 'aestheticism' in this sense: it is a process of 'transforming yourself' in an experience which is 'rather close to the aesthetic experience.' Why else, he asks, should a painter paint 'if he is not transformed by his own painting' (MS, 14).

To give style, to stylize, is to apply the *stylus* to some pliable material: it is to inscribe, to make one's mark, to *own* one's character as one's own. Not only is this a task for our future, it can also be a *grille d'analyse* through which to view our history. In the version of 'On the Genealogy of Ethics' (OGE) which Foucault re-edited and greatly modified for publication in French, he foresees the writing of a modem 'history of human existence' which would be based not on its conditions, or the mutations in its psychology, but would be a 'history of existence as art and as style' (*DE* IV, 629). Such a history could, for example, see the French Revolution not so much as a political project, but as 'a style, a mode of existence with its aesthetic, its asceticism, its particular forms of relation to self and to others' (ibid.). This possibility, Foucault argues, was present in the ancients but disappeared in the Middle Ages; it reappeared with the idea of 'the hero as his own work of art'[7] during the Renaissance and then took on great importance in the nineteenth-century notion of '*la vie "artiste"* ' – the artist's life, or the life of art. The concept of style could become a leading heuristic device in historical interpretation and also a means of conceiving of our present ethical dilemma. What we would need, then, is neither to follow the moral law, nor to foster our virtues, but to formulate and practise new styles of existence – styles which would answer as much to the necessities of our present as to the age-old demands of our 'impatience for liberty'.[8]

The application of the *stylus*, like the practice of all crafts, requires technique (*techne*), feeling (*aesthesis*) and discipline (*askesis*). *Techne* is a skill or a craft that can be applied in any field: the training of horses, the framing of laws, the mastery of the self – even the sculpting of statues. In Foucault's interpretation this is very close to, at times even indistinguishable from, 'art' – that technique whose aim has been defined, since the eighteenth century, as the production of an aesthetic effect. *Aesthesis* is the field of sensation, and aesthetics is 'the science of sensory cognition' (Baumgarten); a form of thinking which occurs through the senses, especially in their perception of beauty. *Askesis* is an exercise, applied to the self, to achieve self-discipline. A form of relation to the self which, for the Ancients (at least in Foucault's interpretation), was very far from Christian asceticism – an asceticism whose guiding principle was self-sacrifice rather than self-care.

It seems inevitable that this adoption of the metaphor of *techne* will lead to the use of the metaphor of art, which in turn must call forth the modern notions of aesthetics and beauty. Foucault's adoption of this aesthetic metaphor in the field of ethics is made possible by a certain reception of ancient Greek thought; a reception which is even more strikingly displayed in Nietzsche's thought. For Nietzsche, the artist operates at the level of surface appearances in order to 'make things beautiful, attractive and desirable for us'.[9] This is the skill, the 'subtle power' which we should learn from them and apply to every detail of our lives. And this is the skill the Greeks *did* apply to their lives. They 'knew how to live'; they knew how to stop courageously at the surface, the fold, the skin, to adore appearance, to believe in forms, tones, words, in the whole Olympus of appearance'. And we – 'we daredevils of the spirit' – we are coming back to this style of existence, we are becoming 'admirers of forms, of tones, of words'. We are becoming Greeks, and 'therefore – *artists*'.[10]

If, as Foucault seems to suggest, ethics is the giving of style to one's existence, and if its primary tools are practices of ascesis, of self-disciplining and self-fashioning, then we might wonder if there is a particular style for which we should be aiming. Nietzsche answered this question in a way which might seem, at best, to be amoral, at worst immoral: 'Whether this taste was good or bad is less important than one might suppose, if only it was a single taste.'[11] Or again: '. . . our ideas, our values – grow out of us with the necessity with which a tree bears fruit – related and each with affinity to each, and evidence of *one* will, *one* health, *one* soil, *one* sun, – whether *you* like them, these fruit of ours? – But what is that to the trees! What is that to *us, to us philosophers!*'[12] While Foucault is certainly a Nietzschean philosopher, he does not necessarily follow Nietzsche in all the detail of his thought, and certainly not in this detail – or at least not in this way of expressing it. In a late interview Foucault refers to his Nietzscheanism in this way:

> . . . I am simply Nietzschean, and I try to see, on a number of points, and to the extent that it is possible, with the aid of Nietzsche's texts – but also with anti-Nietzschean theses (which are nevertheless Nietzschean!) – what can be done in this or that domain. I'm not looking for anything else but I'm really searching for that (RM, 251[704]).

One of those anti-Nietzschean, and yet Nietzschean theses which animate Foucault's work, is that the twofold aim of philosophy, of critical thought and of ethics itself, is the cultivation of practices of liberty which tend to minimize domination. I will argue that the old Enlightenment dream – which strives to combine individual freedom with respect for the freedom of others – continues to drive Foucault's 'Nietzschean' search for an aesthetics of existence. One could even argue that Foucault's ethic is no more – and no less – than a post-conventional, post-Christian, post-Kantian attempt to re-ignite this Enlightenment vision. It is certainly not the case then, for Foucault, that *any* taste will do, so long as it has unity: it is not the case for him that any style has value, so long as it has style.

Perhaps the difference between Nietzsche and Foucault on this point is made possible by the fact that Foucault had the advantage of seeing what the twentieth century had brought. Between Nietzsche and Foucault lies that Nietzschean and anti-Nietzschean novel *Doctor Faustus,* in which Thomas Mann explores the ethical and political implications of what he understands as Nietzsche's aestheticism. Without entering into this debate (until Chapter 7), it can at least be admitted that Foucault inherits Mann's twentieth-century distrust of the notion of a complete and unified work – whether that be a work of art, an individual or a nation:

> ... now the question is whether at the present stage of our consciousness, our knowledge, our sense of truth, this little game is still permissible, still intellectually possible, still to be taken seriously; whether the work as such, the construction, self-sufficing, harmonically complete in itself, still stands in any legitimate relation to the complete insecurity, problematic conditions, and lack of harmony of our social situation; whether all seeming, even the most beautiful, even precisely the beautiful, has not today become a lie.[13]

What *does* matter for Foucault is that we should change our modes of relation to the self. This relation should not be conceived, in Sartrean terms, as either authentic or inauthentic: rather, it should be conceived as a 'creative activity' (OGE, 351). The self is not a foundation, a source or a starting point: it is an end, a task, a work which, although constantly worked, is never completed. Nevertheless, Foucault is still obviously fascinated with the idea of a 'work' in Mann's and Nietzsche's sense; and in his writing – and especially in his late interviews – he still hovers between conflicting understandings of art and the aesthetic. The illustrations he uses: the lamp, the house, the art object, and the examples he chooses: the dandy and the Renaissance self-made hero, all suggest that for Foucault the Classical (and Nietzschean) ideal of unity and harmony and the Romantic (and Nietzschean) ideal of the form-giving creative genius are still alive enough in his thought to give us reason for suspicion. But suspicion of what? Suspicion that in his negotiation of these tensions Foucault has occasionally fallen short of his own standard of critical thought. This is a suspicion that I will explore in several of its possible manifestations in this work. My primary task, however, will be to subject Foucault's thought – especially this notion of an 'aesthetics of existence' – to criticism *without* taking the easy option of rejecting it as impossible, and perhaps immoral, nonsense. The overriding suspicion, then, is that there is a way of understanding the aesthetics of existence which will provide us with an irreplacable tool in the necessary task of re-inventing and re-formulating the work of ethics. *This* art of ethics, this art of self-transformation, may help us to answer Socrates's question – 'how is one to live?'

THE QUESTION

Foucault's suggestion that traditional, code-based morality can only be replaced by an 'aesthetics of existence' appears at first sight to be a highly contentious claim. Even if it could be argued that Nietzsche's prediction – that 'the next two centuries would see the dissolution of traditional moral systems – has already been validated, it is not clear why this lacuna *must* be filled with an aesthetic ethics. My initial motivation in undertaking this work was to try to make sense of this claim; I wanted to know what basis Foucault had for making it, and how it could be made to fit into the framework of his work in general. In particular, I wanted to understand Foucault's appeal to the *aesthetic* in this context. The first question this book tries to answer then, is 'what's *aesthetic* about the aesthetics of existence?' Its central focus is the role played by the idea of the aesthetic in Foucault's ethics. The second question I try to answer is whether such an aesthetic ethics is actually capable of filling the contemporary need for a non-normative morality. If the traditional answers to Socrates's question, 'how is one to live?', can no longer be accepted, does Foucault offer an answer that may be more acceptable today?

In his late work Foucault turns to ancient Greek philosophies of ethics, believing that they may have something to offer in place of modern moral philosophy. He asks if 'our problem nowadays' is not similar to the Greek one, 'since most of us no longer believe that ethics is founded in religion, nor do we want a legal system to intervene in our moral, personal, private life' (OGE, 343[611]). His analysis of the ethical systems of ancient Greek society identifies a broadly diffused idea of the aesthetic construction of the self as a key feature of Greek notions of ethics. It is this idea which, he hopes, can help us to answer Socrates's question today (OGE, 348).[14] In this appeal to the aesthetic Foucault is motivated, as he was in earlier projects, by a concern with a contemporary 'crisis in subjectivation'.[15] In this case the crisis takes one of its forms in the perceived failure of the sexual liberation movements to solve ethical problems relating to sexual practice. When Foucault suggests that our problem today is the same as the problem which faced the ancient Greeks – that is, to constitute an ethics that is founded neither upon social nor legal institutions – he seems to imply the possibility that aesthetics could constitute such a base. This suggestion, that an appeal to the aesthetic is in some sense called for by a contemporary crisis in ethical and political subjectivity, is one which recurs throughout Foucault's late work. However, when he argues that the absence of morality today 'must' be answered by an aesthetics of existence, it is important to note that this 'must' carries the weight of a historical, rather than a moral necessity. Rather than saying that we should make the *moral* choice to develop an aesthetics of existence, Foucault seems to be arguing that such a development is a matter of historical inevitability; because, quite simply, we have no other choice. This is not to deny an element of personal choice, since for Foucault the search for an aesthetics of existence is both an historical *fait accompli,* and a task which we must undertake. If, at this moment in history, and in this socio-cultural context, the self is not 'given' to us, then, according to Foucault, there is only one practical conclusion: 'we have to create ourselves as a work of art' (OGE, 350–1).[16]

One of the most significant limits to individual freedom in this work of self-transformation, according to Foucault, is the array of practices that one's culture makes available for appropriation. Among the practices of the self which are made available in the Western cultural tradition is the practice, or the group of practices, which Foucault investigates in volumes II and III of *The History of Sexuality* (UP, CS) under the names of 'aesthetics of existence' and 'techniques of life'. It is these practices which, in Foucault's view, may be capable of responding to our present need. The aspect of Greek ethical practice Foucault found most interesting, and therefore no doubt found to be the most suitable for a contemporary re-appropriation, was the idea of a non-normalizing ethics based upon personal choice rather than social or legal imperatives. Such an ethics would satisfy what Foucault calls our 'desire for rules [and] ... desire for form' (CT, 262[673–4]), while avoiding the 'catastrophe' of a universally imposed moral code (RM, 254[706]). Such an ethics would be 'a very strong structure of existence, without any relation with the juridical *per se,* with an authoritarian system, with a disciplinary structure' (OGE, 348). It could provide a mode of ethical being which would satisfy what Foucault calls 'our impatience for liberty' (WE, 50[578]).

I will argue here that, despite all its problems (many of which I will explore), there is something in this mobilization of the concept of the aesthetic which can contribute to attempts to work through and deal with the contemporary ethical lacunae. My task, therefore, is twofold: first, to draw out, piece together and critically appraise Foucault's use of the concept; and, second, to explore and elucidate the contribution it might make to thinking about ethics. The overall aim of the work is not only to present a particular interpretation of Foucault's oeuvre, but also to see whether understanding ethics as an aesthetics of existence could make a contribution to our contemporary attempts to answer Socrates's question. I focus on one aspect and one period of Foucault's work, in order to contribute to a more general problem that Foucault was really only beginning to directly address at the time of his death in 1984: How do we begin to develop, both individually and communally, forms of life, modes of behaviour and ways of thinking that can satisfy our need for freedom and form?

One of the key features of Foucault's approach to this problem is his striking modesty about the role philosophy, or critical thought in general, can play in helping us to give shape to our lives. Foucault, like Bernard Williams,[17] insists that philosophy very quickly runs up against its limit: most importantly, it becomes 'ludicrous' as soon as it tries to dictate to others (UP, 15[9]). For Foucault, it is not the task of a philosophy of ethics to tell us what our duty is, to tell us what kinds of action we should perform and what kinds we should avoid. It is not the philosopher's task to engage in what Nietzsche calls the 'moral chatter of some about others'.[18] But what is the task of philosophy in relation to ethics; what does critical thought have to offer? This question, which I will address most fully in Chapter 8, can best be approached by starting with one of Foucault's rare attempts to convey his understanding of philosophical activity itself: 'But what, then, is philosophy today ... if it is not the critical work of thought upon itself? And if it does not consist ... in trying to see how and to what extent it would be possible to think otherwise' (UP, 14–15[8–9]).'[19] For Foucault, philosophy is primarily the critical reflection of thought upon thought; a reflection whose aim is not to 'legitimate what is already known', but to 'free thought from what it silently thinks', thus allowing it to 'think otherwise'. And as I will argue in more detail later, Foucault's understanding and practice of this reflection is distinguished by two defining characteristics. These are, firstly, that critical reflection is historical – it involves thought 'thinking its own history' (UP, 15[9]) – and, secondly, that it must be carried out in relation to a specific 'field of real forces'.[20] Critical thought cannot operate in a vacuum; it must always be related to a particular contemporary concern, to a particular local struggle. It is this 'fundamental' relation between 'struggle and truth' which, Foucault argues, constitutes the very dimension in which philosophy has, for centuries, occurred.[21] Without a relation to a concrete social or subjective concern, then, critical thought could not occur, or could only occur in a meaningless way.

I will argue that the 'field of real forces' within which Foucault's late work occurs is that of the constitution of subjectivity. If Foucault's early work is characterized by a concern with the discursive production of knowledge, and his middle work by a concern with the interconnections between knowledge and power, then his later work introduces the question of subjectivity, or the question of the self's relation to self. In Foucault's later understanding of this trajectory, it is the theme of 'games of truth' (jeux de vérité) which provides its common thread. In the early work (roughly the 1960s) he was concerned with the play of games of truth in relation to each other; in the middle work (roughly the 1970s) he was concerned with the relation between games of truth and power relations; while in the later work (the early 1980s) he investigates the role of games of truth in 'the relation of self to self and the constitution of one's self as a subject' (UP, 12[6]). Truth and subjectivity then, are the twin themes which dominate Foucault's late work.[22] The field of forces which he investigates is, initially, that of sexuality and subjectivity, but finally and more generally that of our self-constitution as subjects per se: that is, the field of ethics.

The general question that frames this work is, then, the same one that Plato attributes to Socrates – 'how is one to live?' Its more particular question is, what can Foucault's appropriation of the ancient idea of an aesthetics of existence contribute to our contemporary attempts to answer this question? Can he justify his claim that, in the absence of traditional moral systems, our only choice is to create ourselves as a work of art?

METHOD

When I began to research this field very little had been published either on Foucault's encounter with ancient Greek philosophy or on his attempts to formulate an aesthetics of existence. Since then, there has been an explosion of interest in these aspects of Foucault's work, particularly in the areas of classical studies, political philosophy and gay and lesbian studies. Apart from James Bernauer, John Rajchman and Thomas Flynn,[23] however, few philosophers have attempted an extensive exploration of Foucault's contribution to philosophies of ethics. In particular, there is still a lack of any major work that specifically focuses on the aesthetic theme in his approach to ethics. The implications of this situation for my work are twofold. Firstly, since there was no standard interpretation of this aspect of Foucault's late work, or even a body of literature discussing it, my research has had to focus almost exclusively on the writings, seminars, interviews and lectures that Foucault produced in the last five or six years of his life. Since 1994, my primary source for this material, apart from the published volumes of *The History of Sexuality,* has been volume IV of Foucault's *Dits er Ecrits* (although I have also had access to the recordings of Foucault's Collège de France lectures that are held at the Bibliothèque du Saulchoir). The result of this focus is a work that does not turn around debates between Foucault's interpreters. It does not, for example, enter into detailed consideration either of the Habermas and Fraser criticisms of Foucault's position,[24] or of debates such as that between Taylor and Patton in relation to Foucault's theory of power.[25] Similarly, Foucault's exploration of 'governmentality', which has been so important to political theorists such as Barry Hindess and Cohn Gordon, is not extensively discussed.[26] While these debates are not a central focus, they are, however, continually present as a frame of reference. My approach – which focuses on the emergence of an aesthetic ethics from Foucault's engagement with ancient philosophy – is intended to complement and extend the kind of positive, creative reception of Foucault's thought that Bernauer, Rajchman, Flynn and Patton exemplify. While pursuing important criticisms of Foucault's late work, the work ultimately gives a positive appraisal of the creative power of his thought and offers an interpretation that is both critical and affirmative.

The second implication of this approach is that it makes it impossible to address all the legitimate concerns that could be raised about Foucault's late work. While many of these concerns are addressed in Part One (principally those relating to his reading of ancient philosophy and his use of history), many others are ignored. Of the latter, one concern deserves mention here; that is, feminist criticisms of Foucault's apparent blindness to the place of women and female sexuality in volumes II and III of *The History of Sexuality.* At many times in the following pages, I have found myself making excuses on Foucault's behalf because of his apparent assumption that in the ancient world all subjects were male. Sometimes I have had to appeal to the fact that the French language consistently assumes that non-gendered subjects are male and that Foucault's English translators usually reproduce this use of male pronouns. At other times, I have appealed to the fact that Classical and Hellenistic discussions of the way that one should form oneself almost always assume that 'one' is a man – and a free one at that. While this kind of special pleading goes some way to answering these concerns, it is clearly not satisfactory. Amy Richlin, for example, has argued convincingly that even if Foucault's ancient sources are themselves blind to female sexuality, the 'vision of ancient sexual systems' that he presents is even more male-centered than what his sources present'.[27] To fully address these criticisms in my own reading of volumes II and III of *The History of Sexuality* would have required such a shift in emphasis that my own substantive criticisms could not have been so fully developed. I have chosen, therefore, to address one set of concerns about Foucault's *History of Sexuality*, without denying that he also has many other equally worrying charges to answer – one of the most important being this charge of gender-blindness.

This work does not, therefore, claim to be a complete critical appraisal of Foucault's late work, nor does it claim to be a complete critical appraisal of his ethics. It aims instead to give a coherent interpretation of Foucault's appeal to an aesthetic ethics; an interpretation which is both critical and positive, which focuses on Foucault's engagement with ancient philosophy, and which situates itself within the larger framework of late modernity's perceived failure to respond to the crisis of morality.[28]

One of the crucial features of Foucault's approach to ethics, the one that makes it possible for him to appeal to an aesthetics of existence, is the fundamental distinction he makes between morality and ethics. According to Foucault, any morality has three aspects; first, a moral code which may be more or less explicitly formulated; second, the actual behaviour of those who are 'subject to' this code; and, third, the way individuals constitute themselves as moral subjects of the code – that is, the way they 'conduct themselves' and 'bring themselves' (*se conduire*) to obey (or disobey) a set of prescriptions (*UP*, 33[26]). It is in relation to this third aspect, the aspect of 'subjectivation' (*UP*, 37[29]), that Foucault uses the term 'ethics'. In this schema, ethics is a sub-set of the category of 'morality', but it is prioritized by Foucault for two reasons. On the one hand, for the methodological reason that it is this aspect of morality which, he argues, is most subject to historical change and, on the other hand, for the reason that the field of relations of self to self is the contemporary field of forces in which his critical reflection occurs. Understanding the history of this field is, there-fore, crucial to the task of its reconstitution. For Foucault, ethics is not a field of rules, principles or precepts, it is the field of our self-constitution as subjects.

According to Foucault's definition, ethics consists of the set of attitudes, practices and goals by which we guide our moral self-fashioning. To wish to found a new ethics is to wish to re-imagine and re-invent the multiple facets of our modes of self-constitution; it is to wish to recreate ourselves. These modes of self-constitution can be divided, according to Foucault, into four principal aspects: the ethical substance, the mode of subjection, the practices of the self and the mode of being, or way of life, towards which the ethics aims.[29] In *The History of Sexuality*, volume II, Foucault describes the sexual ethics of Classical Greece in terms of these four aspects. The first aspect, the ethical substance, is the part of oneself (for example, acts, desires, or feelings) which one takes as the material of one's moral conduct. In the Classical era the ethical substance consisted of the *aphrodisia*; a term which has been translated into French as '*les plaisirs*' and into English as 'the pleasures'. According to Foucault, for the ancient Greeks the term covered desires and acts as much as pleasures; but it referred, specifically, to those pleasures-desires-acts which belong to Aphrodite (*UP*, 38[47]). The object of ethical concern for the ancients was not the vagaries of desire, or the concupiscence of the flesh, but a certain set of pleasures-desires-acts which were problematized because of their intensity and their tendency to excess. Second, there is the 'mode of subjection'; that is, the way one brings oneself to follow a code – whether one does so, for example, in response to a divine command, or perhaps because one recognises oneself as a member of a particular community. In the Classical era, according to Foucault, the mode of subjection was a free 'personal choice' (OGE, 356) – a choice to give one's life a certain noble, perfect, or beautiful form. Third, there are the 'forms of elaboration' of self; that is, the techniques which are used in the work of constituting oneself as an ethical subject – techniques such as memorization of precepts and exemplars, examination of one's daily thoughts and actions, or the deciphering of one's hidden desires. During the Classical era, for adult male citizens, these techniques centred around concerns with the body, with the management of one's patrimony and with one's relations with boys. Finally, there is the 'teleology of the moral subject'; that is, the mode of being towards which one aims in the ethical work which one carries out on oneself. This could be, for instance, the tranquillity of the soul, or a purity which would guarantee one's salvation after death. For the individual in Classical antiquity, however, it was the ideal of self-mastery; a self-mastery which, moreover, ensured one's mastery of others.

It is possible to characterize these four aspects of ethics in terms of the questions they pose to the subject of ethics. The first aspect, the ethical substance, asks what part of oneself should be subject to a work on the self. The second aspect, the mode of subjection, asks why one should engage in such a task. The third aspect, the forms of elaboration of the self, asks what tools or techniques one has at one's disposal in this work. The fourth aspect, the telos, asks what mode of being or way of life constitutes the goal of this work. In Foucault's model, these are the four questions that frame the task of ethics – not only as a theoretical, philosophical undertaking, but also as a practical effort to live well: what part of myself should I address?; why should I engage in such work?; what tools are available to me?; what kind of person do I want to be, or what kind of life do I want to lead? Since one of the primary aims of this work is to see to what extent Foucault's late work can in fact provide a coherent contemporary ethics, I will try, in Part Two, to formulate a Foucaldian view of ethics that answers these four questions. The necessary groundwork for carrying out this test will be laid in Part One.

In Chapter 1, I situate Foucault's late work on ethics in the context of his earlier investigation of the way institutions and practices of power/knowledge construct and impose forms of individuality. This involves clarifying the way Foucault's history of sexuality is transformed, in the late 1970s, into a genealogy of ethics. One of the central themes in Foucault's late work is the idea that the task – the political, philosophical and ethical task – which confronts us today is one of rejecting the forms of subjectivity and the modes of subjectivation which are imposed on us. 'Maybe', Foucault suggests, 'the task nowadays is not to discover what we are, but to refuse what we are' (SP, 216). In this particular case, Foucault is referring to the kind of individuality which is imposed by the 'simultaneous individualisation and totalisation of modem power structures' (ibid.). From a broader historical perspective, however, Foucault argues that our contemporary forms of individuality have been fixed by a technology of the self which grew out of early Christianity, underwent intense development in the early modern period and took on its 'governmentalized' form in the modern state. This is a self which, in Foucault's view, is 'nothing else than the historical correlation of the technology built into our history' (BHS, 222). If we now take the position that this technology must be rejected, we are faced not only with the question of how one could go about doing such a thing but also with the question of what kind of technology, what kind of self, could replace it. In other words, how does one distance oneself and free oneself from oneself, and what kind of self could or should one then become?

It is here, in relation to both these questions, that Foucault introduces the concept of an 'aesthetics of existence'; it is this work of self-transformation (of freeing oneself from oneself) that Foucault understands as aesthetic. In Chapter 2, I argue that Foucault uses the aesthetic metaphor here in two distinct ways. First, to suggest a form of relation of self to self (that is, an ethics) which is neither a hermeneutic relation, nor a relation that attempts to fix a pre-given or natural identity, but is a relation which sees the self as a task, as something which needs to be continuously worked on. In this sense, aesthetic is closest in meaning to the ancient Greek term *techne*, as it is used in expressions such as *techne tou biou* ('the technique/art of life', or in Foucault's rendering, 'the art/aesthetics of life/existence'). In this sense, to understand ethics as an aesthetics of the self is to understand it as a relation which demands a certain attitude towards the self, an attitude not unlike that of an artist faced with his or her material.

Foucault also uses the notion of the aesthetic, however, in contexts which suggest the aesthetic might contribute to the question of what *kind* of self we want our work of self-transformation to result in, and to suggest the criteria we might use to guide such a work. In this sense, his use of the term aesthetic is closest in meaning to the modern use of the term, in particular to its connotation in the nineteenth-century movement 'aestheticism'. Here, it implies the centrality of the category of 'beauty' in all decisions affecting the way that we live. The question this raises is whether Foucault's suggestion is that we should endeavour to make our lives and ourselves more *beautiful*. Is the aesthetics of existence simply a late twentieth-century version of aestheticism? In Chapter 2, I address this concern by developing a critical reading of Foucault's apparent aestheticization of Classical Greek ethics. I argue that even his fourfold characterization of ethics is constructed in such a way as to favour an aesthetic interpretation of the theories and practices he is analysing. This chapter concludes with a section that confronts the problems inherent in Foucault's use of the term 'aesthetic' to translate the Greek preoccupation with *technai* (techniques). I ask what justification there is for Foucault's translation of the Greek term *techne* as 'aesthetic', and to what extent he might be forgetful of, or playing with, the conceptual and historical distance between these two terms.

In Chapters 3 and 4, I subject volumes II and III of *The History of Sexuality* to a close critical reading in order to gauge the degree of distortion that Foucault's 'bias' introduces into his interpretation of Classical and Hellenistic ethics.[30] In these chapters, I argue that this slant shows itself clearly in the rather peculiar story Foucault tells about ethics in the Classical Greek and Hellenistic world. What we see in this history, and in the many interviews which surround them, is a strong tendency on Foucault's part to read the second 'aestheticist' meaning into pronouncements and ethical techniques which, at the most, can only be taken in the former 'technical' sense. While recognizing that the category of 'beauty' was important in ancient Greek conceptions of ethics, and that what I have called the 'technical' and 'aestheticist' senses of *techne* are equally present, I argue that Foucault overstates the case in claiming that beauty was the end, the *telos*, of the practice of these techniques. Finally, in Chapter 4 I argue that this interpretation of the ends of ancient ethics is motivated by Foucault's diagnosis of the end of morality – or, rather, by his project to end and have done with a certain form of morality, a form which is charac- terised by what he calls the 'hermeneutics of the self'. I suggest that the key feature of Foucault's return to the Greeks, like the return of so many others before him, is the wish to find an era which did not appear to be subject, or at least did not appear to be *helplessly* subject, to the harsh demands of a punitive moral code. I argue that what Foucault finds captivating about ancient *ethics* is precisely that it is not modern *morality*; and that his hopes for the 'end of morality' hang upon his analysis and interpretation of the 'ends' of that ethics. It is crucial to note that, throughout this book when I speak of Foucault's relation to the 'end of morality' I take that phrase to mean the end of a *particular modern, Western form* of morality. Foucault's project is not one of immoral, or amoral, nihilism; his aim is to replace a certain form of morality with something which he prefers to call an ethics.

In Chapter 5, I ask whether the many criticisms of historical detail that one can make about Foucault's history of ethics render that history useless for us today. Is it possible to base a contemporary approach to ethics on an historical analysis that has been subjected to such extensive criticism? This question demands that we examine the relationship between historical research and critical analysis in Foucault's work, and also that we think about the way that Foucault's histories can be most fruitfully read. In this chapter, I present two such approaches as illustrative of two of the most common reading strategies adopted in relation to these histories. I argue that ultimately both are inadequate ways of approaching Foucault's works and that what is required is an approach that can balance the 'concern for (historical) truth' with the 'concern for the present'. I develop just such a reading strategy in Part Two.

In Part Two, I take up the challenge of identifying in Foucault's late work a coherent ethics that can be formulated in terms of his fourfold division of ethics. Chapter 6 focuses on the question of the substance of ethics: what aspect of ourselves, in Foucault's view, calls for the interven- tion of ethical transformation? I argue that since, for Foucault, the subject is not a substance but a form, the substance of the work of ethics is the forms of individuality and identity that are imposed on us as subjects. The starting point for a Foucaldian ethics is therefore the refusal of self, the rejection of those forms of identity to which we are tied – both by ourselves and by the institutions, values and practices of the societies we live in. Chapter 7 turns to the second question of ethics: why should I engage in the task of ethical self-transformation? I argue that Foucault's ethics demands what we could call an aesthetic attitude towards the self; an attitude of *autopoesis* which would regard the self as the malleable material for a task of self-transformation. Making such a claim, however, inevitably provokes the charge that basing an ethics on such an attitude is highly dangerous. In this chapter, therefore, I also argue against those misunderstandings of Foucault's ethical project which see it in the context of what Walter Benjamin called the 'aestheticization of politics' – that is, an application of aesthetic categories to political life which leads to manipulative, fascist-style politics. My discussion turns around the question of the extent to which Foucault saw the work on the self as *oeuvre* or as *travail*; as the creation of a beautiful, finished object, or as the continuously renewed effort of a work-in-progress.

One of the advantages of thinking about ethics as the field of relations of self to self, is that it allows us to raise the question of the techniques which are, or could be, employed in the cultivation and transformation of these relations. In his account of the ethics of antiquity, Foucault emphasizes the constitutive role and the historical transformations of ethical techniques such as Stoic self-examination. And while he doesn't suggest that we should adopt these techniques, he does see them as offering a certain vantage point from which we might critically address our contemporary forms of ethical self-constitution. One of the questions that this emphasis on techniques of life naturally raises is what techniques, if any, would Foucault recommend in our present context? In Chapter 8, I argue that one of the most important results of Foucault's engagement with the Classical philosophical tradition is that he found there a model for understanding critical thought as a technique for transforming ourselves, our modes of self-relation and the way we relate to others. In answer to the third question that faces the subject of ethics – 'what techniques are available to me?' – I present philosophy as a unique example of a technique of ethics which can make a significant contribution to transforming the way we live.

In the final chapter, Chapter 9, I turn to the fourth question: 'what mode of being, or way of life, do I aim for?' After discussing Foucault's assessment of the creative potential of the position of gay men in Western societies – both in relation to sexual pleasure and relations of friendship – I conclude that, for Foucault, the ultimate aim of any ethics must be the maintenance of freedom. The maintenance, that is, of the real capacity to modify and transform the ways we think and act, both towards ourselves and others. The emergence of this theme in Foucault's late work, I argue, requires us to reconsider his relationship to the Enlightenment ideals that his earlier work had done so much to undermine. Contrary to the arguments of many of his critics, this affirmation of freedom places him firmly in the tradition of *les lumières*.

Finally, the ethical attitude I draw out of Foucault's late work is one in which the transformation of the self is the central concern. This concern is conceived as an aesthetics of existence because it requires a continuously renewed act of creation: an act that can call upon no given criteria for success, no universally recognized set of rules. Such an attitude will clearly not be universally acceptable, and there may not even be any individuals for whom such an ethics would constitute a *complete* answer. What it does offer, however, is a model of ethics that both avoids the dangers of the search for a universally grounded normativity, and makes available a rich and suggestive answer to the question 'how is one to live?'

PART ONE

CHAPTER I

The Journey to Greece

When we speak of the Greeks we involuntarily speak of today and yesterday.

Friedrich Nietzsche[1]

I do not know what meaning classical studies could have for our time if they were not untimely – that is to say, acting counter to our time and thereby acting on our time and, let us hope, for the benefit of a time to come.

Friedrich Nietzsche[2]

... we have to refer to much more remote processes if we want to understand how we have been trapped in our own history.

Michel Foucault (SP, 210[225])

In a footnote taken from the introduction to volume II of *The History of Sexuality, The Use of Pleasure*, Foucault attempts to justify his return to the Greeks. This justification attempts to counter not only the possible charge that, when it comes to Classical antiquity, Foucault doesn't know what he's talking about (and this is a charge which was subsequently made), but also to justify, in more general terms, the very idea that we today should be interested in anything which the ancients had to say. The passage reads:

I am neither a Hellenist nor a Latinist. But it seemed to me that if I gave enough care, patience, modesty and attention to the task, it would be possible to gain sufficient familiarity with the ancient Greek and Roman texts; that is, a familiarity that would allow me – in keeping with a practice that is doubtless fundamental to Western philosophy – to examine both the difference that keeps us at a remove from a way of thinking in which we recognise the origin of our own, and the proximity which remains in spite of that distance which we never cease to explore (*UP*, 7[13]).

In volumes II and III of *The History of Sexuality*, Foucault, by his own account, is engaging in a task which is 'fundamental' for Western philosophy. Moreover, it is a task for which, he admits, he lacks scholarly training. Neither a Hellenist nor a Latinist, he is returning to the ancients, not with the task of understanding their view of the world, or their philosophy, but with the task of measuring the distance which both separates and joins 'us'. This is a task which Foucault is willing to see in relation to the many previous returns which have characterized Western philosophy. Like his predecessors – take Hegel or Heidegger, for instance – he brings with him in this return his own contemporary concerns. However, to measure the distance that both separates us from and joins us to the Greeks is a very different procedure for Foucault in the 1980s than it was for Hegel in 1805,[3] or for Heidegger in 1935.[4] And to say, as one must, that his return is neither motivated by a search for origins, nor for the moment at which the promise of that origin was forgotten is, in fact, to tell us very little about Foucault's project. What, then, is the nature of Foucault's return to the Greeks? Why does he depart from the historical terrain with which he was most familiar – the period from the end of the Renaissance to the present? Why did he embark on the study of a period and of texts which he 'did not know well enough' (*UP*, ibid.).[5] One of the aims of this chapter is to explore this question of Foucault's motivation in his return to the Greeks. Motivation will be understood here, not only in the sense of his initial reason for turning in that direction, but also in. the sense of the underlying concerns and attitudes towards our present ethical dilemma which determine his reading of ancient ethical practices. In other words, what are the present concerns, what is the contemporary project, which led Foucault to embark on his 'journey to Greece'?[6]

MODERN SEXUALITY

The work of Foucault which, arguably, has had the greatest intellectual and political impact is *The History of Sexuality*, volume I. This work has inspired not only feminist readings of the history of the construction of female sexuality, critical histories of the nineteenth century 'medicalization' of sex and a whole array of studies in the history of queer sexual practices, but it has also become, in the words of David Halperin, the 'bible' of groups such as ACT UP, America's gay activist group on AIDS issues.[7] This impact is probably best explained by the fact that the book can be read as an impassioned, rhetorically sophisticated and theoretically innovative call to battle for all those who find what Foucault calls '*l'intolérable*' in

modern sexuality.[8] It is a book whose style has an almost physical impact
on the reader: in the words of James Bernauer, 'Foucault's style mirrors the
fundamental urgency of his thought, which is less to convince than to
agitate, to compel a desire for flight, to afflict the reader with a pressure or
force'.[9] However, the book is far from being merely polemical; in fact,
despite its sometimes strident rhetoric, it also importantly attempts to open
up a space in which all our accepted everyday and scholarly preconceptions
about modern sexuality can be subjected to critical re-examination and
reflection. It is a book which, according to Foucault, proposes no more than
a 'hypothetical discourse'; it is deliberately 'full of holes'; it simply intends
to provoke discussion, to see to what extent certain arguments can be
pushed. It is full of 'uncertain' hypotheses; as he says, 'whatever is uncertain in what I have written is certainly uncertain'. In this sense, it proposes
a 'game' which, Foucault finds, not many people have been willing to take
up and play.'[10]

Whether or not we can take seriously Foucault's assertion that the book
contains no 'rhetoric' and that he is uncertain of the arguments he is
making, it is certainly the case that it has been read as offering something
approaching a manifesto for people involved in a wide range of political
struggles. This is an effect and an impact which are relevant for my
purposes here because they indicate that *The History of Sexuality*, volume I
is, perhaps, of all Foucault's works the one which is the most clearly
motivated by an ethico-political position. And that position is, in a certain
sense, a 'revolutionary' one – at least insofar as it involves 'cutting off the
king's head'. In one of the central passages of the book, where Foucault
argues against certain dominant understandings of power,[11] he says that
despite the example set by the demise of (absolute) monarchy, political
theory still has not 'cut off the head of the king' (*VS*, 89[117]). Consequently, what he proposes to do in this section, and in fact in the book as a
whole, is to develop a new theory of power at the same time as he writes a
new history of modern sexuality. The theory of power will make possible
the new history, while the examination of the historical data will feed back
to modify and further develop the account of power: 'it is a question of
forming a different grid of historical decipherment by starting from a different theory of power; and, at the same time, of advancing little by little
toward a different conception of power through a closer examination of an
entire historical material' (*VS*, 90–1[120]). What this requires, in Foucault's
view, is a theoretical shift in each domain: we must conceive of power
without the king and of sex without the law. We must recognize both that,
in modern societies, power no longer operates according to the model of
sovereignty and that, in particular, it has ceased to regulate sexuality

through law. Having made these theoretical moves, it becomes possible for Foucault to develop a picture of a power which operates by inciting, cajoling, producing, normalizing and 'governing' sexuality, rather than by repressing, silencing and denying it. However, the 'revolutionary' import of Foucault's history doesn't stop there.

While, on one level, the book certainly is an important 'revolutionary' contribution to both the understanding of power and the history of modern sexuality, on another level it also operates as a call for the reader to engage in an insurrection against the subjective practices which ground these modern forms of sexuality. Employing the same metaphor again, Foucault refers to our subjection to the 'austere monarchy of sex' (VS, 159[211]) and, in an interview from 1977, calls for us to say 'non au sexe roi.[12] Foucault's reconceptualization of power implies that this 'no' is to be directed not so much against the repression or the prohibition of sex, but rather against the entire mechanism of sexuality itself. In other words, if, as Foucault says, 'we are all living more or less in a state of sexual misery' (PS, 112[258]), then the cause of this misery is not to be found in a repressive social mechanism, or in a more general psychological repression. It is, rather, a secondary effect of the way power is exercised through the production of sexuality. It follows that saying 'no' to repression in favour of the liberation of sexuality, or overcoming repression by interrogating and speaking one's sexuality, is simply to remain within that same mechanism which makes one suffer; it is to remain subject to the monarchy of sex. In contrast, Foucault is suggesting that, to the extent that adolescents, women, homosexuals, or anybody 'suffers' from their sexuality, the strategically effective course of action to take is not to look for a panacea within the confines of the very mechanism which brings with it these 'effects of misery', but to undermine and reject this whole 'sexography' (PS, 116[261]) which makes us seek our most intimate and secret truth in our relation to sex. While Foucault's rhetoric certainly suggests a 'revolution', it does not imply a liberation or a freeing of a previously existing but 'enslaved' aspect of our experience: rather, it insists that this 'cutting off of the king's head', this 'end of the monarchy of sex', can only be based on an effort to 'fabricate other forms of pleasures, relations, coexistences, attachments, loves, intensities' (PS, 116[261-2]). It follows that resistance to the modern 'apparatus' of sexuality can only succeed if it attempts to move beyond the limits of the regime and mechanisms of power which invented and continue to police modern sexuality.

Foucault's *History of Sexuality*, volume I, then, is a book which not only proposes a new way of understanding the operations of power, and a new way of reading the history of sexuality in modern Western societies, it is also a book which aims to show those who 'suffer' from modern sexuality how they can most effectively resist and undermine that mechanism of power/knowledge which produces their 'misery'. It is a book which points out the strategic pitfalls of liberatory discourses (at least in the field of sexuality), which counsels suspicion with regard to the 'sexological' discourses of psychotherapy and psychoanalysis, and which, in contrast, urges us to 'counter the grips of power with the claims of bodies, pleasures and knowledges, in their multiplicity and their possibility of resistance' (*VS*, 157[208]). If we are to understand the 'motivation' behind Foucault's journey to Greece, we must begin with the motivation behind this first volume of *The History of Sexuality*. And in order to understand this motivation more fully, we need to examine in a little more detail the story Foucault tells in this volume of the emergence of sexuality in the modern West and the connections that can be made between this emergence and the question of contemporary ethics.

At first glance, *The History of Sexuality*, volume I does not appear to be a book about modern morality: the question of the constitution of the subject of ethics is never raised, nor is the contemporary rejection of previously dominant forms of morality. Instead, we are presented with a rhetorically charged attack on the particular relations between power, knowledge and sexuality that obtain in modern Western societies. It is a book which could easily be seen simply as an attempt to further the cause (by problematizing the cause) of the sexual liberation movements of the 1970s. In what sense can we read it as a work which exposes the price of modern morality? How can it be read as the first volume of what Foucault will later call his 'genealogy of ethics' (OGE, 356)?

The first clue to such a reading is to be found in the French title of this volume – *La Volonté de savoir* (The Will to Knowledge) – which, in the English translation, becomes the uninspiring *An Introduction*. The will to knowledge Foucault is concerned with here is that which accompanies the discourse of sex and its effects of power, as both instrument and support. It is a will to know the intimate truth of the individual's desire, a will which proceeds by exacting 'true confessions'. If modern sexuality has, for Foucault, one essential defining characteristic, it is its relation to speech, or more precisely its relation to true speech. The story that Foucault tells of the history of sexuality, from the Council of Trent to the end of the nineteenth century, is one in which the injunction to 'tell everything' concerning our sex has been both the means and the end of the gradual penetration of the body by the machinery of power. From the Christian pastoral's imperative that 'everything having to do with sex [must pass] through the endless mill of speech' (*VS*, 21[30]), to the 'discursive explosion' (*VS*, 17[25]) that has characterized the modern era, Foucault traces the 'great subjugation' of sex to discourse (*VS*, 21[30]), a subjugation which has facilitated the parallel subjugation of sex to power. One could say that, in Foucault's account, power 'hijacks' the confessional incitement to discourse in order to spread its own networks and intensify its own effects. In the case of childhood masturbation, for example, Foucault argues that it was by relying on this 'vice' as support that power 'advanced, multiplied its relays and its effects ... penetrating further into reality at the same pace' (*VS*, 42[58]). Similarly, in the development of 19th century scientific discourses about sexuality, Foucault sees the escalating operation of a power which increased its effectiveness and expanded its domain by instituting a cycle involving a 'sensualization of power and a gain of pleasure', a power which 'wrapped the sexual body in its embrace' (*VS*, 44[61]). Through the vehicle of true discourses, then, power has invested the body, has organized and increased its pleasures, has defined its pathologies and multiplied its perversions.

The images used here – of power 'penetrating', 'advancing' and 'multiplying' – suggest that a pre-existing sex has been both 'hijacked' and repressed by power. Foucault, however, concludes his argument by suggesting that not only is *sexuality* an invention of the mechanisms of modern power/knowledge, but that *sex* itself – understood as a pre-discursive substance or substratum underlying sexuality – is merely a 'fictitious unity' which artificially combines anatomical elements, biological functions and sensations and pleasures into an 'ideal point' functioning as a kind of anchor for the modern deployment of sexuality (*VS*, 154–5[204–5]). Indeed, this imaginary point has been so successfully constituted, Foucault argues, that it is our desire for it – for 'sex' itself – that has allowed the operations of power to remain hidden. It is this idea of a unified force called 'sex' which has made it possible to view 'sexuality' as a target of a repressive and dominating power: thus, it is the idea of 'sex' which has made it so easy for us to conceive of power as nothing but law and taboo – 'the idea of 'sex' makes it possible to evade what gives 'power' its power' (*VS*, 155[205]). In effect, we have been engaged in the task of exacting 'the truest of confessions from a shadow' (*VS*, 159). Here again is the reason that Foucault cannot adopt the discourse of the sexual liberation movements in response to this modern deployment of sexuality. Since the whole discourse of sex/sexuality (whether 'repressive' or 'liberatory') is intimately connected to the modern forms of power/knowledge, then regardless of how subversive or oppositional such a discourse might seem to be it will necessarily remain within the logic of those mechanisms.

As we have seen, one of the key characteristics of modern sexuality, according to Foucault's account, is its relation to true speech. The 'incite-ment to discourse' which inaugurates modern sexuality is a demand for the production of true discourse, a demand which builds upon and institutiona-lizes a certain relation to self whose paradigmatic form is the confession. Confession, in the broadest sense, indicates for Foucault 'all those proce-dures by which the subject is incited to produce a discourse of truth about his sexuality which is capable of having effects on the subject himself' (CF, 215–16[317–18]). And modern power has inscribed the truthful confession 'at the heart of the procedures of individualisation': not only do we confess in relation to sexuality, but also in relation to 'justice, medicine, education, family relationships, and love relations'. In short, 'Western man has become a confessing animal' (*VS*, 59[80]). However, to think, as we have learned to do, that confessing one's truth is to gain freedom, is a 'ruse' which it has taken Western societies an 'immense labour' to instil in us: it has led, he argues, to 'men's subjection: their constitution as subjects in both senses of the word' (*VS*, 60[81]). And it is subjection – in the sense of the process of making one *a* subject – which for Foucault defines the field of ethics.

'Do we *really* (*vraiment*) need a *true* (*vrai*) sex?' – according to Foucault, modern Western societies have been 'stubborn' and 'obstinate' in their insistence that this question must be answered in the affirmative.[13] In the collection of documents around the case of Herculine Barbin, a nineteenth-century hermaphrodite, he demonstrates the cost which such an answer can exact at the level of the individual. Herculine (known as Alexina) was born in 1838, she was brought up as a girl and educated in a convent school; she became a teacher and worked in an all-female boarding school and had a secret, almost unavowed affair with the daughter of the school's owner. Even though, from the age of puberty, her body was different from those of her fellows (she was gangly, narrow-hipped and had more body hair), no suspicion of a sexual 'anomaly' was ever raised. As Foucault underlines in the 'Introduction' to the collection, Herculine lived in an exclusively female world, one in which the other sex was never present with its demand that one be on one side or the other of a sexual divide. In fact Herculine was very happy, in this monosexual environment, to be 'other' without being of the 'other sex'. It is because she was both the same as her fellows and strangely different that, in Foucault's surmise, Herculine was a source of fascination and attraction to the women who surrounded her:

Neither a woman loving women, nor a man hidden among women. Alexina was the subject without identity of a great desire for women; and for these same women, she was a point of attraction of their femininity and for their femininity, without anything that would force them out of their wholly feminine world (*DE* IV, 121).

At the age of twenty-two, however, Herculine was plucked from this world of 'discretion'[14] and secret, unavowed desires by a doctor's discovery of a genital deformity. Through the intervention of the medical, legal and church authorities she was forced to change her legal status (to that of male); she was sacked from her teaching position, moved to Paris where she wrote a memoir and eight years later committed suicide.

What we see occurring in this case is the operation of a set of mechanisms and techniques by which a 'mistake' in the order of sexuality is corrected and a 'true' sexual identity is imposed on an unsuspecting individual. Herculine's tragedy was that her parents were mistaken about her true sex and that by the time the mistake was recognized it was too late for it to be successfully 'corrected'. The point of the story, however, is not the tragic intrusion of a (masculine) science into an innocent (female) paradise; nor is it to attempt to establish in retrospect whether Herculine *really* was male or female: the point, rather, is to make us question the role which 'truth' has, relatively recently, come to have in the modern 'apparatus' (*dispositif*) of sexuality.[15] The historical significance of the case comes from the fact that two hundred years previously it would not have been a question of 'correcting' a 'mistake'; and Foucault's question is how and at what cost did sex become such a matter of truth. Foucault points out that up until the eighteenth century hermaphrodites were legally allowed to choose which sex to adopt at the age of majority: in other words, it was legally recognized that hermaphrodites were 'truly' neither one sex nor the other. In the modern period, however, hermaphroditism is itself almost seen as a mistake, as a confusing appearance which hides one true sex. Herculine's tragedy is not that a mistake was made, but that the question of her sexual identity was one in which truth was made to play a fundamental role. This is, of course, not only an historical question, it is also a question of our present; because while hermaphroditism itself (and sex changing in general) are treated very differently today, it is still the case that truth is determinant in our relation to our sexuality.

What Foucault is suggesting is that the relation between truth and sexuality that obtains today is a mutually constitutive one: our sexuality has come to be a domain in which a secret truth is hidden, while the truth of our subjectivity has come to be grounded in our sexuality (*VS*, 69[93])[16] What the modern apparatus of sexuality demands is that we both interrogate our sexuality about its hidden truth and that we look to it for the truth of our own subjectivity. It is around this interplay, Foucault contends, that a whole science of the subject has sprung up: 'causality in the subject, the unconscious of the subject, the truth of the subject in the other who knows, the knowledge he holds unbeknown to him, all this found an opportunity to deploy itself in the discourse of sex' (*VS*, 70[94]).

In the final section of *The History of Sexuality*, Foucault links the growth of this apparatus of subjectivation to a transformation in the mechanisms of power in Western societies from a 'sovereign', 'deductive' power to a 'life-administering' 'bio-power'. Before the eighteenth century, he argues, power operated negatively, by deduction: it was characterized by the sovereign's right to *take* life (a right whose contrary was not the right to *give* life but merely to *let live*); it was, 'essentially a right of seizure: of things, time, bodies, and ultimately life itself' (*VS*, 136[179]). In contrast, since the eighteenth century power has come to be a 'life-administering' force: it no longer operates by 'deduction' but by 'addition' and augmentation. It has become a 'positive influence on life', one that 'endeavours to administer, optimize and multiply it'; but all within an orientation towards 'subjecting it to precise controls and comprehensive regulations' (*VS*, 137[180]). And it is within the context of these controls that sexuality takes on its modern importance, because it comes to be situated at the intersection of the two axes along which bio-power operates: that of the *'anatamo-politics of the human body'* (the disciplines) and the *'biopolitics of the population'*.[17] In modern societies sexuality comes to be a 'crucial target' of power (*VS*, 147[193]); it is subjected to a whole range of administrative mechanisms, an 'entire micro-power' involving 'infinitesimal surveillances, permanent controls, extremely meticulous orderings of space' (*VS*, 145[192]). So close is this link between sexuality and modern mechanisms of power that one could say that sexuality was simply 'invented as an instrument-effect in the spread of bio-power'.[18] And it was an 'instrument-effect' which gradually, from the nineteenth century, became 'the stamp of individuality'; that is, it became what enabled one both to 'analyse' individuality and to 'master' it (*VS*, 146[192]); it became a crucial element in the modern political technology of the individual.

Linking this theme of bio-power to Foucault's slightly later interrogation of 'governmentality',[19] we can see that the question of sexuality has a significance far beyond the field of sexual practices. By governmentality, Foucault means, on the one hand, the ensemble of 'institutions, procedures, analyses and reflections, calculations and tactics' which allows the exercise of what we could call bio-power; and, on the other hand, the process by which this type of power has become pre-eminent in Western societies, leading to the formation of a whole series of governmental 'apparatuses' (*appareils* not *dispositifs*) and 'knowledges' (*savoirs*) (*OG*, 102–3[655]). What we need to recognise, then, is that 'our' sexuality is a battleground in which a whole array of 'governmental' forces combine (not, of course, without resistance) to produce particular kinds of individual: it is one of the key channels through which modern individuals are subjectivized and governed. Through the mutual relation between sex and truth, through the legal and medical administering of sexuality and through the private and public regulation of sexual practice, we have become individuals who are fixed to particular forms of identity; and it is these forms of identity which could be said to be the 'cost' of the Western *scientia sexualis*.

In the long development of this *scientia sexualis*, which doubles as a science of the subject, Foucault isolates one element of the apparatus, one technique which has been of central importance: the technique of confession (*aveu*). According to Foucault's 'broad historical perspective' (*VS*, 67[90]), the technique of confession has, since its beginning in the thirteenth century, become 'one of the main rituals we rely on for the production of truth' (*VS*, 58[78]). Where an 'avowal' (*aveu*) initially involved a guarantee of the value or status of one person by another, it came to be a question of guaranteeing *oneself* by virtue of the truthful discourse which one could pronounce *about* oneself; in this way confession, the truthful confession, came to be 'inscribed at the heart of the procedures of individualization by power' (ibid.). In other words, it came to be one of the principal ways we are constituted (and constitute ourselves) as individuals. One of the reasons that confession has been so successful a technique of individualization is that it 'pretends' that the truth it exposes has been hidden by a repressive power; confession is always understood as a 'liberation' of truth, a truth which does not belong to the order of power, but of freedom. What this 'revelation' successfully hides is that even this production of truth is 'thoroughly imbued with relations of power' (*VS*, 60[81]). This is what Foucault calls the 'internal ruse of confession' (ibid.): it has made us subject to the 'millennial yoke' (*VS*, 61[82]) of its demand, thus fixing us to forms of identity which arise from the complex formations of power/knowledge prevailing in modern societies.

To return to the point with which we began this section, it is clear that Foucault is not just analysing or describing this phenomenon; indeed his rhetoric alone should be enough to convince us of his 'political' project. Confession is a 'millennial yoke' which is responsible for our subjection 'in both senses of the word'; it is enforced by 'a power that constrains us' (*VS*, 60[81]), it proceeds by a 'many-sided extortion' (*VS*, 64[86]) and, contrary to the 'repressive hypothesis', it has led to 'too much rather than not enough discourse' (ibid.). How, then, should we characterize – or 'quantify' – the cost which these techniques of subjectivation/individualization exact?

We would have to differentiate between two aspects of this cost: firstly, there are the actual forms of subjectivity themselves which are made possible within, and enforced by, modern apparatuses of subjectivity. These are forms which, as we have seen, frequently entail what Foucault calls 'effects of misery'. Secondly, Foucault clearly implies that there is something particularly effective, and therefore pernicious, about modern Western techniques of subjectivation: these techniques force individuals back on themselves and fix them to their own identities 'in a constraining way' (SP, 212[227]). Not only are we 'fixed' to forms of subjectivity which 'entail effects of misery', but more importantly, we are fixed to them in an extremely effective and thoroughly 'naturalized' way: they have become a 'second nature'[20] from which it will require a massive labour to free ourselves.

We can now say that *The History of Sexuality*, volume I deals with ethics because it deals with the ways we are constituted and constitute ourselves as subjects; and the task of understanding the historical forces which have made us the kinds of individuals that we are is, for Foucault, one of the most important tasks of ethics. If Foucault's aim is always 'to increase our freedom with respect to a specific way in which we are determined',[21] then in this case his aim is to allow us to open up a space between us and the forms of sexual identity which the modern 'apparatus of sexuality' imposes: *this* is a task of ethics. And, precisely in order to do this, Foucault thought it necessary to understand the emergence, the historical development, and the ultimate secularization of Christian confessional practices. It is for this reason that the second volume of the original 'History of Sexuality' project was to be a volume dealing with the 'confession of the flesh' in Christianity from the Middle Ages to the eighteenth century.[22] This was the first step in Foucault's 'journey to Greece'.

CONFESSING THE SELF

While the originally projected second volume of *The History of Sexuality* (later announced as a forthcoming fourth volume) has never been published, other sources are available to us which offer an insight into Foucault's reading of what he comes to call the 'hermeneutics of the self'. The first volume already defines the 'broad historical perspective' (*VS*, 67[90]) of Foucault's approach to the development of the techniques of confession from the Lateran Council of 1215 up to the twentieth-century practice of psychoanalysis. Although the story he tells about this development, especially in its modern phase, is one he recognizes here as requiring further, more detailed 'historical inquiry' (*VS*, 72[97]), it is possible to fill in some of these details using other, later texts.

In the specific context of *The History of Sexuality* volume I, Foucault's concern is to map out the prehistory of the modern era's *scientia sexualis*. He postulates a 'continuous' line of development from the formalisation of the Catholic sacrament of penance by the Lateran Council of 1215, through the secularization and proliferation of confessional techniques after the Reformation, to the domination of our contemporary forms of self-understanding by the techniques of modern psychoanalysis, 'sexology' and pop psychology. This development of a Western *scientia sexualis* is contrasted with a supposed 'Eastern' *ars erotica* in 'China, Japan, India, Rome, the Arabo-Moslem societies' (*VS*, 57[76]). The Western science of sexuality, we are told, is a procedure for producing the truth of sex which is founded on the extraction of self-avowal; it has become one of the key elements in the power/knowledge apparatus that moulds modern subjectivities. In contrast, the 'Eastern' *ars erotica* is founded on the transmission of a knowledge concerning the cultivation of pleasure; the initiated gain mastery of the body, they are transfigured through a 'singular bliss' and they receive the 'elixir of life' (*VS*, 58[77]).[23] Unlike the relation between the master and the initiate in the *ars erotica* (in which it is the master who holds the 'secrets' and the initiate who demands to know), in the Christian confession it is the confessing individual who is compelled to speak by a confessor who not only has the power to impose an obligation to speak, but who also interprets and judges the proferred speech. In contrast with the *ars erotica*, the science of sexuality compels a discourse (which must come 'from below') in which truth is guaranteed by the number of obstacles and resistances which have to be overcome, and the mere utterance of this truth effects a modification in the speaking subject. It is a 'ritual of discourse' which harnesses a particular power relation (between confessing subject and confessor) in order to compel the confessing subject to 'articulate their sexual peculiarity' (*VS*, 61[82]).

It was during the seventeenth century, particularly in the context of the Catholic Counter-Reformation, that this technique came to be centred increasingly around the weaknesses of the 'flesh'; the required frequency of confession was increased, renewed effort was given to imposing 'meticulous rules of self-examination', and all the deceitful movements of desire and the flesh had to be pursued and brought to light (*VS*, 19[28]).[24] In the seventeenth century, the confessional techniques and procedures of self-examination which had been developed in Medieval monasteries became an ideal to be practised by everyone; and even though, as Foucault recognizes, only a tiny elite would have fully complied with this demand, the important point is that the imperative was established. This establishment is crucial because, during the next two centuries, the techniques became separated from their religious context and began to function at the core of the modern apparatuses of individualization; in effect, the injunction to confess achieved a general application in a new secularized form.

While, in *The History of Sexuality* volume I Foucault traces the history of confessional techniques back to the beginning of the thirteenth century (the Lateran Council of 1215), he later turns his attention to the origin of these same techniques of self-examination and confession in the early centuries of Christianity. It is in the context of this investigation that he first addresses in detail the shift which occurred between pagan antiquity and the Christian Middle Ages. Foucault now conceptualizes this as a shift towards the 'hermeneutics of the self': that is, a shift towards the requirement that the self – its thoughts, desires and drives – be subjected to a (continuous) *interpretation*. In a series of seminars,[25] he outlined the key features of this move away from the constitution of the self in Late Stoicism towards the discovery and deciphering of the self in early Christianity.

In one seminar (BHS), Foucault plots this transformation by comparing Seneca's technique for the examination of conscience[26] with the status and practice of the penitent in early Christian communities. For Seneca, in Foucault's reading, the objective of daily self-examination is, firstly, to measure the distance between what has been done during the day and what ought to have been done (this *ought* is founded on the precepts and principles of reason); and secondly, to bring about a fuller integration between the subject of knowledge and the subject of the will – that is, to ensure that knowledge of the rules of conduct will in future be implemented in right conduct. The aim of this practice, then, is to remind the subject of a truth which has been forgotten and to remobilize that truth in the individual's life. Its aim, in short, is to constitute a self through 'the force of truth' (BHS, 210) – not through self-discovery or self-interpretation.

In contrast to Late Stoicism, early Christianity developed two techniques for the 'diagnosis' and 'treatment' of such lapses from right conduct – techniques which involved an important shift both in the object and the aim of self-examination and confession. The first and, for Foucault, the least important of these techniques was the *exomologesis*. This practice involves the purification of the individual through the physical and dramatic showing forth of the truth of their sinfulness: the penitent performs public acts of self-punishment, such as the wearing of sack-cloth and ashes, in order to obtain absolution from their transgression and allow their reintegration into the community. The practice is based, Foucault argues, on a kind of 'ritual martyrdom': it is a form of self-destruction which effects a 'breaking away from self' and a rupturing with 'one's past identity' (TS, 43).[27]

The second technique, which Foucault isolates as the 'small origin' (BHS, 221) of our contemporary culture of confession, is the *exagoreusis*: a procedure for examining and verbalizing thoughts in the context of a relation of obedience to a director of conscience. In this practice the confessant submits wholly to the authority of the confessor, endeavouring to uncover the source, whether from God or Satan, and value of every thought, impulse and movement of the 'flesh'. This search has two crucial characteristics which distinguish it from the earlier Stoic techniques: firstly, verbalization itself has the effect of both confirming the truth of the discovery and effecting an absolution of the transgression; secondly, the subject is constituted as being susceptible to a permanent inner deceit and is therefore obliged to continuously engage in self-interpretation, thus giving rise to the endless task of the 'hermeneutics of the self'. On the one hand, then, *exomologesis* consists of the physical, dramatic showing forth of the truth of one's sinfulness, while *exagoreusis* involves the constant search for and verbalization of the truth of the hidden sinfulness of one's thoughts. While the two techniques differ in their aims and procedures, they share a common characteristic Foucault sees as being of central significance in the subsequent development and transformation of the confession: in both cases, the price which must be paid for the discovery of the truth of the subject is self-renunciation – there is no truth of the self without self-sacrifice. Ultimately, it is this feature of confession which Foucault wishes to combat.

In the 'broad historical perspective' adopted by Foucault in *The History of Sexuality*, volume I, confession features as the technique which provides the basis for the modern apparatus of sexuality. Therefore, it can be seen as being at least partly responsible for the 'effects of misery' which that apparatus necessarily produces. As Foucault pursued the history of these techniques further, however, he came to view their development as a key moment, not only in the history of sexuality, but in the history of the self – in the emergence of the Western subject. And if the modern apparatus of sexuality brings with it 'effects of misery', then the modern forms of subjectivation are no less open to critique. What occurs in this broadening of Foucault's historical perspective is a corresponding widening of the scope of his critique; and this widening is reflected in the way Foucault reformulates his project during this same period (the early 1980s): from a history of sexuality to a genealogy of the subject, or a genealogy of ethics.

In several of the seminars I have discussed here,[28] Foucault tells the story of a nineteenth-century French psychiatrist (François Leuret) who 'cured' a patient by using a shower to force him to admit to his own madness. What is distinctive about this therapy, for Foucault, is that it simply requires the verbal affirmation 'Yes, I am mad' in order to effect a cure. The psychiatrist is not in the least interested in what happens in the patient's head – only, we could say, in what happens in his speech. And what happens in his speech, Foucault suggests, is the opposite of a performative speech act: because, in this case, the affirmation destroys the condition in the subject which made the affirmation true. Thus, the anecdote can be taken as an illustration of the 'bizarre' relations which have developed in Western culture between 'individuality, discourse, truth and coercion' (BHS, 201). Or, to be more precise, it leads one to ask what relation between truth and subjectivity could give rise to such a 'strange and yet widespread practice' (SS, 8). The formulation of this question can be taken as indicative of the change of focus which occurs in Foucault's work: from a concentration on techniques for dominating others (*Discipline and Punish* and *The History of Sexuality*, volume I) to an investigation of techniques for the government of the self.[29] And what his initial work in this field showed him was the importance of investigating the precise ways Western societies have linked subjectivity and truth together 'with the tightest bond'.

Foucault's use of this expression can be taken as a clue to the reason for his critical attitude towards the hermeneutics of the self: for, not only does this technique demand a sacrifice and renunciation of self, but it has become an almost inevitable 'second nature' – in fact, it has been so widespread in Western culture for so long that it has become difficult for us to 'isolate and separate it from our own spontaneous experience' (TS, 17). This, for Foucault, is the reason the modern human sciences failed to found the truth of subjectivity on a *positive* emergence of the self (on an 'identity technology of the self, HL).[30] In response to this failure, Foucault asks whether we should not rather reject this whole model according to which the self is that which must be discovered in its truth, and replace it with a model according to which 'the self is nothing more than the correlate of technology built into our history' (HL). In this way we would not only get rid of the sacrifice which has been linked to the hermeneutics of the self, but we would also get rid of that entire technology itself. It is this project, of doing away with the hermeneutics of the self, which I argue is central to Foucault's entire subsequent reading of the ancient Greek and Hellenistic techniques of the self: not only do these ancient techniques come to fill the role of critical counterpoint to our modern secularized Christian technologies; but this critical project fundamentally determines the story which Foucault tells about those ancient practices.

WHY GREECE?

Drawing on this discussion of Foucault's attitude towards the hermeneutics of the self, and on our reading of *The History of Sexuality*, volume I, it is now possible to deal with the question of the motivation behind Foucault's account of ancient ethics. Foucault gives his own answer to this question in the introduction to *The History of Sexuality*, volume II, *The Use of Pleasure*,[31] where he speaks of the fundamental change his project underwent in the years between the publication of volume I in 1976 and the publication of volumes II and III in 1984. The two key elements of this explanation are, firstly, the account it gives of the three axes of 'experience' (*UP*, 4[10]) and, secondly, the way that it redefines the history of sexuality project as a history of the ethical 'problematization' of sexual conduct through an investigation of the history of 'techniques of the self' (*UP*, 11[17]).

The sexuality Foucault wishes to investigate in these volumes (as was also the case in volume I) is a sexuality which is, importantly, 'in quotation marks': he wants to write the history of our experience of something that we call 'sexuality'. And this experience is made possible by the intersection of three constitutive axes: a field of knowledge, a type of normativity and a form of subjectivity (or, a formation of sciences, a system of power and a mode of relation to self).[32] While these three axes constitute 'any matrix of experience' (PHS, 338), it is not the case that their relative importance is always the same: indeed, in the field of sexuality, it is the third axis which (at least prior to the modern period) is of most importance. Foucault considered that, based on his work from the 1960s, he already had the methodological tools with which to investigate the first axis (knowledge), and that his work from the 1970s gave him the tools to investigate the second axis (power), but that the third axis (the self) required the development of a new methodological approach. The approach Foucault adopted was to analyse the practices through which individuals constituted themselves as sexual subjects, or as subjects of desire. His aim was to understand how individuals were led to practise a hermeneutics of the self and to experience themselves as subjects of a sexuality. In the most general terms, then, what was required was a genealogy of the subject; an investigation into the 'forms and modalities of the relation to self by which the individual constitutes and recognizes himself as subject' (*UP*, 6[12]).

As a result of this methodological change of focus, the project of the history of sexuality now becomes one chapter in the genealogy of the subject; the history of the self-constitution of the subject in relation to sexual conduct becomes one element in the history of the self-constitution of the subject per se. Consequently, Foucault becomes interested in the forms of relation to the self 'in and of themselves' and the essential emphasis of the work shifts to what originally had been merely its 'historical background' (PHS, 339[583–4]). The way that this particular aspect of self-constitution is now related to the more general genealogy of the subject is through the concept of 'problematization'. The questions Foucault now asks about sexuality are 'how, why, and in what forms was sexuality constituted as a moral domain?' (*UP*, 10[16]). He rejects the possibility of explaining this problematization of sexual conduct as a straightforward result of the strong social taboos and interdictions which are commonly associated with it; on the contrary, he suggests, the moral problematization is often strongest where obligations and prohibitions are weakest. Against the former kind of response, then, he develops an answer which is based on the hypothesis that the problematization (at least in ancient Greek and Roman culture) is inextricably linked to the ancient 'arts of existence'. These arts he defines as:

> those intentional and voluntary actions by which men not only set themselves rules of conduct, but also seek to transform themselves, to change themselves in their singular being, and to make their life into an *œuvre* that carries certain aesthetic values and meets certain stylistic criteria (*UP*, 10–11[16–17]).

What Foucault is arguing here is that in Classical Greece and imperial Rome (adult male) individuals were concerned with their sexual conduct not because this field was subject to social or religious control, nor because it was a field where the truth of their subjectivity would be discovered, but because it was *one* of the fields where one could (and should) practise the art of transforming one's life into a *work*. There are two reasons for Foucault's interest in this model. In the first instance, it is a useful counterpoint to the modern hermeneutic model of relation to the self. It serves to make visible the historical formation of the later model, by demonstrating its non-universality. However, it also comes to function as what we could call a critical indictment of our modern modes of self relation: in the comparison between the two it is the ancient model which, for all its faults, triumphs. Hence, Foucault is interested in Classical Greece arid imperial Rome because there 'the effect of scientific knowledge and the complexity of normative systems were less' (PHS, 339[583]) and the arts of existence thus enjoyed a greater 'importance' and 'autonomy' (*UP*, 11[17]). Subsequently, these arts were integrated into the development of Christian pastoral power and into the disciplines of modern government; they lost both their autonomy and their importance, reappearing occasionally only, in figures such as the Renaissance man and the nineteenth-century dandy.[33] What I will suggest in the following two chapters is that this second reason for Foucault's interest, this second motivation for his journey to Greece, often slides into a certain nostalgia for an age in which individuals were not tied to their forms of identity by the 'tightest bonds' of power/knowledge-apparatuses; but were to an extent free to engage in a work of self-constitution whose guiding principles were not interpretative but aesthetic. My argument is that, for Foucault, the modern hermeneutics of the self is both historically preceded and normatively surpassed by the ancient aesthetics of the self.

My aim in this chapter has been to lay the groundwork for showing that if there is a type of sexual ethics at the centre of volumes II and III of *The History of Sexuality*, it is neither that of Classical Athens, nor that of the imperial era; rather, the ethics which dominates these volumes – as much by its absence as its presence – is the sexual ethics of Christianity. Despite the fact that Foucault's historical schema comprises (at least) three phases, it is the Christian phase, both politically and philosophically, which ultimately defines and negatively determines Foucault's genealogical project. On the one hand, it is the 'Christian' elements of the modern *scientia sexualis* – that is, its tendency to codify, to normalize, to relentlessly pursue the vagaries of our hidden desires and to demand a renunciation of self – that Foucault takes greatest exception to. On the other hand, in the account he gives of the two pre-Christian modes of sexual ethics, we will see that it is always the 'un-Christian' aspects which he emphasizes. No matter that there are great similarities in the code, he tells us, what is important are the differences at the level of *rapport à soi;* the fact that this ethics is characterized by an aesthetics of existence rather than a hermeneutics of desire; the fact that it valorizes the care of the self rather than demanding a renunciation of self; the fact that it sees sexual desire and pleasure as, at worst, dangerous but never as evil. My suggestion now is that if we read *The History of Sexuality*, volume I in this way – that is, as part of a 'manifesto of anti-Christian sexuality', or an 'introduction to the non-devout life'[34] – we will be able to understand the provenance of many of the highly particular features Foucault's account of the ethics of antiquity subsequently displays.

CHAPTER 2

Alcibiades Goes Wilde

This elaboration of one's own life as a personal work of art ... was at the centre, it seems to me, of the moral experience, of the will to morality in Antiquity.

Michel Foucault (AE, 49[731])

In the history of the slow demise of Christianity as the moral standard-bearer of Western societies, many figures and many movements have been chosen as scapegoats by the defenders of the faith. One figure, Oscar Wilde, represents a movement which embraces both the Baudelairean dandy and the pre-Raphaelite aesthete – a movement which represents not only the rejection of traditional moral codes, but also the reduction of religious symbolism and iconography to mere aesthetic phenomena. In the figure of Wilde this moral and religious transgression is coupled with a transgression of nature – the practice of 'unnatural deeds' – which threatens not only the moral law, but also the laws of social propriety.[1] It is not by chance, then, that for Foucault the prime example of what he calls 'the attitude of moder-nity' is Baudelaire's dandy – that figure who, rather than trying to discover his secrets and his hidden truth, tries to 'invent' himself, to make of his life a work of art (WE, 41–2). Neither is it by chance that the picture Foucault paints of ancient Greek discourses and practices of sexuality conjures images of a Baudelairean *dandysme* which is very much *avant la lettre*.

In volume I of *The History of Sexuality*, Foucault urges us to 'counter the grips of power with the claims of bodies, pleasures, and knowledges' (*VS*, 157[208]); in volume II he seems to be saying, 'counter the grips of modern subjectivity with the claims of a Hellenized aestheticism and an aestheticized Hellenism'. In this chapter, I will begin to explore the possi-bility that Foucault's reading of the ancients imports a decidedly modern sensibility into the presentation of ancient erotic practices. I will present the prima facie case that Foucault 'aestheticizes' the Greeks of the Classical period by presenting their sexual ethics primarily in terms of their desire to create an aesthetic effect, rather than in terms of their desire to achieve and maintain political mastery in the *polis*. In doing this, Foucault would be presenting ancient sexual ethics more as a contribution to modern attempts to formulate a 'non-devout' life than as a working out of the social, political and personal parameters of sexual practice in fourth century BC Athens. Whether this tendency should be taken as a weakness or a strength is a question I will turn to in Chapter 5.

AESTHETIC ENDS

In his late work, Foucault develops a model (or a *'grille d'analyse'*) which is purportedly capable of mapping and ordering the diverse ethical practices in which a particular society engages. This analytic grid emerges out of his research into the ancient Greek 'use of pleasure', but it is one which in principle can be used to analyse and chart the practices in any ethical system. While any such grid is, of course, permanently open both to external evaluation and internal re-adjustment, my argument here will not relate to either form of evaluation.[2] Rather, I will focus on the relation between the details of the model and the ethico-political project of which it is a part. In particular, I will suggest that the model is constructed and used in such a way as to prioritize the aesthetic dimensions of ancient ethical practice; and that it does so in order to provide Foucault with a more effective counter-ideal to the modern secularized Christian hermeneutics of the self. What Foucault's argument suggests is that if the self is not given to us, if it is not there to be discovered or interpreted, then of course we must make it for ourselves; we must mould it, fashion it, perfect it – just like the Greeks used to do. However, the question that must be asked is, how exactly *did* the Greeks do this? Or, perhaps, how can they be made to appear as if they did?

Foucault's characterization of ancient ethics begins to respond to these questions, at a methodological level, by implementing a crucial distinction between 'ethics' and 'morality'. Early in *The Use of Pleasure* (*UP*, 25–8[32–5]), he distinguishes between three aspects of 'morality'. These are, morality proper; that is, the moral code, or the set of values and rules of action which are prescribed to individuals in a given social, cultural and religious setting. Secondly, the real behaviour of individuals, or the margins of variation and transgression which individuals take in relation to the code. Finally, and for Foucault most importantly, the way one makes oneself conform to, or vary from, the code; that is, the way one conducts oneself (*UP*, 26[33]). Here, Foucault plays on the possibilities of the French verb *'se conduire'*, which may mean 'to behave' – as in the second aspect, real behaviours – but can also mean literally 'to guide oneself', or 'to lead oneself'. Hence, we could say that, if the first aspect concerns the code itself, then the second concerns behaviour in relation to the code, while the third concerns behaviour in relation to oneself. The third aspect is the realm of the way in which one, literally, 'brings oneself' to either obey or transgress a moral code. It is this third aspect which, from the point of view of Foucault's genealogy of ethics, is of most importance. It is in this field, the field of ethical self-constitution, that Foucault discerns enormous historical changes – whereas the elements of the moral code itself appear to remain remarkably stable. The object of study of volumes II and III is, then, these changing modes of ethical self-constitution, particularly as they relate to sexual conduct.

As we saw in the Introduction, Foucault divides this third realm of morality – the realm of 'ethics' – into four aspects; and it is here that we first encounter the model, or *grille*, with which he will analyse and map ancient ethics.[3] For Foucault, if we wish to analyse a system of ethics, and especially if we wish to understand its history, we must divide it into these four constitutive elements: the ethical substance; the mode of subjection; the forms of elaboration of self (or the techniques of the self); the telos (or the mode of subjectivity towards which the ethics aims).

But are there any specifically aestheticizing elements in this way of dividing up the field of ethics? In a central section of *The Use of Pleasure* (*UP*, 89–93[103–7]), Foucault presents one important version of his aesthetic interpretation of Greek sexual ethics. Here, he states that Greek moral reflection on the *aphrodisia* leads neither to a codification of licit and illicit acts, nor to a hermeneutics of the subject, but rather to an 'aesthetics of existence' (*UP*, 92[106]). Far from culminating in the imposition of a universalizing code, this reflection leads to a sort of 'open demand' (*'exigence ouverte'*, ibid.), a non-obligatory call to stylize one's sexual practice by limiting and rarefying one's activities (ibid.). In contrast to the sexual ethics of Christianity, Foucault tells us, the ancients were less interested in the nature of the acts themselves, than in the attitude one adopted in relation to them. Indeed, the whole work of becoming an ethical subject in relation to the *aphrodisia* involved establishing a relation of mastery with these pleasures. 'Stylization' involved the cultivation of the ability to control and limit the dangerous excesses to which the *aphrodisia* could lead. It involved the cultivation of a way of life which owed its moral value not to the acts which it excluded, but to the form or the 'general formal principles' (*UP*, 89[103])[4] which governed the way in which one used one's pleasures. It was a way of life which manifested its moral value in its reasoned and harmonious form, a form which participated at the same time in beauty and truth; a moral value which was also an aesthetic value and a truth value (*UP*, 93[107]).

Both crucial elements of Foucault's aesthetic reading are present here: first, concerning the mode of subjection, the individual embarks on a particular path of self-constitution, not because it is prescribed by a universally imposed code, but because they have made a free, personal choice; and, secondly, concerning the telos, the aim of this work of self-constitution is a self which is remarkable for its beauty, its harmony and its perfection. I would suggest that it is through his account of the mode of subjection and the telos of Classical ethics that Foucault succeeds in aestheticizing the practices which are described in *The Use of Pleasure*. That is, it is in his account of these aspects, as opposed to the aspects of ethical substance and the forms of elaboration of the self, that Foucault's picture of ancient ethics manifests its highly particular characteristics.

Turning firstly to the mode of subjection, Foucault argues that the ancients developed an ethics which is characterized by its openness to individual differences and its refusal to impose itself universally. One cannot fail to notice, Foucault remarks (*UP*, 92[106]), that the ancient authors never try to establish a table of forbidden acts. However, while they did not consider the sexual act itself to be an evil, they did insist on the necessity of modulating its use according to a whole series of variables. For example, before acting upon the desire to have children, it was necessary to consider the age of both parents, their state of mind at the moment of coitus, the time of year, the time of day and whether there were any overriding reasons for temporarily abstaining from sexual activity – such as, for example, a strict regime of athletic training (see, generally, *UP*, Part 2 'Dietetics'). The point, for Foucault, is that one did not go to a 'dietician' in order to find out which acts should or should not be performed. One went, rather, to learn the general principles which must govern the right 'use' (*chresis*) of the *aphrodisia*. As for specific cases and applications, only the person involved could judge when and in what way to apply the general rules. The first element of Foucault's reading, then, which contributes to his 'aesthetic' interpretation, is this emphasis on the individualizing characteristics of ancient ethical practices.

Indeed, it is this non-universalizing and non-normalizing characteristic which, in the first instance, makes Classical ethics attractive for Foucault.[5] And the reason why Foucault maintains that it has this characteristic is, precisely, because the aim of this ethics is not universal salvation, but simply giving a beautiful form to an individual's life. In this ethics, one makes a personal choice to restrict, for example, one's sexual activity, and the choice is motivated by 'the will to live a beautiful life and to leave to others memories of a beautiful existence' (OGE, 341). For Foucault, then, ethical practices in Classical Greece arise out of a concern to elaborate and stylize one's conduct 'in the exercise of one's power and the practice of one's liberty' (*UP*, 23[30]). Having introduced the question of the aims of this ethical practice, we have now come to the second crucial element of Foucault's 'aesthetic' reading; that is, the contention that the telos of these practices was to give one's life the brilliance, the *éclat*, of beauty.

One of the central questions Foucault tries to answer in *The Use of Pleasure*, is why is it that it was in the field of the *aphrodisia*, a field in which the adult Greek male enjoyed relative freedom, that there developed in the Classical era a whole thematics of austerity? Why was it that, precisely in regard to an area of their lives where there were very few prohibitions, these free adult males were concerned to restrict their own behaviour? In relation to this question, Foucault's text gives a basis for two seemingly incompatible answers. These are, either that the telos of this 'will to austerity' was a life which, because of its beautiful form, would be remembered after one's death, or that its telos was a state of mastery over others, a state which would be guaranteed by one's mastery of oneself. While the latter explanation of this telos is supported by much of Foucault's research, it is nevertheless clear that the version which Foucault prefers, or tends to prioritize, is the 'aesthetic' explanation. In the 'On the Genealogy of Ethics' (OGE) interview, for example, we see Foucault moving from the characterization of Classical ethics as an ethics whose primary concern is with establishing and maintaining relations of domination with one's inferiors, to its characterization as 'a philosophical movement coming from very cultivated people, in order to give their life more intensity, much more beauty' (OGE, 349).

Again, in his many discussions of the four aspects of any system of ethics, Foucault tends to allow these two interpretations, while at the same time privileging the aesthetic one. In his first discussion of this distinction, for instance, in *The Use of Pleasure*, Foucault suggests that 'mastery of the self (*UP*, 28[35]) is one possible aim of ethical practice, and, indeed, that this was the aim which motivated Classical ethics. This state of self-mastery, however, was more than simply a state of non-slavery in relation to one's passions; it was also, in its 'fullest and most positive form', a 'power which one exercises over oneself through the power which one exercises over others' (*UP*, 80[93]). It was this state of self-mastery (*enkrateia*), which was the moral condition of possibility of one's mastery over others. As Foucault recognizes, this was an ethics which was resolutely 'virile' in character; if one was a 'man' in relation to oneself, one could be a 'man' in relation to others – and this, presumably, is what free Greek males wanted. So, when Foucault says that the telos of this ethics was *self-mastery*, we would be justified in wondering if it would not be more accurate to say that its telos was mastery of others. Despite the fact that he does recognize this 'isomorphism' (*UP*, 76[88]) between mastery of self and others in Classical Greece, Foucault in fact tends in the vast majority of cases to privilege, as we have seen, a surprisingly apolitical aesthetic account of this telos. If there is no trace of normalization in Greek ethics, he suggests, it is because 'the *principal* aim, the *principal* target of this kind of ethics was an aesthetic one' (OGE, 341).[6]

It should be clear on the basis of this overview of Foucault's aesthetic characterization of the telos of Classical ethics that, despite recognizing the relative importance of the contrary characterization, Foucault consistently favours and privileges the aesthetic interpretation. Setting aside, for the moment, the question of the extent to which these two accounts may in fact be incompatible, I will now put this model to the test, by applying it to a figure who was renowned in antiquity *both* for his youthful 'dandyism' and his precocious political ambition. Focusing on the pseudo-Platonic dialogue *Alcibiades I*, I will ask how adequate is Foucault's model when applied to the ethical motivation of a figure such as Alcibiades? Does the application of that model not tend to produce a picture of Alcibiades as 'aesthete', a picture which can give little space to Alcibiades as 'Machiavellian Prince'?

A PERICLEAN DANDY?

One important lesson which can be learned from volumes II and III of *The History of Sexuality* is that to speak globally of 'the Greeks', 'the ancients', or 'ancient ethics' is potentially very misleading. Despite the fact that both Foucault and his commentators have a tendency to speak of his late work in these terms, we should bear in mind that it is not by chance that this work is divided into two separate volumes – each dealing with an historical period that is separated from the other by up to five hundred years, and with a social and political context that, in terms of history, culture and institutions, is even more distant. While one of Foucault's aims in these volumes is to show us to what extent 'ancient ethics', considered globally, is both distant from and related to Christian ethics, it is also the case that the whole point of his charting of the shift from ethics as 'use of pleasure' to ethics as 'care of the self' is to demonstrate the enormous changes in ethical subjectivity which occurred within the 'ancient world' itself. We should be cautious, then, of thinking that 'Greek' or 'ancient' ethics forms a more or less homogenous whole, even when contrasted with the more immediate heritage of Western Christianity. Notwithstanding this caution, there are nevertheless many elements of continuity, not only between Classical and Hellenistic ethical reflection, but also between 'ancient' and Christian modes of reflection.

The single most important of these elements, and one which gives a certain similarity of style to the Classical and Hellenistic eras, is the theme of 'care of the self'. When Foucault uses this expression as the title of volume III of *The History of Sexuality*, this is not so much because the theme is newly developed in late antiquity, as because this was the element of Classical ethical reflection which had come to dominate the thought of the imperial era. As a theme, however, it had been of importance throughout the Classical Greek world and, in fact, it is in texts from this era that it first receives a philosophical treatment. The most important of these texts, for Foucault, is the *Alcibiades I* – a text which, traditionally, was considered to be a genuine work of Plato.[7] Foucault discussed this dialogue extensively in his course at the Collège de France in 1981/2[8] and in a seminar, from the same year, which he gave at the University of Vermont (TS). It is clear, from both these sources, that Foucault sees Socrates's interrogation of Alcibiades in this dialogue as crucial for a history of the theme of the care of the self, especially in its relation to political life. In his lecture of 12 January 1982 at the Collège de France, for example, he emphasizes the fact that the specifically *philosophical* treatment of the theme which Socrates instigates here, raises very important questions about the techniques of the care of the self – techniques which had been familiar to Classical Greek males for some time.

The subject of *Alcibiades I* is an encounter in which Socrates convinces the young Alcibiades that, in order to undertake a successful political career, he must first of all begin to 'care for himself'.[9] The dialogue, as Foucault points out (*RC*, 149–55; TS, 23–6), centres around three questions. These are: what is the relationship between care of the self and political life? what is the role of care of the self in pedagogy? and, what is the link between care of the self and knowledge of the self? These questions are explored through the dramatic frame of an encounter between Socrates and the young Alcibiades, in which Socrates, the erstwhile 'lover' (*erastes*) of the noble and beautiful Alcibiades, seeks to reverse his role to that of 'beloved' (*eromenos*) by convincing his friend that it is he, Socrates, who alone can ensure the satisfaction of Alcibiades's political ambitions. As Socrates says, 'Without me it is impossible for all those designs of yours to be crowned with achievement; so great is the power I conceive myself to have over your affairs and over you' (105d). But what is the nature of this power which Socrates, the penniless sage, holds over Alcibiades, the heir to one of Athens' most wealthy and prestigious families? It is, as one might expect, even in a pseudo-platonic dialogue, that Socrates knows the limits of his own knowledge. Accordingly, his first task is to demonstrate that Alcibiades does not possess the knowledge he thinks he possesses; that is, the knowledge which would give him the right to stand before the Athenian Assembly and advise it on matters of war and peace, justice and injustice. By his usual method, Socrates succeeds in getting Alcibiades to admit that not only does he not have the requisite knowledge of justice, but that he was about to embark on a political career with the false conviction that he did have this knowledge. To Socrates's insistence that, 'you are not only ignorant of the greatest things, but while not knowing them you think that you do', Alcibiades can only reply 'I am afraid so'. And Socrates drives home the point, 'you are wedded to stupidity, my fine friend, of the vilest kind; you are impeached of this by your own words, out of your own mouth' (118b). Having reduced Alcibiades to this state of self-confessed ignorance, it is now Socrates alone who has the power to restore to him the confidence which, he says, is necessary for Alcibiades's ambitions to be 'crowned with achievement' (105d). And the route to this success is, as Socrates reveals, the care of the self, a practice which Socrates alone can teach.

Socrates's next task is to convince Alcibiades that his noble birth and his 'natural powers' (119c) will not be sufficient to ensure his political success. Through an account of the lineage and education of Alcibiades's 'natural enemies' – the kings of Sparta and Persia – Socrates demonstrates that, so far as birth and upbringing are concerned, Alcibiades is much their inferior. What can he rely on, then, in this contest for ascendancy? Nothing, says Socrates, except 'care and skill' (*epimeleia* and *techne*) (124b). The education of Alcibiades, Socrates suggests, needs to be supplemented by the acquisition of this skill, or what Foucault would call this 'technique', which is the art of caring for the self. Needless to say, Alcibiades's first reaction is to demand to know what this care is which he must take; because Socrates's words are 'remarkably like the truth' (ibid). Before answering this question, however, Socrates insists that we need to know the true nature of the 'self'.[10] Appealing to the injunction to 'Know Thyself', which is inscribed over the temple at Delphi, Socrates argues 'if we have that knowledge we are likely to know what pains to take over ourselves; but if we have it not, we never can' (129a).

In a lengthy discussion, Socrates establishes the duality of body and soul, demonstrating that it is the latter which is the best, highest and truest part of ourselves; in fact, for Socrates man is 'nothing else but soul' (130c). However, knowing that the self for which one should care is the 'soul', and knowing the nature of that soul are two different matters. And in order to gain such knowledge, Socrates proposes a technique for knowing the nature of the soul, a technique which consists of self-contemplation through the medium of a reflective surface – in this case, another soul, and especially that most 'divine' part of the soul which is 'the seat of knowledge and thought' (133c). According to Socrates, what one learns in this contemplation of the soul is that its most 'divine' part finds its excellence in temperance and justice, and, what is more, that 'it is impossible to be happy if one is not temperate and good' (134a). The proper task of 'care of the self' then, to answer Alcibiades's question, is precisely the cultivation of these 'excellences' of temperance and justice. And it follows that the statesman, if he is to 'impart virtue [and hence happiness] to the citizens' must first 'acquire virtue himself' (134b–c). It is the statesman, therefore, who must be practised above all others in the arts of the care of the self; and if Alcibiades wishes his designs to be 'crowned with achievement' (105d), argues Socrates, it is not 'licence or authority' which is required, but 'justice and temperance' (134c); neither should he seek 'despotic power,' but rather 'virtue' (135b).

The three questions which, in Foucault's reading,[11] structure this text circle around the issue of the relationship between care of the self and broader cultural practices. The answers the text offers to these questions are, in Foucault's view, indicative of the Classical culture of the self, and also serve as useful points of comparison with later developments, especially in the imperial era. In answer to the first question – 'what is the relation between care of the self and political life?' – the dialogue suggests that in the Classical era (or, at least in the Socratic tradition), being practised in caring for the self was a necessary prerequisite for political life. It was this, as Socrates indicates, that guaranteed that the statesman would show, for instance, the wisdom of a Pericles. Foucault notes, however, that emphasis on the care of the self as *pre*requisite gives way in the imperial era to the idea of care of the self as a lifetime occupation. As Epicurus says, 'It is never too early or too late to take care of one's soul' (cited, *RC*, 149–51). In this eclipsing of the idea of the political motivation for the care of the self, Foucault sees the growth of the very new idea of caring for the self for its own sake. With regard to the second question around which the *Alcibiades I* turns – that is, 'how does care of the self relate to pedagogy?' – the text suggests that this technique should be seen as a supplement to the education of those with political ambition. It is Socrates's task to compensate for the 'defective pedagogy' (TS, 25) which now threatens Alcibiades's future.[12] Thus, the care of the self in the Classical era is itself, as Foucault says, *'une formation'*, an education (*RC*, 151). In contrast, during late antiquity, when the care of the self no longer applies exclusively to the young, other functions come to the fore; it becomes a set of techniques which have a life-long 'critical', 'combative' and 'curative' function (*RC*, 151–3). Finally, the *Alcibiades I* answers the third question – 'what is the relation between care of the self and knowledge of the self?' – by suggesting that the knowledge which is a necessary element of the care of the self can only be achieved in and through an 'erotic' attachment between a disciple and a master. It is Socrates's great love for Alcibiades which – even in its purified, 'platonic' form – is the driving force behind bringing Alcibiades to virtue and temperance. In late antiquity, in contrast, even though these relations between disciple and master maintain their importance, according to Foucault they lose their 'amorous' character (*RC*, 153), becoming, we could say, relations more of profound *philia* than intense *eros*.

The importance of this dialogue for Foucault is that it permits him to specify some of the key changes which occurred in ethical self-constitution between the Classical era and late antiquity. In particular, it allows him to attribute this change, not to the tightening of a code, but to an intensifica-tion and an increased valorization of 'relations of self to self (*CS*, 43[57]). It is this increased emphasis – on techniques already present in the Classical era – which gives rise, in late antiquity, to what Foucault calls a 'culture of the self';[13] that is, to a new form of ethical subjectivity which calls upon new principles of application, new ways of working upon the self and new goals for ethical life – all of which are based, to a great extent, on the application of ever more sophisticated 'practices of the self'.[14]

While it is undeniable that Foucault's reading of *Alcibiades I*, along with his subsequent account of this historical shift, makes an important contribu-tion to the history of ethics, it is nevertheless possible to question the picture presented here, especially in the light of the more general model or *grille* presented in *The Use of Pleasure*. Because what we find when we apply Foucault's model to the Alcibiades of this dialogue is the over-estimation of an 'aesthetic' motivation and the under-estimation of a 'political' one: Alcibiades emerges more as Wildean aesthete than as Machiavellian operator. I should stress that this is not a picture which is made explicit by Foucault in his own discussions of the dialogue; it is rather a picture which emerges if we apply Foucault's general model to the text. However, the advantage of putting Foucault's model to the test in this way is that it makes it possible to see the extent to which Foucault may be said to 'aestheticize' ancient ethical practices. In other words, it allows us to see exactly how Foucault goes about ensuring that the aesthetic interpretation finally seems to win out over the alternative version; a version according to which the primary concern of the practices which are analysed here would have been to guarantee the mastery of the *aristoi* – both in the *oikos* and in the *polis*.[15]

For anyone familiar with the life of the historical Alcibiades (*c.* 450–404 BC) – who appears in both the *Alcibiades I* and Plato's *Symposium* – it will come as no surprise to hear this figure spoken of as an aesthete. Plutarch, for example, recounts the description of an Alcibiades who was 'effeminate in dress and would walk through the market-place trailing his long purple robes'.[16] He also tells how Alcibiades refused to learn the flute, because using a wind instrument distorted the features of one's face – features which, in the case of Alcibiades, were universally agreed to be of 'extraordinary grace and charm' (ibid. 1). However, whether Alcibiades, the historical figure, was or was not a Periclean dandy, isn't the question we are addressing here. The question, rather, is does Foucault's characterization of Greek ethical practices, when applied to the Alcibiades of this dialogue, lead to a picture of him as, at least, what one could call an 'ethical dandy'?

Alcibiades, as we saw, is faced with a dilemma about the kind of preparations which he must make before he enters into public life. With the help of Socrates he comes to recognize and accept that this preparation consists of 'taking care of the self' – that is, an ethical practice which takes the 'divine' part of the self as an object of investigation and uses the knowledge of the truth of this divine principle as a basis for future conduct. Alcibiades must finally acknowledge that licence, authority and despotic power will bring happiness neither to him nor to the people of the city. Looking at this ethical practice – the 'care of the self' – using Foucault's fourfold division of ethics, would suggest that its 'mode of subjection' was a free, personal choice, while its telos was the creation of the self as a work of beauty. Alcibiades's decision to follow Socrates would come from a personal choice, rather than from the imposition of an external prescriptive code. Similarly, his aim in adopting Socrates's recommendation that he 'care for himself' would essentially be to give his life a certain form, perfection and beauty. Alcibiades, then, would be a figure who decides, of his own volition, to embark on a particular 'philosophical' path, in order to give his life an accomplished brilliance. But how accurate is this picture? How much evidence is there in the dialogue itself to support such an interpretation?

So far as the mode of subjection is concerned, it does appear that Socrates's task is to convince Alcibiades to *choose* the care of the self. Similarly, it does appear that Socrates cannot appeal to any universal principles according to which every individual should 'take care of himself'. On the contrary, Socrates appears to assume that it is only those who are to lead the people who must engage in this activity of care. It is only those who are 'free' (that is, citizens, non-slaves) who need to be virtuous; while 'virtue becomes a free man', Socrates says, 'vice is a thing that becomes a slave'. The question, and indeed the challenge, he poses to Alcibiades is 'are you on the side of the free, or not?' (135c). It would seem, therefore, as Foucault's model suggests, that Alcibiades is free to choose either virtue or vice, freedom or slavery. However, things are not quite as simple as that; for, not only was it impossible in the Classical era to choose to be either a free citizen or a slave, it is also clear from the beginning of the dialogue that Alcibiades is considered, both by himself and by others, to be destined to lead the people. It is never a question, for him, of choosing between a position of authority and a position of subjection. Hence, Socrates's strategy in his encounter with Alcibiades is to convince him, first of all, that this 'choice' is in his best interests, and secondly, that it is the duty of every free man, in so far as he is free, to make this choice. Far from allowing Alcibiades to express his personal preference in this matter, it is Socrates's task to show him that his personal preference – which is, for 'licence, authority and despotic power' – would in fact militate against his aims.

The 'choice' Alcibiades makes is determined by his consciousness of his position as free adult male. To the challenge, 'are you a slave, or are you free?', Alcibiades had no choice but to reply 'free', since there was no greater dishonour for a free man than to be called a 'slave'. Foucault recognizes this necessity when he explains the Greek male's 'choice' of self-mastery as 'a mastery made *obligatory* by his status or by the authority which he had to exercise in the city'.[17] Once Socrates demonstrates that virtue is on the side of freedom and vice is on the side of slavery, Alcibiades, in effect, has no further choice. As he says at the end of the dialogue, he must 'begin here and now to take pains over justice' (135e). But what, for Alcibiades, is the aim of this care? Can we really accept, as Foucault's model would suggest, that his aim is to fashion a self and a life which would have the qualities of harmony and beauty? Or, must we not recognize that, while beauty was indeed an important criterion for judging a life in Classical antiquity, it was not because it was important for its own sake. It is quite clear, for example, in the case of Alcibiades, that his final aim in engaging to 'care for himself' is to win power in the city, to gain, as he says, 'ascendancy'. Recognizing this motivation, Socrates's first move is to appeal to Alcibiades's enormous ambition, and to convince him that it is Socrates alone who has the power to help him realize his hopes of winning 'unlimited power' (105d). Against the picture Foucault's model would generate, then, Alcibiades appears to be no aesthete; he is interested more in power for its own sake than beauty for its own sake – in fact, he would seem to have more in common with Machiavelli's Prince than with Oscar Wilde.

WHAT IS 'AESTHETIC' ABOUT THE 'AESTHETICS OF EXISTENCE'?

To present ancient Greek ethics as oriented towards 'aesthetic' ends, is also to raise the inevitable question of the distance which separates modern concepts of the aesthetic from their ancient counterparts; it is to raise the question of whether there *are* any such counterparts. One could endlessly debate whether the figure of Alcibiades is closer to the pole of Machiavellian Prince or Wildean dandy; but what of the suspicion that 'Wildean dandy' is a category which can only be applied anachronistically to Classical Greece? Surely the aesthete has had a much shorter history in Western societies than the ambitious political operator?[18] It follows that if Foucault is to translate *techne tou biou* as 'aesthetics of existence', then we must ask 'what is *aesthetic* about this technique?'

In the middle of the first century AD, Seneca enjoined his friend and correspondent Lucilius to cultivate a style of life which would mark him out from the crowd; a style of life which would not be 'contrary' to the way of the crowd, but 'better' than their way. And this mark of distinction, he assures his friend, will be visible to all who look closely: 'Anyone who enters our home,' he writes, 'will admire us rather than our furniture.'[19] In the late 1870s, at Oxford, Oscar Wilde began to cultivate a style of life which was dedicated to beauty and he quickly became notorious (and notoriously admired) for his reported complaint: 'I find it harder and harder every day to live up to my blue china.'[20] The question I now wish to address is the difference between Seneca's and Wilde's concern to outshine their furniture; and whether Foucault takes this difference sufficiently into account when he speaks of the ancient 'aesthetics of existence'. In other words, when Foucault translates the Greek term *techne* by 'art' or 'aesthetic', and the Greek phrase '*techne tou biou*' as 'aesthetics of existence', is he reading too modern a notion of art and creativity into the Greek conception of 'craft'?

The first point that must be made is that ancient Greek and Roman thought, especially ethical thought, makes much use of the semantic possibilities of the terms *techne* (craft, skill, knowledge, art) and *kalon* (fine, beautiful, worthy – and therefore 'good'). I will suggest, however, that interpretations of this strand of ancient thought all turn on the kind of aesthetic theory one attributes to its proponents. And I will ask whether Foucault's success in making the ancients appear to be an early chapter in the history of the 'arts of the self' – in other words, in making them appear to be precursors of Wilde – may not be because he interprets their 'aesthetic' pronouncements through the lens of a modern aesthetic sensibility.

Is it as a result of such an interpretation that Alcibiades, for example, can be presented more as aesthete than as Machiavellian political operator?

Foucault's claims about the aesthetic motivation of Greek practices of the self rest primarily on his interpretation of two key terms in Greek thought: *techne* and *kalon*. If we follow Foucault in straightforwardly translating *techne* as 'art' and *kalon* as 'beautiful' then we might be led to believe that the aim of ethics in antiquity was indeed the 'elaboration of one's own life as a personal work of art' (AE, 49[731]). If we look more closely at the way these terms were used, however, we might come to see that Foucault's interpretation is open to doubt.[21] In Classical Greek thought, for example, Plato draws extensively on the concept of craft or skill in his discussions of virtue – and especially in his discussion of justice. This is an approach which is made possible, initially, by the fact that Socrates regularly treats the virtues as 'crafts' or 'skills' which can usefully be compared to other crafts, such as horse-training, shoemaking or medicine. And, since this type of comparison is never met with by any surprise on the part of his inter-locuters, we can assume that to treat courage or piety as 'skills' comparable to, say, shoemaking was to remain well within the possibilities of the term *techne*. This mobilization of the notion of *techne* takes on even more impor-tance in the dialogues Plato wrote in his 'middle period'. Here, Plato develops most fully what has come to be called the 'craft analogy': the idea that the practice of virtue, in general, can be usefully considered as anala-gous to the practice of any other 'craft' or *techne*.[22]

In the most general terms, we can say that what this analogy makes possible is the conceptualization of the good man as he who knows his 'materials' (since *techne* always implies knowledge, or a particular relation to truth), and as he who possesses the skill required to put his life together in such a way that it will bring its 'craftsman' both happiness and prosperity. When put in these general terms, this is a framework for understanding ethics which can be detected not only in Socratic philosophy, but also in Aristotle, Stoicism and even neo-Platonism. In the *Nichomachean Ethics*, for example, Aristotle compares the good man's adaptation to circumstances to the shoemaker who 'makes the neatest shoe out of the leather supplied to him'.[23] And he compares virtue to an art which, like other crafts, aims to hit the mean – although in a 'more exact and more efficient way'.[24] Similarly, the late Stoic authors continuously draw on the possibilities of the craft analogy. So, Epictetus explains the 'art of living' in this way: 'For as wood is the material of the carpenter, bronze that of the statuary, just so each man's life is the subject matter of the art of living'.[25] And in his role of teacher, Epictetus presents himself as a craftsman who will mould his students: he wishes 'to make of [them] a perfect work' – 'Here also then is the craftsman, and here is the material: what do we yet lack?'[26] Seneca, working in the same tradition as Epictetus, both equates philosophy with the other 'arts' and places it far above them: 'She [philosophy] is not, say I, the artisan of the appliances of our daily use; why attribute such trifles to her? In her you see the artificer of life.'[27] And by the training in philosophy which he has given to Lucilius, through their correspondence, he claims him as his very own 'handiwork'.[28] The idea that virtue is a 'skill in living' (*techne tou biou*) is, then, not only a central tenet of Stoicism, it is also an idea which appears in myriad forms throughout Classical and Hellenistic antiquity.[29]

This claim is in itself quite unexceptional: not even Foucault's most trenchant critics would deny that this theme maintains a constant presence in ancient thought. But what of the suggestion that this craft, this art of living, has as its end an 'aesthetic' effect? How easily can Foucault be allowed to maintain this? In order to respond to these questions, we must firstly recognize that there is a great deal of overlap, particularly in the Classical era, between the ideas of beauty and of moral worth. Indeed, a single word covers both meanings – *kalos*. One of the best illustrations of the ambivalence of this term is provided in Plato's early dialogue, the *Hippias Major*.[30] Here Socrates is seeking a definition of *to kalon* – which Woodruff translates as 'the fine' but which could just as easily be translated as 'the beautiful'. In this case, the difficulty of finding a satisfactory definition comes not only from the nature of Socrates's demand, but also from the fundamental ambivalence of the term itself: hence the suggested definitions for *to kalon* range from 'a fine [beautiful] girl' (287e4), through 'the appropriate itself' (293e5) and 'the beneficial' (296e6), to 'that which is pleasant through hearing and sight' (298a6). In other words, it oscillates between the morally good and the aesthetically beautiful. It is a term, therefore, which is rich in semantic potential, and this potential is fully exploited by Greek thought.

In the aristocratic concept of the *kaloskagathos*, for example, we find the combination of the value judgements 'fine' (*kalos*) and 'good' (*agathos*) with the notion that such a person will necessarily also be 'beautiful' (*kalos*).[31] However, not only are the good and the beautiful combined in this concept, they are also made to coincide. Plato, for example, points out the 'obvious' fact that: 'The good, of course, is always beautiful, and the beautiful never lacks proportion. A living creature that is to have either quality must therefore be well-proportioned' (*Timaeus*, 87c). And in the discussion of the best education for the Guardians of his Republic, Socrates asks 'is not the fairest sight of all ... for him who has eyes to see it, the combination in the same bodily form of beauty of character and looks to match and harmonize with it?' (*Republic*, 402d). This idea, that moral character can (although not necessarily) manifest in bodily form is a basic assumption of the Classical ideal. As Jean-Pierre Vernant points out, the term *kaloskagathos* underlines the idea that 'physical beauty and moral superiority being indissociable, the latter can be evaluated simply by looking at the former'.[32]

In late Stoicism we again encounter this idea. Seneca reprimands the Epicureans, who have mistakenly given pleasure precedence over reason, with the 'aesthetic' crime of having elevated 'a thing spineless and ignoble, a monstrous hybrid ... compounded of ill-assorted and badly joined members' to the status of supreme good.[33] And Epictetus exhorts his followers to abandon fine clothes and cosmetics in favour of adorning their reason, their 'moral purpose': 'if you get that beautiful, then you will be beautiful'.[34] Perhaps the best example of this aestheticism of late antiquity is Plotinus's neo-platonist discussion of 'care of the self' in terms of 'modelling one's own statue':

> And if you do not find yourself beautiful yet, act as does the creator of a statue that is to be made beautiful: he cuts away here, he smooths there, he makes this line lighter, this other purer, until a lovely face has grown upon his work. So do you also: cut away all that is excessive, straighten all that is crooked, bring light to all that is overcast, labour to make all one glow of beauty and never cease chiselling your statue ... When you know that you have become this perfect work ... nothing now remaining that can shatter that inner unity ... When you perceive that you have grown to this ... strain, and see ... This is the only eye that sees the mighty beauty (Plotinus).[35]

No other ancient vision of the self as a work of art could correspond so closely with the passage from Nietzsche which I quoted in the Introduction (p. 2) – in which the self is a scene from which some features are removed, some are added and others are modified and 'realigned', in order to produce an effect of beauty for the eye.[36] But does this imply that these two visions are essentially the same? Or, more importantly, does it imply that the ancient themes of virtue as an 'art' and the good as 'beautiful' justify an aestheticist reading of that tradition?

On the one hand, there is some evidence to suggest that it does. Arnold Hauser, for example, suggests that Plato's hostility towards the arts is merely a sign of his opposition towards the 'prevalent aestheticism' of his day. Plato's attack – the 'first example of "iconoclasm" in history' – appeared along with 'the first signs of an aestheticising outlook on life in which art not merely has its place, but grows at the expense of all the other forms of culture.'[37] According to this interpretation, Plato's expulsion of the poets from his ideal city was no more than a protective measure against the encroachment of the 'aesthetic' on the political and the ethical realms. If Plato is reacting against a growing emphasis on what for him is the illusion of empirical phenomena, and a growing valorization of sensation (*aesthesis*), then it is perhaps not surprising that certain forms of philosophy today are also unwilling to grant sensory experience – especially of the beautiful – equal status alongside reason and the ideal. Perhaps this is what is at stake when, for example, Julia Annas insists that the best translation of *techne* is not 'art' but 'craft';[38] and when English translators consistently give 'fine' for *kalos*, whereas their French counterparts prefer 'beautiful'.

This latter phenomenon, which is also clear in the work of French commentators on ancient philosophy and ethics,[39] appears most strikingly when we compare Foucault's French texts with the English translations. In *The History of Sexuality*, volume III, for example, Foucault speaks of a certain Thrasea Paetus who, according to Foucault, committed suicide with the help of a philosopher in order to give 'a son existence sa forme la plus belle et la mieux achevée' ('to give to his life the most beautiful and most accomplished form') (*CS*, 52[68]). However, this is translated by Robert Hurley as 'give his life its finest and most accomplished form'. Similarly, in *The History of Sexuality*, volume II, Foucault quotes Plato's *Laws* (783e) as: parents must give to the city 'les enfants les plus beaux et les meilleurs possibles' ('the most beautiful and the best children possible') (*UP*, 123[140]). The English translation has: 'the noblest and best children possible. The question naturally arises here as to why English translators of ancient texts and commentaries automatically translate *kalos* and its derivatives as fine or noble, while French translators seem to consistently prefer beautiful.[40] 'While this question is beyond our present scope, it can at least be said that Foucault, in emphasizing the 'aesthetic' dimension of ancient thought, is perhaps doing no more than exploiting possibilities inherent in that thought and, particularly, in its reception by French-speaking philosophers and historians. The question might then become, not 'why does Foucault aestheticize the Greeks?', but 'why have English speaking philosophers been for so long blind (or hostile) to this theme?'

If we suppose that Foucault is quite right to draw attention to the 'aesthetic' theme in ancient thought, and that the ancients did indeed conceptualize ethics as a form-giving work on the self, we are still faced with a question about the difference between *their* conception of a 'work of art' (which could be a chair, a table, an athlete, a virtuous character, or one's life) and 'our' conception of such a work which, as Foucault points out, can be few of these things: 'Why should the lamp or the house be an art object, but not our life?' (OGE, 350). The core of the problem is that to call such a work 'aesthetic' as Foucault does is, firstly, to prioritize the idea that the work's value comes from its appearance, its form, the effect it produces in the viewer or the listener through sensation – *aesthesis*. And, secondly, it is to prefer that approach to the practice and reception of art which has ensured that, precisely, only objects can be considered as works of art.

The distance traversed between Plato's early discussion of the multiple meanings of *kalos* in the *Hippias Major*, and the array of philosophical and critical assumptions which, for example, Wilde had at his disposal is enormous. For Plato the serious attempts to define 'the beautiful/fine' ranged from 'the useful', through 'that which is beneficial', to 'that which is pleasant to hearing and sight'. The 'beautiful/fine' is as much an aesthetic as a moral phenomenon – and one which is not confined to lamps and houses. Indeed, its highest manifestations are in those individuals whose bodily form and moral character combine in the most pleasing, most useful and most beneficial excellence. Not only did the Greeks have no conception of an 'aesthetic sphere' as opposed to a 'moral sphere', but in their art practices they did not rely on a specialized notion of the 'fine arts' as opposed to utilitarian craft.[41] It would seem that they had too much respect for *techne* and *poesis* to leave it entirely in the hands of 'artists'. In the modern period, however, art has been transformed both theoretically and practically. The idea that the artist is the specialist producer of non-utilitarian objects of aesthetic pleasure is, despite the best efforts of avant-garde art movements, still dominant. And the Baudelairean and Wildean concepts of an art of the self – which Foucault associates with ancient Greek ethics – embraced most of the assumptions of nineteenth-century aesthetics. That is, despite the fact that their approach was necessarily an attack on the autonomy of the aesthetic sphere, it is arguable that the aesthetic principles which they wished to apply to the self were not significantly different from contemporary approaches to art. Wilde, for example, wanted to produce a self and a style of life which could be aesthetically appreciated – just as one would appreciate a painting by Whistler or a vase from Sèvres. But is this what Alcibiades wanted? And is it what Foucault wants for us today?

The question we must ask is whether presenting the Greek idea of a *techne tou biou* as an 'aesthetics of existence' does not align it too much with a practice and a philosophy of art to which it is completely alien. And, in so doing, does it not tend to produce an excessively 'distorted' view of Greek ethical practices? Now that we have a clear question, we shouldn't be too disappointed to find that a clear answer becomes impossible. On the one hand, it is undoubtedly the case that this theme was present, in varying forms, throughout Classical and Hellenistic antiquity. On the other hand, we have already seen that an overly 'aestheticizing' reading of these practices can lead to the presentation of a power-hungry, ambitious 'politician' like Alcibiades as something of an aesthete *avant la lettre*. However, we may find that somewhere between these two extremes, somewhere between the technical form-giving of the Greeks and the aesthetic pleasure-giving of Wilde, there is a conception of ethics which conceives of a form-giving art without object. And such an art, when applied to the self, might be what Foucault intends when he speaks of an 'aesthetics of existence'.

To investigate this possibility, in the next two chapters I will engage in a close reading of *The History of Sexuality*, volumes II and III, in order to determine not so much how aestheticist were the Greeks, but how aestheticist is Foucault. In other words, notwithstanding all the striking formulations of the interviews, is Foucault's reading of ancient ethics really a 'distortion' of the truth, or is it simply an interpretation which picks out certain 'neglected' themes, connects them with present concerns, and thus says something of both historical and contemporary importance? That is, that our present modes of relation to the self are not only historically specific (and therefore changeable), but that they have blinded us to the possibility that other societies (in this case Greece) may have cultivated other modes of subjectivity – a knowledge of which might be useful to us today. The apparent anachronism in Foucault's 'aesthetics of existence' then, may be no more than an effect of the shock which a new interpretation inevitably brings. Indeed, the problem may not be that Foucault reads the Greeks through the lens of modern aesthetics, but that standard interpretations persist in reading them through the lens of modern subjectivities. In that case, we might find that Foucault's understanding of aesthetics is neither Greek nor modern – nor even Nietzschean.

CHAPTER 3

The Style of Domination

One recognizes the superiority of the Greeks ... but one would like to have them without the causes and conditions that made them possible.

Friedrich Nietzsche[1]

It's a good thing to have nostalgia toward some periods on the condition that it's a way to have a thoughtful and positive relation to your own present.

Michel Foucault (TPS, 12)

Volumes II and III of *The History of Sexuality* span seven hundred years of history; they deal with a period which is at an enormous cultural and historical remove from us; they focus, like all Foucault's histories, on texts from fields as diverse as philosophy, medicine, 'economics', and literature; they attempt to give an account, both in overview and in a certain amount of detail, of a major transformation in the way that individuals in Western culture relate to themselves as subjects of ethics; consequently, they lay themselves open to endless re-evaluation on the grounds of historical 'accuracy'. In this chapter, I will begin to explore the possibility that any 'misinterpretations' Foucault's account includes are not due to unconnected misunderstandings or isolated errors on his part. In this analysis of Foucault's ancients, it will not be a question of locating and cataloguing a series of minor lapses of scholarship in Foucault's work; rather it will be a question of suggesting that his interpretations are all determined by the same motivating factor and that, through a close reading of the texts, we can observe the precise way in which he arrives at them. In short, I will explore the extent to which Foucault's interpretation of ancient ethics may be said to be coloured by his commitment to 'a new form of dandyism'.[2]

THE ABSENCE OF POWER

One way of formulating the peculiarities of Foucault's picture of Alcibiades is to say that it neglects the question of the way in which relations to self intersect with power relations. This idea, that power is, in an important sense, 'absent' from Foucault's late work is a familiar one. Martha Nussbaum, for example, notes with dismay that Foucault seems to have retreated from his earlier views about 'the inseparability of ideas and institutions'.[3] Foucault's account, in her view, is 'disappointing' and 'mediocre' due, in part, to its neglect of the social and political context of the authors whose writings it discusses. David Halperin, although he is far from sharing Nussbaum's hostility towards Foucault's work, concedes that in Foucault's readings of ancient texts the 'relative neglect of the authors' social context or purpose in writing' is a cause for 'justifiable alarm'.[4] This perception, however, is not confined to classical scholars. Thomas Flynn, for example, recognizes that if it were not for his 'insistent nominalism', one would perhaps be able to see Hegel replacing Nietzsche as the inspiration for Foucault's late work; in other words, Foucault's Nietzschean genealogies are dangerously close to becoming Hegelian histories.[5] Similarly, Jon Simons notes the uncharacteristically 'apolitical' position which arises from Foucault's determination to 'separate ethics as much as possible from the axis of political power in his analysis of Greek and Hellenist [sic] arts of the self'.[6] This kind of argument about the 'absence of power' commonly serves either to undermine or deny the value of Foucault's account of Greek ethics – Nussbaum's strategy – or to argue for an incoherence or inconsistency on Foucault's part – the strategy of Peter Dews.[7]

There is, however, a strong textual basis for arguing that Foucault's relative neglect of key issues, such as the institutional bases and the political motivations of ancient ethical practices, should be understood as a shift in perspective in relation to earlier principles, rather than as a rejection of those principles. In several of the late interviews (RM, ECS, OGE), as well as in the introduction to *The Use of Pleasure*, Foucault offers an interpretation of his entire intellectual development which tries to integrate and explain his latest turn – towards the question of subjectivity – in terms of his concern with the way human subjectivity is constituted through 'games of truth [*jeux de vérité*]' (ECS, 112[708]). It was only in his work from the early 1980s, he claims, that he began to deal with this problem 'in its generality', and that he came to recognize how each phase of his work hitherto had been concerned with a different aspect of this general problem. In *The Order of Things* he had looked at the way in which the human subject is defined through scientific discourse as a working, living, speaking individual, while in *Madness and Civilization* and *Discipline and Punish* he had examined the way in which coercive practices produced the truth of mad or deviant subjects. Finally, in volumes II and III of *The History of Sexuality*, he looked at the relation between subjectivity and truth through the way in which subjects constitute themselves using certain techniques or practices of the self (ECS, 113[709]). Corresponding to each of these aspects is what Foucault, by the early 1980s, calls a 'domain', or an 'axis', of genealogy (OGB, 351–2). Each axis corresponds to one possible way of analysing and understanding the games of truth through which our experience is constituted; through which 'being is historically constituted as experience' (*UP*, 6[13]). Genealogy, in this schema, becomes a threefold mode of analysis which can be applied to any field of human experience, whether it be our experience of ourselves as living beings, as deviants, or as subjects of desire. Depending on which axis is being pursued, its privileged domain will be either truth, power, or relations to the self; or, using different terminology, its domain will be theoretical games of truth, practices of power, or practices of the self (ECS, ibid.).

For our present purposes, the important point to be made about this new conceptualization, is that Foucault sees his late work as investigating the third of these axes and, hence, it may be thought to be unreasonable to expect the analysis he develops there to include a consideration of the other two domains. In other words, if, in previous works, he has practised a genealogy along one or other of the first two axes, then in his late works he is practising a genealogy which concentrates almost exclusively on the axis of relations to the self, to the exclusion of relations of coercion, or relations between different truth games. On this account, we would excuse Foucault for his apparent neglect of issues of power in volumes II and III of *The History of Sexuality* on the basis that these volumes are by necessity partial and incomplete genealogies of the subject of ethics.

But Foucault cannot be so easily excused. We cannot so easily assume that he saw his work in such a 'compartmentalized' way; we cannot conclude from his discussion of the three axes of genealogy that he saw each of his works as operating *exclusively* along one of these axes. In relation to *Madness and Civilization*, for example, Foucault says that 'all three' axes were present, although 'in a somewhat confused fashion' (OGE, 352). Despite the fact that he goes on to say that *The Birth of the Clinic* studied the axis of truth, while *Discipline and Punish* developed the axis of power, he nevertheless maintains the inextricability of the three domains. In his last interview, no doubt with the benefit of hindsight, Foucault insists that 'these three domains of experience can only be understood in relation to each other and they cannot be understood without each other' (RM, 243[697]). Indeed, what bothered him about his previous books was that because they did not take the third domain into account they had to resort to 'somewhat rhetorical methods' in order to cover up this exclusion. His hope now is that, with the inclusion of the axis of relations to the self, this form of evasion will no longer be necessary. It is clear that Foucault's ideal is a work which would incorporate all three axes, a genealogy which would not have to deny any of the fundamental domains of experience. And the question arises, then, of whether or not the last two volumes of *The History of Sexuality* do indeed operate along the three possible axes of genealogy, or whether it is possible to discern here also the operation of certain 'rhetorical methods' which compensate for the exclusion of one of the domains. In the section which follows, I will suggest that in his emphasis on the axis of relations to the self, Foucault does indeed seem to exclude (or, at least, to downplay) a consideration of the axis of power relations.

MASTER MORALITY

In his discussion of the theme of self-mastery (*enkrateia*), Foucault recognizes that self-mastery, both as a theme and as a social practice, is inseparable from the mastery of others; the *askesis* of the self, or the individual, is inseparable from the *askesis* of the citizen, or the individual aristocrat in the polis.[8] The inseparability of these two forms of mastery is underlined by Jean-Pierre Vernant, who argues that the Classical practice of moral training 'is born, develops and only makes sense, within the framework of the city'. Therefore, it is impossible to separate 'training in virtue' from the 'civic education' which prepares one for the life of a free man.[9] Similarly, Walter Donlan, in his study of aristocracy in Greek society,[10] points out that while the *aristoi* considered themselves to be above the common people (including the less wealthy free citizens), they never considered themselves to be apart from the polis. Indeed, 'aristocrat and non-aristocrat alike agreed that a man existed to serve the community. The disagreement was over who did this best, which element should hold which relative position'.[11] The training in virtue, self-control and temperance which the cultural and political elite embarked on, was intimately connected with their role in the polis, and it was intimately connected for a very precise reason. As Plato warns in the *Laws*, those who are not practised from an early age in the arts of self-mastery will find themselves not only slaves of their own passions, but, more shamefully, they will be slaves of 'those who *can* remain strong in the midst of pleasures, those who are masters of the art of using them' (635c–d).[12] What is at stake in the ethical self-constitution of the subject is not only one's *rapport à soi*, but also and perhaps most importantly, one's relation to others. It is impossible to distinguish – at least in the case of Classical Greece – what Foucault, in another context, calls 'the government of the self' from 'the government of others'[13] – and Foucault was well aware of this impossibility.

As I have insisted, Foucault is by no means unaware of this aspect of Greek sexual ethics. Readers such as Simon Goldhill can remark, as if it was self-evident, that the 'cornerstone of Foucauldian analysis of ancient sexuality' is the focus on 'the violence and power-play of penetration'.[14] In a similar vein, David Halperin argues that 'Foucault ... sees the Greek moralists in terms of a will to power, a strategy for achieving domination of self and others';[15] and this, he suggests, is the 'key' to Foucault's view of ancient ethics. Foucault certainly recognizes that the mode of being, or telos, towards which the work of ethical self-constitution aimed, was a state of active freedom which was made possible by the 'power that one exercises on oneself in the power that one exercises on others' (UP, 80[93]). The contrary of this mode of being was the state of slavery – whether vis-à-vis oneself or others. Consequently, the principle that only those who can govern themselves are worthy of governing others was applied in every area of life. In Plato's Republic, for example, the artisan who cannot control the 'animal part' of his soul must be placed under the authority of those who can (cited in UP, 80[93–4]). Similarly, despite the fact that women do participate to an extent in the virtue of temperance (sophrosune), according to both Plato and Aristotle (see Foucault's discussion, UP, 84[97–8]), they participate in it in a subordinate way and must therefore, like the artisan, be subject to the superior virtue of the temperate man. At the political level also, the polis (if it is to be well ordered) must be governed by those who can govern themselves. It is for this and no other reason that Plato looks forward to the advent of philosopher-kings – because, of all men, it is philosophers who exercise the most perfect self-mastery and who, therefore, are most worthy of being entrusted with public office.[16]

This isomorphism between self-mastery and mastery of the other is a feature of Greek ethics which takes on central importance in the field of sexuality. As many historians have pointed out, this entire field is governed by the primary opposition active/passive, penetrator/penetrated and dominator/dominated. One of Foucault's most sustained discussions of this opposition occurs in volume III, The Care of the Self, in relation to a text which comes not from the Classical Greek era but from the second century AD. Foucault opens volume III with a discussion of this text, the Dream Analysis of Artemidorus, in order to point to the continuities between Classical and Hellenistic sexual ethics. In this text, he says, we find 'the principal characteristics of the [Classical] moral experience of the aphrodisia' (CS, 36[49]).[17] Artemidoros's treatment of dreams of sexual activity clearly corroborates the view that, in Classical Greece, sexual activity was understood primarily in terms of the active/passive dichotomy. For Artemidoros, to penetrate a sexual partner is, in general, good (it augurs well for the future), while to be penetrated is, in general, bad. If a man dreams of having sex with his wife or his slave (whether male or female), this is a good omen since it signifies the pleasure/profit one takes in one's possessions. This is the case even if the act, in waking life, is subject to a strong social prohibition. Hence, 'to penetrate one's brother, whether older or younger, is good for the dreamer; for he will be above his brother and will look down on him'.[18] Conversely, to be penetrated by a slave, or by any other social inferior, is bad since, as Artemidoros says, 'it is the custom to give to such' and not, presumably, to 'take'.[19] Similarly, Kenneth Dover, in his *Greek Homosexuality*,[20] discusses the Classical use of sodomy as symbolic of domination or victory over an adversary. In particular, he refers to an attic red-figure vase which depicts a Greek soldier holding his half-erect penis as he approaches a Persian soldier who is bending over and saying 'I am Eurymedon, I stand bent over.' This vase refers to the Greek victory over the Persians in the fifth century and Dover glosses its caption as 'We've buggered the Persians!'[21] The practice of certain sexual acts, then, especially between males, clearly signified relations of domination.

However, not only does Artemidoros's text attest to an unquestioned assumption of the active/passive distinction, it also attests to the close connection which was drawn between this distinction as it operated in the domain of the *aphrodisia* and in the social domain. Indeed, in Foucault's view, there is in this regard a 'consubstantiality' between the sexual and the social domains (*CS*, 28[42]). Put simply, one could say that those who occupied a politically and socially dominant role were 'obliged' to be equally active and dominant in their use of the *aphrodisia*. In one of the most revealing studies of this aspect of the Greek use of pleasure, John Winkler demonstrates that the Greek male – or, at least, the aristocratic male who was interested in vying for power in the city – was subject to a complex set of 'manhood rules' which were imposed not only by public legal procedures, but also by gossip and close, critical observation by one's peers.[22] These rules were based on the assumption that in the practice of the *aphrodisia* there is always an active/dominant partner who 'does things to' and 'takes pleasure in' the passive/submissive partner. While it might be tempting here to assume that this active/passive distinction mapped directly onto the male/female gender distinction, Winkler argues that at least from the point of view of the dominant male culture there was no such absolute distinction. Rather, 'maleness' or masculinity was a hard-won achievement, an achievement which one was always in danger of losing through the temptation to 'desert one's side' (ibid., 182). Hence, male and female are two poles of a continuum and the slightest relaxation can lead to a slide towards the lower end of the scale, towards the *kinaidos*, the male of effeminate and cowardly character. Another way of making this point would be to say that, at least for politically elite males, the distinction which ultimately governed all social relations was not that between male and female, but that between ruler and ruled. In relation to sexuality, then, it was not because one was a man that one had an 'obligation' to be the active partner; because, in fact, that 'obligation' was only ever enforced in the case of those who wished to rule. Rather, it was only those who wished to convince their peers that they were worthy of public office who had to be able to show that they were active and dominant in all areas of their private lives. Two examples will serve to illustrate this point.

Firstly, Foucault, Winkler and Dover[23] all discuss a speech which Aiskhines delivered at Athens in 345 BC, in order to prevent a certain Timarchos from becoming a *rhetor*. The rank of Speaker (*rhetor*) was informally 'awarded' to those members of the Assembly who wished to take a leading role in the city's affairs; that is, to those who not only listened and voted, but also spoke in favour of proposals and had the opportunity to introduce new legislation. It was, therefore, a crucial step for anyone with political ambitions, and anyone who wished to take this step could be subjected to a *dokimasia*, or a 'test'. One of the conditions of this test was that the person in question should not have accepted money from another man in return for sexual favours. And, since to prostitute oneself in this way was, clearly, to accept a submissive role in relation to another man, to allow him to 'take' his sexual pleasure, it was equally clear – to Classical Athenians – that such a person was unfit to manage the city's affairs. Even though such practices were never strictly speaking illegal in Athens, they were specifically prohibited for those who wished to be political leaders. What Aristophanes mockingly calls 'anus-surveillance'[24] was only ever applied to this group, and to the extent that members of this group *did* limit their sexual activity, they did so primarily out of a concern to maintain their reputation and thus to ensure their prospects for political advancement.

The second example comes from *The Use of Pleasure* and also concerns sexual relations between men – or, in this case, between men and boys. Foucault's discussion of the *aphrodisia* as they are used between men centres around what he calls the 'antinomy of the boy' (*UP*, 221[243]). Foucault, following Dover, shows that the practice of erotic relations between adult and adolescent males was extremely problematic for the Greeks. In fact, it was this form of sexual relation, more than any other, which gave rise to concern, anxiety and, hence, philosophical and ethical reflection. The reason for this problematization was that at the centre of this form of relation – which was not only socially valorized, but also involved a high degree of social ritual – the boy (the free-born boy, that is) occupied a paradoxical and dangerous position. On the one hand he was expected to take the submissive and passive role of object of pleasure for the older man (he was not even 'allowed' to enjoy the experience); while, on the other hand, he was expected, as soon as he reached manhood, to adopt the role of active mastery in his own *oikos* and in the city. In other words, the fact that sexual relations were viewed according to a model of domination/submission, and that social relations were viewed in the same way, implied that a boy who had been rendered submissive in sex could not, later on, become dominant in society. If one wished to rule, then, it was important never (or, at least, only under special circumstances) to submit to the will of another.

It is precisely the uncovering of this relation between domination of the self and domination of others that is one of Foucault's major contributions to the understanding of Classical sexual ethics. If one is always in danger of being taken over by desire, then one must engage in a whole series of techniques and practices which help one to master oneself – one's appetites and one's drives. The state of being towards which these techniques aim is a state of temperance (*sophrosune*), but it is a state which is in no way static. Rather, it is an active mode of being in which one governs that which ought to be governed in oneself (appetite), in order to govern that which ought to be governed in the city (one's social and political inferiors). There was, Foucault says, 'a close connection between the superiority which one exercised over oneself, that which one exercised in the context of the household, and that which one exercised in the field of agonistic social relations' (*CS*, 94–5[116]). Indeed, it was the mastery which one exercised over oneself that guaranteed one's right and ability to exercise mastery in the other two domains. As Foucault insists, this is a thoroughly masculinist ethic; it is an ethic which is created 'by men' and 'for men'. Its supreme virtue, temperance (*sophrosune*), is in the fullest sense a 'man's virtue' (*UP*, 83[96]). It is nothing more than the ability to act as a 'man' towards oneself, just as one acts as a 'man' towards others. There is, then, a continuum between 'sexual virility', 'social virility' and 'ethical virility' (ibid.); or, we could say, between sexual mastery, social mastery and ethical self-mastery. It is for this reason that Foucault, along with Dover, argues that the principal dividing line between virile and effeminate men was not the gender of their sexual partners (that is, their 'hetero-' or 'homosexuality') but the degree to which they were active or passive, dominant or submissive. Hence, 'active homosexuality' was not only accepted but was culturally valorized, while 'passive homosexuality' was both against nature (*para phusin*) and a betrayal of one's status as free male; 'what constitutes, in the eyes of the Greeks, the ethical negativity par excellence ... [is] to be passive in relation to the pleasures' (*UP*, 85–6[99]).

It is crucial for Foucault that this was not only a question of making sure one was always 'on top of' the other, it also – as he goes to great pains to show – involved a work of getting 'on top of' oneself. In other words, the form of relation to self which was required by the Classical use of the *aphrodisia*, was one of combat, struggle and eventual domination. Taking the third aspect of Foucault's fourfold division of ethics – the forms of elaboration of self – we can say that this elaboration was characterized by an agonistic attitude towards the self, or at least towards that part of the self which was unruly. That is, the required attitude was one of hostility and opposition towards one's pleasures (*hedonai*, not *aphrodisia*) and desires (*epithumiai*).

Foucault's reading of Xenophon, Plato and Aristotle suggests that, despite varying theorizations of the status and origin of these unruly drives, the metaphors used to represent this struggle with oneself invariably came either from the domain of military activity or from wrestling. Hence, there was general agreement that the virtuous (that is, temperate) subject must gain and maintain control and mastery over that part of himself (different expectations functioned in the case of women) which threatened to usurp the role of reason. In effect, the individual was engaging in a battle or contest and was expected to be victorious; and the most glorious of victories was that which one gained over oneself, while the most shameful and cowardly of defeats was when one was vanquished by oneself (*UP*, 69[80]). In short, virtue and temperance require that one maintain with oneself a relation of ' "domination–submission", "command–obedience", "mastery-docility" ' (*UP*, 70[82]); in this ethical system, the ethical subject takes on an ' "heautocratic" structure' (ibid.).[25]

We have seen that, in the Classical era, sexual practice itself functioned as a 'game' of domination–submission; that social relations were seen (at least by the political elite) in the same way;[26] and that in the philosophical elaboration of questions of ethics, individuals were enjoined to adopt the same attitude in relation to themselves. The question we must now ask is *why* did anyone (no matter how small a number) adopt the 'heautocratic' relation to self that (at least) the Socratic tradition proposed? In the previous chapter we saw that Foucault, at least some of the time, suggests that this attitude of ethical self-constitution was adopted for aesthetic reasons; that one worked on oneself *in order to* give oneself a certain style, a certain brilliance, a certain beauty. But, does not the close connection which the Greeks themselves drew between domination of the self and domination of others force one to suspect that there was a more 'political' (and more unsavoury) motivation for this work on the self? It is clear from Xenophon, Plato and Aristotle – if not from Foucault's presentation of them – that active mastery was the aim, not only of the *chresis* of the *aphrodisia* and the *techniques de soi*, but also of the modes of regulating relations with others. It would even appear that self-mastery was the aim of the techniques of the self simply because of the contribution it could make to the mastery of others. Isn't it the case that the 'style' which Foucault says the Classical Greeks wished to cultivate was more a 'style of domination' than a politically neutral or, from a contemporary perspective, an ethically useful 'style of life'? Why does Foucault insist that the Classical Greek male practised an austerity inspired by the will to give his life a certain beauty and grandeur – rather than an austerity inspired by the will to maintain what we can call the isomorphism between sexual and social domination? That is, to put it crudely, the will to make sure that one was not 'fucked with', either in the home or in the polis.

In the light of these questions, we can no longer consider Foucault's central question ('why did the Greeks develop a sexual austerity?') without taking account of: the fact that those who cultivated this austerity were a tiny minority, not only of the entire (Athenian) population, but even of the political elite; and that they did so consistently in terms of a reflection upon what it is that makes one fit to rule. Such a consideration would almost inevitably recall the analysis Nietzsche develops in *The Genealogy of Morals* of the emergence of the aristocratic value judgement 'good'. Surely it is not by chance that, in Athens, the 'good' man was, necessarily, a member of the political elite – at least until the middle of the fourth century BC. And surely Nietzsche's characterization of the general features of the 'aristocratic value equation' fits perfectly the ethical experience of Classical Greece. Nietzsche's characterization of the values of the pre-Christian master morality – 'good = noble = powerful = beautiful = blessed'[27] – is a perfect match with the values of the Classical Greek aristocracy. Here, too, the good (*agathos*) man is necessarily noble (well-born, *eugenes*), powerful (*dynatos*), beautiful (*kalos*) and blessed (*eudaimon*).

This is particularly clear, for instance, in the fifth century emergence of the term *kaloskagathos* as an epithet exclusive to the nobility. As Donlan points out,[28] this term combines the traditional, but contested, idea that the aristocrat is the *agathos* (good man), with the indisputably aristocratic quality of *kalos* (fine, beautiful, distinguished, elegant). If, in the fifth century, it was no longer the case that all aristocrats (*aristoi*/best) were 'good', it was at least the case that they could claim to be *kaloikagathoi* (the beautiful-good, or as Donlan and others suggest, 'gentlemen' in the eighteenth-century sense of the term). Along with this claim, Donlan shows, there went the necessary development of a 'cult of aristocratic exclusiveness that permeated every aspect of social behaviour' (ibid., 156). In every arena, from the all-male *symposia* of which Plato writes, to the elaborate rituals of the courtship of boys; from the cultivation of male physical beauty (*gymnastike*), to the development of a 'liberal' education (*mousike*); from the valorization of temperance (*sophrosune*), to the discourse of self-mastery (*enkrateia*), the adult male aristocrat proved his worth in the polis and justified his claim to authority.

If, as Nietzsche argues in *The Genealogy of Morals*, a critique of moral values must investigate 'morality as result, as symptom, as mask, as tartuffery, as sickness, as misunderstanding; but also morality as cause, remedy, stimulant, inhibition, poison' (Preface, 6), we are surely justified in wondering if Foucault's reading of Classical Greek ethics does not excessively downplay the political motivations and aims of the 'use of pleasure'.[29] How is it that, having detailed the intimate and necessary connection between the discourses and techniques of self-mastery and the social practices of domination, Foucault can then characterize the telos of self-mastery as an 'aesthetics of existence' (*UP*, 89[103]); how can he maintain that 'the principal aim, the principal target of this kind of ethics was an aesthetic one' (OGE, 341)?

My aim in this chapter has been, firstly, to establish that Foucault does indeed emphasize one aspect of Greek reflection on ethics at the expense of an aspect which is of equal if not more importance; and, secondly, to suggest that it is not by chance that the neglected aspect is less 'noble' than the one which is emphasized. In *The Use of Pleasure*, Foucault seems to be trying to distract our attention from those necessary but unsavoury 'causes and conditions' which, in Nietzsche's view, made Greek 'superiority' possible.[30]

CHAPTER 4

The Ends of Ethics

I don't think one can find any normalization in, for instance, the Stoic ethics. The reason is, I think, that the principal aim, the principal target of this kind of ethics was an aesthetic one.

Michel Foucault (OGE, 341)

I am a little afraid that in focusing his interpretation too exclusively on the the culture of the self, on the care of the self, on the conversion towards self ... Foucault is proposing a culture of the self which is too purely aesthetic ... a new form of dandyism.

Pierre Hadot[1]

In the previous chapter, I argued that Foucault's account of the ethics of Classical antiquity is open to a charge of one-sidedness. His reading of the ethics of this period seems to under-emphasize one crucial aspect of that ethics – its 'heautocratic' structure which is motivated by a will to maintain personal and political domination. In this chapter, I will argue that his reading of the ethics of the Hellenistic period would appear to be similarly one-sided, insofar as he neglects the normative role of reason and nature in Stoicism. In this chapter, I will examine Foucault's reading of the ethics of imperial Rome in *The Care of the Self* with the intention of measuring the distance between the account he presents there and an alternative one based both on the work of his critics and on my own reading of Stoicism. I will suggest that Foucault tends to over-emphasize the free, creative, form-giving aspects of Hellenistic ethics, at the expense this time of the role of Stoic ideas of reason and nature played in this era's conceptions of the ethical subject. Ultimately, I will argue that Foucault's desire to bring morality to an end constrains him to give a particular reading of the telos of Hellenistic ethics; and that this reading not only clashes with the historical data, but is also subject to internal inconsistencies. I will argue that it is Foucault's wish to hasten the end of morality which ensures that his account of the ends of Classical and Hellenistic ethics is so often unsatisfactory.

THE CULTURE OF THE SELF

In his choice of title for *The History of Sexuality*, volume III – *The Care of the Self* – Foucault announces which element of the sexual ethics of late antiquity he will take as determinant; that is, the theme of *epimeleia heautou* or *cura sui* – the 'care of self'. In choosing to emphasize this theme, rather than for instance the theme of the life lived 'in accordance with nature', Foucault is not necessarily committing a sin against historical accuracy. After all, even a leading historian of Stoic thought such as A. A. Long can recognize that, 'any creative discussion of Stoic philosophy requires a distinct focus, but there is always a risk of distortion by omission or emphasis since the system was peculiarly holistic'.[2] In this reference to the peculiarly 'holistic' nature of Stoic philosophy, Long is referring to the close connection which prevails in this system between the areas of logic, physics and ethics.[3] Despite this, however, there has always been a tendency on the part of commentators to emphasize one of these areas at the expense of the others, in accordance with their own philosophical interest. Hence Foucault, along with Hadot and Veyne, prefers to emphasize the *practical* nature of this philosophy, to prioritize its ethics, to read it as a philosophical *technique de soi* and 'way of life'.[4]

Foucault's account of the ethics of the Hellenistic period, then, is inevitably a partial one – in both senses of the term: it is neither complete nor objective. It does not intend to give an encyclopaedic view of its subject; such a pretension would itself constitute, at least from Foucault's point of view, an even greater failing than any number of possible distortions. However, to point out that Foucault's picture of Hellenistic ethics is no more complete than any other such picture, is not to say that there is nothing to be learned from Foucault's particular form of partiality. In this section, I will show in precisely what way Foucault constructs his particular account of late antiquity and, more importantly, I will argue that this account displays sufficient peculiarities to justify our treating it with a certain amount of circumspection.

In recent years, many classical historians and historians of ancient philosophy have addressed themselves to the last volumes of *The History of Sexuality*. As was the case with the 'professional' reception of Foucault's previous works, a great effort has been spent 'correcting' Foucault's interpretations and emphases. This is particularly true of volume III, which has recently been the subject of several expert and often convincing critiques. Parallel to this negative reception, however, these volumes have been welcomed by other classical scholars – especially those working in the field of sexuality and gender. In particular, David Halperin and John Winkler[5]

have consistently defended the contribution Foucault's late work has made
to the project of historicizing desire. I would include here French historian
Paul Veyne, whose influence on volumes II and III Foucault recognized as
considerable (*UP*, 8[14]). Foucault's account of marriage and the family,
especially in volume III, *The Care of the Self*, is heavily indebted to
Veyne's work, and Veyne has reciprocated by consistently referring to these
volumes in his recent writings on Hellenistic philosophy and social
practices.[6]

Those readings which develop criticisms of Foucault's account offer
several possible lines of further investigation, which I will look at briefly
now before adopting a slightly different approach. The first, and perhaps
the most telling, of these critical readings came from Pierre Hadot[7] – a
classical scholar whose work greatly influenced Foucault's interpretation of
ancient ethics. Hadot raises some serious misgivings about the way Foucault
treats some of the central themes and concerns of Hellenistic ethical
thought. In particular, Hadot argues that Foucault – in his account of the
imperial *culture de soi* – places excessive emphasis on the self, or at least on
a certain conception of the self. This is most clear, Hadot argues, in
Foucault's treatment of the Stoic theme of the pleasure one can have in
oneself. Referring to Epictetus, Seneca and Marcus Aurelius, Foucault
argues that an important feature of the Stoic 'care of the self' was the desire
to become, for oneself, 'an object of pleasure (*plaisir*)' (*CS*, 66[83]). This
pleasure (*gaudium*) was opposed, Foucault points out, to the type of
pleasure (*voluptas*) which is external, precarious and potentially violent or
excessive. He suggests that the former pleasure (*gaudium*) acts as a sort of
substitute for the pleasure (*voluptas*) which the Stoic forgoes (*CS*, 66[84]).
Hadot contends, however, that *gaudium* is not so much a special type of
pleasure as an entirely different phenomenon. The pleasure (*gaudium*)
which one takes in the full possession of oneself is, he suggests, better
understood as 'joy' (*joie*); that is, it is not so much a substitute or reward
for those who refuse *voluptas*, as the state one attains through an (almost
Kantian) dedication to morality for its own sake.[8]

Hadot's second, and more important, misgiving about Foucault's reading,
is that it tends to mobilize a notion of self which is very far from either the
Hellenistic or Classical ideas of what it is that one 'cares' for. As we have
already seen, when Socrates enjoins Alcibiades to 'care for himself' he
specifies that he means he should care for that best and highest part of
himself which is 'the seat of knowledge and thought' (*Alcibiades I*, 133c);
or, as Seneca would say, the seat of 'Divine Reason'.[9] In other words, the
'self' which is worked on, cared for and ultimately enjoyed is a transcendent
self which has little in common with the personal and individualized 'self'

of modern self-understanding. Hadot, therefore, suspects Foucault of imposing a modern, individualist idea of self on the ancient texts, in order to be able to read them as what we could call *avant la lettre* guides to dandyism. Hence, Hadot judges Foucault's account to be unsatisfactory 'from an historical point of view'.[10]

Faced with such criticisms, sympathetic readers of Foucault have developed various reading strategies. Arnold Davidson, for example, admits that Hadot's reading is 'the historically accurate interpretation', but insists that Foucault's account, as a 'conceptualization of ethics', remains unaffected.[11] David Halperin, rather than defending Foucault on the grounds that the Stoic conception of self is closer to the modern notion than Hadot allows, argues instead that Foucault's conception of the self is in fact closer to the Stoic transcendent, impersonal self than it is to the modern personal, individualized self.[12] One could pursue Hadot's criticisms of Foucault even further by adding to them the voices of, for example, David Cohen, Richard Saller and Simon Goldhill.[13] Cohen and Saller argue that Foucault's belief in an increasingly practised and valorized equality of spouses in the Hellenistic era is a result, firstly, of his reliance on a 'mistaken' argument of Paul Veyne's and, secondly, of his selective and often unjustifiable choice of authors and texts. They argue that to compare Xenophon's *Œconomicus* with Pliny's 'love letters', is not to compare like with like. Through a choice of different texts, they argue that the new and the old views of marriage in fact existed side by side, and always had done so, even in the Classical period. Simon Goldhill, on the other hand, problematizes Foucault's interpretation not so much by concentrating on his choice of texts, as by suggesting that his way of reading these texts is inadequate to the task.[14]

Clearly, the task of pursuing all the possible historical weaknesses in Foucault's account could be endless; as endless as the task of defending or modifying Foucault's thesis in the light of such criticisms.[15] As factually to the point as these criticisms may be, they fail to adequately address the logic that underpins Foucault's argument. If we turn our attention from the factual weaknesses in the story Foucault tells, towards the relation between that story and the ethico-political project which underlies it, then we can begin to understand the logic behind the particular interpretations that form Foucault's reading. This approach, which I will adopt here, seeks to place the particularities of Foucault's version of ancient ethics in the context of his attitude towards modern morality. It is a reading strategy which offers a way out of the ultimately sterile exchange of factual claim and counter-claim between 'expert' and 'non-expert' – a way out that will force us to come to terms with the *contemporary* significance of Foucault's

history. In the remainder of this section, therefore, I will address the particularities of Foucault's account of the end of Stoic ethics, in order to see
how those particularities, or *peculiarities*, are driven by his attitude towards
the end of morality.

'caring for the self ...'

In *The Care of the Self*, Foucault is interested in tracing the changes which
occurred in modes of ethical subjectivation between the Classical and the
imperial eras. In one of the several accounts which he gives of these
changes,[16] Foucault plots them along the lines of his fourfold analysis of
ethics. Firstly, at the level of the ethical substance, the 'material' of sexual
ethics (the *aphrodisia*) remains, in the imperial era, a force which must be
combatted and controlled. However, there is a new emphasis on the
weakness of the individual and on the necessity of avoiding, or at least
arming oneself against, this force. Secondly, while sexual ethics still
requires that one subject oneself to a 'certain art of living' (*CS*, 67[85]),
this requirement now takes on a universal application. Since it begins to be
founded on an appeal to the universal principles of reason and nature, it
comes to be demanded of everybody – regardless of social or political
status. The third change is that greater importance is given to the ascetic
techniques of abstinence, self-scrutiny and self-control; and, in addition,
that within these techniques the question of truth comes to take a central
position. Finally, at the level of the telos of this ethics, self-mastery remains
the aim, but, according to Foucault, it is a self-mastery which now takes the
form of a relation in which one can take an untroubled pleasure in full
self-possession.

These modifications in the substance, mode, techniques and telos of
sexual ethics lead inevitably to changes in sexual practice (for adult male
citizens) – at the level of the body, marriage relations and relations with
boys. Generalizing, one could say that these practices come to be characterized by an increased anxiety and austerity; anxiety about one's ability to
remain in control, coupled with a vastly increased demand for marital
fidelity and abstinence in relations with boys. While these changes can
be explained in terms of the imposition of a new and more rigorous moral
code – such as, for example, Augustus's attempts to control marriage and
divorce through legislation – Foucault argues that it is, rather, the changes
at the level of ethical subjectivation which are responsible for this new
austerity. In other words, this shift in sexual ethics was not the result of a
change in the *code* of ethics, but was the result of a change in the forms of
ethical subjectivation; that is, a change in the importance which was given

to relations with the self and the *intensity* with which these relations were cultivated.[17] As for the traditional question about the 'proto-Christian' nature of this austere ethics, Foucault – again drawing on his basic methodological distinction between ethics and morality – argues that while there are indeed similarities between the moral *codes* of late antiquity and Christianity, there are nevertheless crucial differences at the level of ethics in the way the individual constitutes him/herself as an ethical subject.

Perhaps the most general of these differences between Hellenistic and Christian ethics is that – at least for Foucault – the ethics of late antiquity was dominated by a culture of the care of the self, while Christianity was characterized by a culture of self-renunciation and self-denial. In 'The Culture of the Self' (*CS*, Part 2), Foucault gives his account of the Roman culture of the self of the first and second centuries AD. He shows how this culture developed by drawing on a tradition which had been well established in Classical Athens – that of the *epimeleia heautou*, or the care of the self. As we have seen, the notion that one must care for the self was central in certain representations of Socrates's teaching – even to the extent of being more fundamental than the familiar demand that one 'know oneself' (*gnothi seauton*). In late Stoicism, for example, which claimed Socrates as its spiritual father, this early emphasis is maintained. And we must remember that Stoicism dominated the philosophical scene of the early Roman empire. In fact, this was a period in which Stoicism practically became the 'official philosophy' of the Roman senatorial class,[18] and it was in the context of this philosophical tradition that the culture of the self experienced what Foucault calls a 'golden age' (*CS*, 45[59]). The key difference, however, between the practice of the care of the self in Classical and late antiquity, is that while in the Classical era the *epimeleia* tended to be justified with reference to the exigencies of one's position (of power) in the city, in late antiquity the *cura sui* became something of an end in itself. It no longer constituted a preparation for one's entry into public life, rather it was something which, as all the Stoic authors insist,[19] one had to practise throughout one's life. In late antiquity, then, the sexual ethics of those whom Foucault calls the 'bearers of culture' (ibid.), developed in the context of this overriding emphasis which was given to the care of the self.

In Foucault's reading, however, this 'self' had changed considerably since the Classical era. Whereas in Classical Athens it was a question of showing oneself to be stronger than one's unruly passions, in late antiquity it was a question of recognizing that one was sick, and that philosophy offered the best means of both curing and caring for the self.[20] In the field of sexual practice this new emphasis meant that it became important to closely monitor the effects of one's passions. Hence, a greater anxiety about the dangers of sex and the weaknesses of the individual characterize Stoic reflection on sexual practice. In effect, as sex gains in power and the individual loses, so sex itself begins to lose its ethical neutrality – it begins to be seen as something which constitutes a permanent threat to the balance and health of the individual. In response to this threat, Stoicism made available a whole arsenal of techniques of the self which helped to guide the individual towards health and tranquillity. These included techniques for testing one's independence from the superfluous and potentially disturbing elements of life (CS, 58–60[75–7]). Seneca, for example, recommended training the self to be able to do without the luxuries which wealth brings. In this way an individual would be better able to maintain tranquillity of soul in a possible reversal of fortune. Similarly, Seneca recommended the practice of a daily account-giving of one's actions and thoughts. This examination served both to determine what progress had been made and to spur one on – by awareness of one's failures – to renewed efforts (CS, 60–2[77–9]). Epictetus recommended a technique of self-examination which, rather than being practised on an occasional basis (whether daily or less frequently), was ideally to be engaged in continuously. This technique involved what Foucault calls a 'work of thought upon itself' (CS, 62[79]) and its aim was to permanently filter and verify all of one's mental representations. Epictetus suggested that each mental representation should be challenged as to its nature and one's attitude towards it should be determined accordingly – in particular, one should cultivate indifference towards all those things which do not 'depend' on oneself. In this way, one could avoid the pursuit of things which are beyond one's control; things such as, for example, political power and wealth.

I will not enter into a critical reading of the details of the account which Foucault gives of these and other techniques of the self, since his description, which closely follows Hadot's, also concurs largely with Nussbaum's version of the same material.[21] It is not Foucault's account of the Stoic techniques of self-elaboration which I wish to question here; rather, it is his account of the mode of subjection and the telos of this form of ethics which, I think, demands closer scrutiny. We have already seen that, according to Foucault, the mode of subjection of Hellenistic ethics differs from that of Classical ethics in that the requirement that one subject oneself to a 'certain art of living' (CS, 67[85]) is now founded on a universal principle which is applicable to all human beings: it is 'founded for all human beings both in nature and in reason' (CS, 238[272]). While in the Classical era one's adoption of a certain style of life was based on personal choice, in late antiquity it came to be founded on a universally binding principle. As for the telos of this auto-subjection, we have seen that in addition to the

Classical mastery of the self, comes the added aim of a 'pure enjoyment (*jouissance*) of the self' (*CS*, 239[273]). According to Foucault the aim of Hellenistic ethics is to establish a certain relation with the self which would have as its result a pure enjoyment. This ethics was, Foucault says, an art of existence that was 'dominated by the care of the self' (ibid.).[22] The principal aim of this ethics was to be found, he says, precisely in this '-relation of self to self' (*CS*, 64–5[81]); this relation was 'the final objective of all the practices of the self' (*CS*, 65[82]).

Foucault's account elevates the theme of the care of the self (*epimeleia heautou, cura sui, le souci de soi*) to the position of principal aim and target of Hellenistic ethics. At the same time, it places the Stoic appeals to nature and reason (as guarantors of a universal ethical norm) in the role of mode of subjection; that is, one aims for full possession and enjoyment of the self because, in some sense, this is natural for human beings. If we were to imagine the way this system of ethics addresses the individuals who embrace it, in Foucault's account it would say something like this: 'the universal principle of nature and reason directs you to use these techniques (of abstention, self-examination, etc.) in order to achieve a pure enjoyment of your self'. The subject of ethics is asked to pursue the cultivation of the self (as his/her telos) because, as rational human beings, they occupy a certain position in the universal order (mode of subjection). The problem with this reading, however, is that it overlooks the central normative role which Stoicism gave to 'reason' and 'nature'. By relegating these concepts to the role of mode of subjection, Foucault fails to take into account the fact that they also functioned as essential measures of the ethical value of an individual life.

'. . . in accordance with nature'

Foucault's tendency to downplay the role that notions of reason and nature play in Stoic conceptions of the ethical life is significant, not because it is yet another example of the historical weaknesses of his work, but because it indicates very precisely the concerns that motivate his engagement with ancient ethics. If we contrast his reading of the ends of Hellenistic ethics with a reading that gives weight to nature and reason as constitutive of that ethics' telos, then in the distance that separates these two readings we will see a mirror image of the contemporary project that motivates Foucault's historical research. Against Foucault's reading, which suggests that a pure enjoyment of the self is the aim of Stoic ethics, I propose an alternative reading; one which, I suggest, accounts at least as effectively – if not more so – for the material Foucault is analysing.

In my alternative reading, the Hellenistic system of ethics would address its adherents in this way: 'there is a universal principle of nature and reason: use these techniques to live in accordance with it and, hence, to be "happy" (*eudaimon*)'. In this version, the subject of ethics is asked to live a life of *eudaimonia* through the cultivation of harmonious relations with the rational order of nature (*telos*), because as rational beings they occupy a privileged position in relation to that order (mode of subjection). The crucial difference here is that, in Foucault's account, it is a particular form of relation to the self (one of enjoyment, possession and cultivation) which is the *aim* of Hellenistic ethics, while nature and reason merely serve to extend the application of this aim. In the alternative that I suggest, *eudaimonia*, understood as the life lived 'in accordance with nature or reason', is the *aim* of ethical practice; here nature and reason perform the double function of both extending the application of this ethics and providing a normative model (albeit a purely formal one) of what constitutes *eudaimonia*. So, while Foucault consigns nature and reason to the level of mode of subjection, thus effectively leaving the care of the self as the only aim, I would suggest that this forgets that Stoicism – like all the Hellenistic schools of philosophy – understands the 'happy life', the ethical life, as the life which is lived in some sense 'rationally' and 'naturally'.

In *The Care of the Self*, Foucault gives an account of the ethics of late Stoicism, rather than an account of the sexual ethics of the Roman Empire or late antiquity in general. The second and third volumes of *The History of Sexuality* do not pretend to offer a history of sexual *behaviours* in particular societies. Foucault is concerned with the ways in which sexual practice is reflected upon, understood and modified in the process of ethical self-constitution; he examines the 'moral problematization' of sexual practices (*UP*, 3[9]), rather than those practices themselves. And if, in his account of the Classical era, Foucault relies largely on the Socratic and Hippocratic traditions as a source of such 'problematization', then in his account of the imperial era he confines his analysis predominantly to Stoicism – or, more specifically, to the late Stoicism of Epictetus, Seneca and Marcus Aurelius. This choice is clear, for instance, in the crucial section of volume III ('The Culture of the Self'), in which Foucault relies almost exclusively either on the writings of the authors just mentioned, or on one of the standard later sources of Stoic thought – such as the writings of Plutarch. To the extent that Foucault refers to any of the opposing schools of Hellenistic philosophy (Epicureans, for example), it is only in relation to shared characteristics, such as the principle that *epimeleia heautou* is to be practised throughout one's life.[23] Even in the section on 'The Body', where he draws mostly on Galen's writings, Foucault makes a point of insisting that Galen's attitude towards the pleasure of the *aphrodisia* is 'clearly Stoic' (*CS*, 139[163]). In the same section, Foucault also points to the 'considerable' Stoic influence on Athenaeus's definition of the role of the soul in the health of the body (*CS*, 133[158]). Again, in the section on 'The Wife', the main sources used, in addition to Plutarch, are the Stoic writings of Musonius Rufus, Hierocles, Epictetus and Seneca. It is only in the last section, that on 'Boys', that Foucault departs from the canon of late Stoicism to consider, in addition to Plutarch's *Dialogue on Love*, the much later narratives of Pseudo-Lucian and Achilles Tatius.

To suggest that *The Care of the Self* is, for all intents and purposes, an account of Stoicism's moral problematization of sexual practice, rather than a more general account of sexual ethics in 'late antiquity', is not itself a criticism. In the first place, as we have seen, Foucault never pretends to be describing general social behaviour. As he admits, he is speaking only of those he calls the 'bearers of culture' (*CS*, 45[59]). His concentration on Stoicism is further justified by the fact that, at this time, the 'bearers of culture' (both philosophical and medical) were, as we have seen, thoroughly 'stoicized'. In a history of *moral problematizations*, then, Stoicism is bound to dominate any account of the imperial era. But, what can we say of Foucault's particular version of this Stoic problematization; what emphases does *this* exhibit?

We have already seen that Stoicism, like the other Classical and Hellenistic schools of philosophy, was eudaimonistic in form. Following Aristotle, it assumes that the ethical purpose of a life is to achieve the active state of *eudaimonia* ('happiness'/'well-being'). But what constitutes 'happiness' for human beings? In relation to this question many widely divergent answers were given in antiquity. Aristotle argued that the happy life is the life which is lived according to virtue and which is adequately provided with external goods (wealth, position and friends[24]), while Epicurus held that pleasure was the end of life. As for Stoicism, the earliest definition of the end of life, which comes purportedly from Zeno,[25] is 'living in agreement [or, harmony]' (*homologoumenos zen*). Zeno's successor, Cleanthes, later modified this definition to 'living in agreement with nature' (*homologoumenos tei physei zen*).[26] And, in the long history of Stoicism, the definition was restated many times – often in varying forms. However, what must be acknowledged is that whether the end of life was defined as living in agreement with 'nature', 'reason' or 'virtue' in fact made little difference – because each of these were merely different ways of considering that active state of human being which we can designate '*eudaimonia*'.[27] The good person, the happy person, the sage, does not have to choose *between* nature and reason; rather, they live a life which embodies and harmonizes human nature (*logos*) and universal nature (*cosmos*) in the practice of virtue.

Scholarly debates about whether the basis of Stoic ethics is to be found in its idea of 'nature', or in its idea of 'virtue', often obscure the fact that nature, reason and virtue *all* figure in the happy life. While Julia Annas, for example, may be justified in giving priority to 'virtue' as the end of life,[28] Gisela Striker's reading is equally justified in its emphasis on the normative role of the Stoic concept of nature.[29] Perhaps a good indication of the non-mutually exclusive character of these apparently opposing interpretations is the fact that, while Annas argues that 'nature' really only became an important part of the definition in late Stoicism,[30] A. A. Long argues that in early Stoicism, on the contrary, 'nature' functions as both a source and a ground of ethics.[31] All three terms, then, 'nature', 'virtue' and 'reason', are key terms throughout the history of Stoicism, and while specific authors or sources may emphasize one term at the expense of the others, it remains the case that all three are taken in some way to define the end of life.

One reading of Stoic ethics which allows such an interpretation is the highly nuanced account which Nicholas White gives of the question of the normative role of nature in this ethics.[32] According to White, the real import of the call to live life 'according to nature' is not that one should use one's knowledge of 'physics' to deduce one's moral principles (thus incurring 'Humean' disapproval); rather, it is that virtue consists in giving one's life and one's actions the rational, ordered pattern which we can observe in the world around us – in the world, that is, as it was seen by Stoicism – a world in which providence ensured that all things, no matter how apparently evil, contributed to the universal good. The aim, he suggests, was to live a 'natural' life, not in the sense of obeying all one's natural impulses, but in the sense of understanding, and hence living in accord with, the highest part of both human and universal nature – that is, reason. The value of White's account is that it brings out the fact that, in the Stoic approbation of universal nature, it was the overall *pattern* of the whole which gave it its value. To live 'in agreement [*homologoumenos*] with nature' was not to simply conform to the natural order, it was to make one's own *logos* consonant with the *logos* of the natural world; it was to bring these two *logoi* into harmony with each other – *homologoumenos*.[33] And this harmony, the Stoics held, comes about through understanding the natural order, the pattern and organization of the universe. The life of *eudaimonia* is the life whose form is consonant with universal nature; it is the life which is in agreement with nature, or with virtue.

Turning to Foucault's account of this same ethics, it would be no exaggeration to say that anyone whose sole source of information on

Stoicism was *The Care of the Self* would be surprised by White's emphasis on the role of nature, reason and virtue as the telos of ethical activity in Stoicism. While Foucault allows reason to enter into this ethics as its mode of subjection, there is little recognition of the central role either of reason or nature as constituting the *ends* of Stoic ethics. Notwithstanding the fact that Foucault *does* frequently refer to reason and nature as key themes in Stoic ethics, the overwhelming impression one receives from *The Care of the Self* is that the aim of Stoicism was simply to cultivate a relation with the self which would, from itself, produce ethical forms of life. A first reaction to this disparity might be to defend Foucault's account on the grounds that the Stoicism with which he is dealing (Roman Stoicism[34]) is very different from the early Greek Stoicism of Zeno, Cleanthes and their followers. However, a reading of the texts of Epictetus, Seneca and Marcus Aurelius strongly suggests that the Roman Stoics had an even greater sense of the normative role of the rational, natural order in ethics.

The *Discourses* of Epictetus, for example, are pervaded with a profoundly religious respect for the natural order of the universe; an order into which it is the aim of every virtuous man to integrate himself:

> We should go to receive instruction, not in order to change the constitution of things ... but in order that, things about us being as they are and as their nature is, we may, for our own part, keep our wills in harmony with what happens (*Discourses*, I, xii, 17).

Here, we are not being asked to engage in an open work of self-creation, whose aim would consist simply in the *relation* which one forms with oneself; rather, we are being asked to follow what Epictetus calls the 'rule of life' – 'we must do what nature demands' (*Discourses*, I, xxvi, 1). And, in even stronger terms:

> He [Zeus] has delivered your own self into your keeping, saying, 'I had no one more faithful than you; keep this man for me unchanged from the character with which nature endowed him – reverent, faithful, high-minded, undismayed, unimpassioned, unperturbed' (*Discourses*, II, viii, 23).

If we turn to Seneca, we find the same sentiment in regard to the guiding role of reason and nature. For example, 'man is a rational animal, and his good is realized if he implements the potentiality for which nature gave him being. And what does reason demand of him? A very easy thing: to live according to his nature.'[35] Or, again, 'What is best in man? Reason ... When this is right and perfected his measure of happiness is full ... this perfect reason is called virtue' (*Letters*, 76). And, the end of ethics, the 'happy life', he says, 'depends solely on our reason being perfect' (*Letters*, 92). Indeed, Seneca holds that it is only with the advent of reason, at seven years of age, that morality as an art of living begins; *reason* is what makes ethics possible (see *Letters*, 117). Marcus Aurelius, in his *Meditations*, also views the universe as a benevolently ordered whole which, in a sense, 'gives the rule' to man. He urges us to 'constantly think of the universe as one living creature, embracing one being and one soul',[36] and to think of this 'Whole' as a moral guide:

> Always remember the following: what the nature of the Whole is; what my own nature; the relation of this nature to that; what kind of part it is of what kind of Whole; and that no man can hinder your saying and doing at all times what is in accordance with that nature whereof you are a part (*Meditations*, II, 9).

Following the common Stoic metaphor that the universe is a city, a 'cosmopolis', Seneca holds that our end, insofar as we are 'reasonable creatures', is to 'obey the rule and ordinance of the most venerable of all cities and governments' (*Meditations*, II, 16). For Marcus Aurelius, as for Seneca and Epictetus, we are rational beings whose end is to willingly submit to the laws of the rational whole of which we are an integral part. It is this freely willed submission, they hold, which constitutes virtue and happiness.

THE END OF MORALITY AND THE ENDS OF ETHICS

This discussion of the Stoic conception of the end of life suggests that Foucault's picture of late antiquity, where individuals engage in an open work of self-creation, is seriously misleading. There are more than sufficient grounds for arguing that one of the major themes in Stoicism – the theme of reason as model and end of life – is either ignored or excessively downplayed in *The Care of the Self*. How, then, are we to approach – or reproach – his account? Are we to argue that Foucault was a careless scholar who simply missed the point of the texts he was analysing? Or, does he simply fall prey to that age-old fascination with an era that does not seem to share the constraints of our modern, Christian morality? Is he simply a contemporary representative of that tradition, stretching from Schiller and the Schlegels to Nietzsche and Wilde, a tradition for which

'Greece' represents freedom from narrow bourgeois morality, the freedom to create oneself anew as a work of art?

Even if we stop short of using the term 'distortion' in relation to Foucault's account of ancient ethics, we can still be concerned that his interpretation exhibits far too many distinctive characteristics. And yet, that is precisely what we have come to expect from Foucault's histories – they have always had the distinctive characteristic of being avowedly motivated by present concerns rather than a disinterested curiosity about the past.[37] The emphasis here should fall on the 'avowedly', however, because there is no history which is *not* motivated by the present, it is just that it is not always 'avowed'. In this regard, one of the great merits of Pierre Hadot's criticism of Foucault is that Hadot recognizes the impossibility of distinguishing between any given historical narrative and the ethico-philosophical project which informs that narrative. Hadot recognizes that a large part of his opposition to Foucault's interpretation comes from his hostility towards what he perceives to be Foucault's ethical project – a project which, he 'fears', is a new form of dandyism. However, more importantly, he also recognizes that his own interpretation, the one which he opposes to Foucault's, is itself informed by an ethical outlook. Hadot admits that his own account is more than a simple historical narrative; it also, like Foucault's, comprises 'the definition of an ethical model which modern man (*l'homme moderne*) can find in Antiquity'.[38] For Hadot this would not be a new form of dandyism, but an openness to the 'universal', an attempt to live, concretely, in 'the universality of the cosmic perspective, in the wonderful and mysterious presence of the universe'.[39] The crucial point for our purposes, therefore, is that it cannot simply be a question of confronting Foucault's 'amateur' interpretations with those of the 'professionals', the serious scholars; it cannot be a matter of correcting the details – or even the broad outlines – of Foucault's account in order to make it more reliable or accurate.

The explanation for the peculiarities of Foucault's reading, as I have already argued, has to be sought in his concern to develop a contemporary, post-Christian ethics of self-transformation. So, rather than condemning Foucault for his 'inaccuracies' I want to re-focus attention on the motivations for this genealogy of ethics. If we use the foregoing reading of the specific features of Foucault's account we can give more substance to this motivation, or at least to that part of the motivation which pertains to ethics. As we have seen, the form of Foucault's return to the Greeks is largely determined by his long-felt and avowed hostility towards modern, which is to say Christian, morality. Hence, the key feature of Foucault's return to the Greeks, like the return of so many others before him, is his wish to find an era which did not appear to be subject, or at least did not appear to be *helplessly* subject, to the harsh demands of a punitive moral code. What Foucault finds captivating about ancient *ethics* is precisely that it is not modern *morality*; and his hopes for the 'end' of this morality, for its termination, hang upon his analysis and interpretation of the 'ends', the aims, of that ethics. The account he gives of these ends, however, may prove to be unequal to the task which he sets for it.

As I have outlined previously, the realm of ethics, the field in which subjectivation occurs, is divided by Foucault into four segments or aspects: the ethical substance, the mode of subjection, the practices or ascesis employed and the mode of being towards which the subject aims.[40] Foucault, as we have seen, differentiates this realm of ethics proper from the realm of the code – a more or less coherent and systematic set of prescriptions which are capable of being fixed, institutionalized and explicitly formulated. While there can be no moral action which is not analysable into both aspects, Foucault suggests that the relative importance of each aspect is subject to historical variation. Hence, he would say that Christian morality, of the Middle Ages for example, was largely focused on morality as coded and codifiable, whereas Classical Greek morality was almost exclusively centred around 'ethics' – that is, the way that one brings oneself to conduct one's own conduct. My argument here, however, is that when it comes to speaking about the ends or aims of this ancient ethical practice, Foucault is either deliberately misleading (for a 'rhetorical' effect) or else he is inconsistent in attributing a telos to these practices.

As I have already pointed out, Foucault is very careful not to present ancient ethics as an alternative or a solution to the ethical impasse of today. He is more interested, he says, in 'problems' than 'solutions' (OGE, 343), and in any case he finds the Classical Greek ethics of pleasure 'quite disgusting' (OGE 346).[41] He is careful not to contrast a relatively free mode of sexual ethics – in Classical antiquity – with a relatively repressive and intolerant sexual ethics in Christianity: the point is not 'they were free, we are not, so let's regain what they had'. And yet, in a sense, that is precisely what he *is* saying – if not directly, at least as an implication of the story he tells about the modifications in (sexual) ethics across two millennia. This implication is clearly recognized by commentators such as Giuseppe Cambiano, who – even though he insists that Foucault has undermined the old 'simplifications' according to which Christian repression has replaced ancient liberty – goes on to say that the difference between the Classical and the Christian ethics of austerity is that for the ancients sexual austerity 'assumes a free form, without being codified in norms or interdictions'.[42] Similarly, in a discussion of power and freedom in Foucault, Paul Patton points out that for Foucault Classical sexual ethics 'presupposes a freedom on the part of the men to whom it was addressed, a positive freedom in relation to their own character as sexual beings'.[43] And this certainly is the impression that Foucault gives. But if Foucault denies that this is the sort of comparison he wants to draw, then where does the impression come from? And is it consistent with the details of his own historical research?

One way of summarizing Foucault's three volume history of sexuality would be to characterize it as the story of our loss of freedom, as the story of how we, in Western societies, came to be not only 'trapped in our history', but forcefully 'attached to our own identity'. In Classical antiquity, in the Athens of the fourth century BC, a small group of politically dominant men made the unforced 'politico-aesthetic' choice to limit the exercise of their liberty in order to achieve a form of self-mastery which would both guarantee and (morally) justify their position in the polis. Their aim, the telos of their ethical practice, was a mode of being which could be characterized as an active form of freedom (UP, 92[106]). Later, in the Hellenistic period, an equally small but less politically dominant group of men, recognizing themselves as subject to the universal demand of reason and nature, developed a mode of behaviour towards themselves and others which would lead to the 'perfect tranquillity of the soul' (UP, 28[35]) and a 'pure enjoyment of oneself' (CS, 238[273]). In Christianity, however, *everybody* is expected to subject themselves to a code which derives from a personal God and requires us to firstly decipher and then renounce ourselves and to sacrifice our pleasures in order to attain salvation (CS, 239–40[274]). In Foucault's view this model is still, or was until very recently, dominant in Western societies – even for those individuals who no longer adhere to Christianity. What we see here is a gradual shift from the 'singular' choice of the Classical male, through the 'universality without law' of Stoicism,[44] to the rigidly codified universality of Christianity. As the ethical system becomes more generalized in its application it becomes more ruthless in its individualizing; the emphasis in the process of ethical subjectivation shifts away from the subject as centre of deliberation and activity and towards the subject as 'subjected', as unfree. It is not surprising then, that while Foucault denies that the ancients can provide an alternative model for us today, he nevertheless insists that their example can be an inspiration to our own efforts. There is a sense in which we should actualize their notion of *epimeleia heautou* against our modern forms of ethical subjectivation – as long as we recognize that this re-activation is not a repetition, but the creation of something new.[45]

This story of a descent from relative freedom to relative repression, the story of the forgetting of the possibilities of a certain relation to self, is given much of its rhetorical force by Foucault's characterization of the ends – of the *teloi* – of the Classical and Hellenistic models. Yet his various presentations of these ends frequently contradict each other. There is often a confusion, or an elision, between the accounts he gives of the ends (the fourth aspect of any ethics) and the modes of subjectivation (the second aspect). The suspicion which arises here is that Foucault does not sufficiently distinguish between the 'how' and the 'why' of ancient ethics. In the introduction to volume II, he sets out the questions he will address there and divides them into two groups. Firstly, *why* did free Greek males choose to moderate and limit their sexual behaviour according to an 'austere style'? Secondly, *how* was sexual behaviour reflected upon and problematized as a 'domain of moral experience'? (*UP* 24[31]). There is no doubt that Foucault addresses and answers the second of these questions – the 'how', the mode of Classical (and Hellenistic) ethics. But he would seem, at least occasionally, to downplay the 'why' question – or at least he seems occasionally to give the same answer to the 'why' as to the 'how'. That is, he seems to attribute to this ethics both an aesthetic mode and an aesthetic aim, thus eliding the second and fourth aspects and confusing the mode of subjectivation with the telos or end.

Throughout *The History of Sexuality*, volume II, Foucault consistently characterizes the first aspect of Classical ethics – or the 'material cause'[46] – as the *aphrodisia*; the second aspect – or the 'formal cause' – as the choice to conform to 'criteria of brilliance, beauty, nobility, or perfection' (*UP*, 27[34]); the third aspect – or 'efficient cause' – as the techniques of self-control and regulation; and the fourth aspect – or 'final cause' – as an ever more complete mastery of self (but one which makes possible the mastery of others). In the Hellenistic period the first of these aspects, the material cause, remains largely unchanged – although the danger of the *aphrodisia* increases; in the second aspect, the formal cause, the choice of austerity is now premissed on one's recognition of oneself as subject to a universal demand of reason and nature; the third aspect, the efficient cause, remains largely unchanged – although there is an increasing emphasis on knowledge of the truth of the self, coupled with an increasing sophistication in the techniques used; in the fourth aspect, the final cause, the aim now becomes an assured self-possession in which one can attain an unbroken enjoyment of self, thus doing justice to one's nature as a creature of reason. In each case, the Classical and the Hellenistic, the second aspect – the mode of subjectivation, or the formal cause – is characterized as a more or less free choice made by more or less free individuals in order to give their lives a certain *form*: it can, therefore, be characterized as a more or less aesthetic, or 'politico-aesthetic' choice (OGE, 357). Similarly, in each case, the fourth aspect of these ethical models – their *teloi* or final causes – are characterized as a certain kind of self-mastery: in the Classical model a self-mastery which finds its *raison d'être* in the mastery of others, in the Hellenistic model a self-mastery which relates to one's own rationality – albeit a rationality which one also recognizes in others. And yet, as we have seen, Foucault often makes the rhetorical point that, on the one hand, the *aim* of Classical ethics was an aesthetic one and, on the other hand, that the *aim* of Hellenistic ethics was the *rapport à soi* itself: in each case he regularly presents the formal cause as the final cause – he ascribes as an end of these ethics something which, on his own account, is simply their *mode*.

As I showed in Chapter 3 and Chapter 4, Foucault engages in a double game in which he both recognizes the fundamentally 'heautocratic' structure of Classical ethics, and the 'reason-oriented' structure of late Stoicism, and yet he insists on their *aesthetic* aim, and on their principal concern with cultivating a particular form of relation to self. And this despite the fact that his own most considered accounts of these ethics clearly show that while their modes may be called aesthetic (although only in the sense of a *techne*), their ends are very far from being the cultivation of the *éclat* of beauty. So, contrary to some of the more unguarded statements he makes in interviews, we would have to say that a close reading of volumes II and III of *The History of Sexuality* shows that according to Foucault's own research the 'aesthetics of existence' is *aesthetic* by virtue of its mode (which is 'ascetic/poetic/technical') rather than by its aim (which is certainly not a simple cultivation of beauty). My suggestion is that the more 'aestheticist' interpretation – which is principally, although not exclusively, presented in interviews – arises from Foucault's wish to produce a shock-effect which will jolt his listeners (and ultimately readers) out of their habitual acceptance of a particular form of morality. Foucault may not exactly be a 'rebel in the name of beauty', but he is a rebel who uses beauty's name to advance the same cause which animated both Nietzsche and Wilde – the end of a particular form of modern, Western morality.

CHAPTER 5

Strange Stories and Queer Stoics

All those who say that for me truth doesn't exist are being simplistic.

Michel Foucault (CT, 257[669])

What then is truth? a movable host of metaphors, metonymies, and anthropomorphisms ... Truths are illusions which we have forgotten are illusions.

Friedrich Nietzsche[1]

In a way which was rather empirical and maladroit, I envisaged a work which was as close as possible to that of the historians, but in order to pose philosophical questions about the history of knowledge (*la connaissance*).

Michel Foucault (*DE* IV, 652)

One of the stories that is told about Foucault's late work is that as his interest shifted from politics to ethics, 'he became attracted to the notion, which he encountered in ancient Greek and Roman writers, of *an aesthetics, or stylistics of existence*'.[2] The possibility I have been pursuing, however, is that this 'encounter' may have been as much a creation as a meeting. If I have succeeded in maintaining, or at least in making plausible, the claim that there is at least as much invention as encounter involved, then the question arises as to what difference this should make to our reading of Foucault.

If Foucault's history of ancient ethics is open to serious criticism, if the 'truth content' of his genealogy of the subject is found to be lacking, then how are we to approach these works? Perhaps the easiest response would be to say that it really does not matter whether Foucault gets, say, the Stoics 'wrong'; that his 'histories' have never really been about finding out 'what actually happened'; and that what really counts is the usefulness of his books for contemporary political debates and struggles. Indeed, there is no shortage of evidence one could bring from Foucault's writings to support such an interpretation. In the opening section of *Discipline and Punish*, for example, he insists that he is not writing this history of the prison 'because [he is] interested in the past', but because of his concern for the present (*DP*, 31[35]). Or again, in an interview from 1977, he makes the unequivocal statement 'I am well aware that I have never written anything but fictions' (HS, 193[236]). Similarly, Foucault insisted on many occasions that his work was to be read as providing tools which could be used in contemporary political struggles: it was to be judged more for its 'effects' than its 'truth content'. Hence, in an interview from 1977, he suggests that a theory should be understood as a 'tool kit':[3] it is to be used to achieve a certain end, and it is according to its efficacy in achieving this end that it must be judged. Similarly, in a 1978 lecture at the Collège de France, he warns his audience that all his work does is offer *tactical* advice (*indicateurs tactiques*) – advice which must be judged subsequently by its practical effects, rather than by its success in 'polemics' which are merely 'interior to theoretical discourses' (*DG*). There is ample evidence, therefore, which would allow one to argue that for Foucault what mattered in his work – especially in his histories – was not accuracy but efficacy; that these works are, as he suggests, political fictions.

On the other hand, however, Foucault's historical researches have always been motivated by what he calls a 'concern for truth'.[4] They start from 'certain historical facts' and make use of 'true documents';[5] they are 'meticulous and patiently documentary', they demand 'relentless erudition', a 'knowledge of details and ... a vast accumulation of source material' (NGH, 139–40[136]). In short, they must be true in terms of 'academic truth', they must be 'historically verifiable'.[6] My aim in this chapter is to make possible a reading of Foucault's histories which recognizes both his 'concern for the present' and his 'concern for truth'; a reading which recognizes that in Foucault the Nietzschean 'use' of history (as 'fiction') is coupled with an historiographical 'concern for truth'. I argue that while Foucault, quite justifiably, refuses to develop an historical methodology which naively pretends to objectivity and truth, he also avoids a straightforward fictionalizing of history, a reckless historical theorizing in the interests of a philosophical argument. Rather, what we see in his historical research is the combination of a 'concern for truth' with a 'concern for the present'; a combination which can give rise not only to new 'discoveries' in the historical field, but also to new possibilities in the field of contemporary philosophical debates about ethical subjectivity. Such a reading should allow us to sustain a critical reading of Foucault's *History of Sexuality*, while maintaining its value as a critical intervention in contemporary debates about ethical subjectivity.

VIRGINS AND SAINTS

Two apparently contrary, yet surprisingly complementary, approaches to the question of the truth of Foucault's histories are Simon Goldhill's *Foucault's Virginity*[7] and David Halperin's *Saint Foucault*.[8] Goldhill suggests that Foucault is a 'virgin' in relation to the academic field of Greek erotic literature – he reads the ancient texts 'like a good Christian', because he does not 'know' the pleasure of the erotic narrative;[9] while Halperin 'confesses' that, 'as far as I'm concerned, the guy was a fucking saint' – indeed, the 'patron saint' of queer activism.[10] These statements and the books from which they come are emblematic of two opposing ways of reading Foucault's history of ancient sexuality: on the one hand, an 'academic' reading (Goldhill's) which brackets the political motivations and uses of his work and on the other hand, a 'political' reading (Halperin's) which brackets, or glosses over, questions about the sustainability of some of Foucault's interpretations. While these are, in a sense, two 'ideal types' (which inevitably elide the complexity of the readings in question), the advantage of making such a contrast is that it shows us, firstly, how the two approaches are closer than they would appear and, secondly, it gives us some indication of how the competing demands of academic accuracy and political efficacy can be, if not reconciled, at least held in a more productive tension.

If we begin, where readers always begin, with the dustcover comments by 'critics', we see an immediate contrast between Foucault's virginity and his sainthood. Goldhill's book, we are told, is a 'corrective supplement' to Foucault's history of ancient sexuality; it, presumably, shows us where Foucault has gone wrong, it subjects the historian of the prison to the discipline of history. In contrast, Halperin's book, we are told, 'delivers Foucault at last from the pedants and the purists'. Foucault is freed from the constraints of academic purity; he is put 'back on the streets' where he belongs. In this opposition, Foucault is constructed, on one side, as a naive wanderer in the field of ancient literature; a wanderer whose path needs to be corrected. On the other side, he is presented as having blazed a political and theoretical path for queer activism; his life is constructed as an 'exemplary' combination of the intellectual and political concerns of the queer community. These opposing evaluations, however, are not necessarily contradictory: it could be argued that Foucault's sainthood in relation to queer activism depends on his virginity in relation to classical scholarship, as much as his virginity depends on his saintliness. In other words, one could argue that the reason Foucault's history is so useful in political activism is precisely because it is 'wrong'; and that the reason it is so 'wrong' is because his political motivation skews his vision. But what if we were to read Foucault as neither virgin nor saint?

Turning firstly to the reading of Foucault as virgin, Goldhill's central argument is that Foucault's account of ancient erotics is driven by a teleological project which inevitably leads to omissions, distortions and oversimplifications. Foucault, along with Peter Brown and John Winkler, is said to be interested primarily in demonstrating that late antiquity was a crucial moment in a development which has led ultimately to 'roughly this order of things which is ours today'.[11] In order to make this demonstration Foucault, like Brown, focuses on 'didactic texts' whose aim is to promote a normative model of the erotic self; in so doing, he ignores the multiple ways in which the normative 'emerges from, is inscribed in, and is manipulated by erotic narrative'.[12] It is this question of the role of erotic narrative in the constitution and contestation of sexual norms which is the central focus of Goldhill's book; and it is this question which, we are told, Foucault ignores. The problem here is not so much that Foucault fails to discuss erotic narratives,[13] it is rather the way that he discusses them that Goldhill criticizes. Goldhill argues that Foucault's approach to the narratives he discusses is motivated by an exclusive interest in the explicit 'moral' of the tales. His concern to construct a line of development from late antiquity to the present, requires the elision of the humour, irony, ambiguity, and playful cynicism which characterize late Greek erotic literature. In taking these texts at face value, Foucault sacrifices their complexity to his own historical teleology. To do justice to Goldhill, then, he is not criticizing Foucault for a lack of expertise in classical scholarship; rather, he is suggesting that the 'sweep of Foucault's vision' is undermined by the 'fundamentally distorting gap' in his approach to erotic narrative.[14] If we conclude that Foucault's virginity detracts from his broader historical vision, however, we must also recognize that it is one of the conditions of possibility of that vision. This becomes particularly clear in Halperin's account of 'Saint Foucault'.

Halperin's aim in *Saint Foucault* is twofold: firstly, to explain how Foucault came to play a key role in contemporary queer activism; and secondly, to justify his claim that 'the guy was a fucking saint'.[15] The book, therefore, is both a discussion of the current state of queer politics and theory, and an attempt to write a gay hagiography.[16] The approach it adopts to Foucault's work is, therefore, inevitably very different from that adopted by Goldhill: not only does it emphasize political application and efficacy over questions of historical interpretation, but it is motivated by the wish to canonize its subject. In the introduction, Halperin justifies this approach in terms of the politics of the reception of Foucault's work in the

American academy, and the broader context of the position of gay men and lesbian women within educational institutions. He explains his growing identification with Foucault in terms of his increasing marginalization as a gay academic: Foucault's life, as a gay man, provides him with a model of a theoretically and politically engaged intellectual practice. In the context of an institutional politics of truth, then, Foucault is transformed from 'interlocuter' (a thinker with whom one engages critically) into 'exemplum' (a figure one emulates). Halperin illustrates this transformation by quoting part of a review he had written of *The History of Sexuality* volume I:

> Volume One, for all its admittedly bright ideas, is dogmatic, tediously repetitious, full of hollow assertions, disdainful of historical documentation, and careless in its generalizations: it distributes over a period spanning from the seventeenth to the twentieth centuries a gradual process of change well known to Foucault only in its later, mid-nineteenth-century manifestations.[17]

Today, he says, he would not write such a sentence. Having been accused of worshipping Foucault, by critics wishing to delegitimize his work on ancient sexuality, Halperin now, in a familiar tactic of appropriation and reversal, adopts the very position of which he was falsely accused.[18] The canonization of Foucault now appears to be an effective political manoeuvre. If academic or scholarly criticisms of Foucault can be used by those who are hostile to Foucault's political and ethical position, Halperin asks, then why should he, as a politically engaged gay scholar, contribute to such a process?

In a conference presentation of the material which now constitutes Chapters 2 and 3 of this thesis I was confronted with a similar dilemma. Having, perhaps foolishly, presented my reading of Foucault's history of ancient sexuality in terms of its peculiar distortions, certain members of the audience at first happily assumed that I was taking up a position on the ethico-scholarly high ground; a position from which I, with their help, could comfortably attack Foucault's false scholarship. When I made it clear that I was interested in using a Foucaldian ethic more to undermine than to occupy this ground, I was warned that any thinker as unscholarly and untrustworthy as Foucault was obviously incapable of making a contribution to ethics. The irony of my position was that my own critique of Foucault's historical account was being used as a basis for this argument. When Halperin says that he would no longer publicly criticize Foucault's scholarship, then, I can understand his motivation. What I would like to suggest here, however, is that such a strategy can be no more than a temporary solution.

In *Saint Foucault*, Halperin pushes this kind of solution to its extreme logical conclusion: he declares Foucault's sainthood and undertakes to Write a hagiography which will install Foucault as the patron saint of queer activism. The first objection that one might make to such a strategy would be to insist on the contradiction between Foucault's understanding of the intellectual's role in political practice and the idea of a 'patron saint of . . .'. What, we may ask, would Foucault think of his political canonization? But perhaps this kind of objection is not really relevant here. In the first place, it is actually a part of saintliness that the saint should proclaim his or her unsuitability for such an elevation; the saint should have a heightened awareness of their own sin. Secondly, Foucault's own approach to the thinkers who influenced him implies that what *they* would have wanted is irrelevant – apart from being unknowable. In a discussion of his relation to Nietzsche, for example, Foucault explains that for him 'the only valid tribute to thought such as Nietzsche's is precisely to use it, to deform it, to make it groan and protest' (PT, 53–4[753]). Those who Foucault revered most, therefore, were the ones he didn't revere: and while Halperin's metaphor of sainthood implies reverence, his reverence too is of a special kind. In the second part of *Saint Foucault*, 'The Describable Life of Michel Foucault', Halperin argues that we must not canonize Foucault as 'the exponent of some authoritative doctrine'.[19] Rather than revering him in this way, we should see him as 'an instructive example' of someone who, in their life as much as in their work, devised ways of understanding and resisting the conditions in which they lived and worked. Saint Foucault cannot be made the support of a doctrine, he can only provide an example of a practice. So what exactly is wrong with canonizing Foucault – in the way in which Halperin does it? The short answer is that there is nothing wrong with it: it is a potentially fruitful theoretico-political tactic which even Foucault might have appreciated. The long answer, however, is that it tends to elide questions about the 'truth' of historical interpretations; questions which, I will argue in the next section, are of central importance to Foucault's own concerns. The second problem is that in claiming Foucault exclusively for queer politics, Halperin risks reducing rather than promoting the significance and potential of Foucault's contribution to the politics of ourselves.

Turning to the first of these problems – the question of historical inter-pretation – Halperin defends Foucault against two related charges which have been made against his account of the history of the Greek self. The first charge, which is most forcefully made by Pierre Hadot,[20] is that Foucault attributes an anachronistically modern notion of the self to Greek and Roman Stoicism. For Foucault, the ancient self is, supposedly, the object of a personal work which one reflects on and in which one is reflected; a self which is both the ground of one's being and the source of ethical pleasure. In opposition to this view, and against Foucault, Hadot argues that for Greek and Roman thinkers of this period the self is neither 'personal' nor a source of 'pleasure'. The second criticism is that Foucault's project for a contemporary ethics involves a concept of the self which is 'tainted' by nineteenth-century dandyism and aestheticism; it is, supposedly, tainted by a Romantic and elitist dilettantism which makes it an unsuitable source of a contemporary ethics. This charge, which is also made by Hadot (although not in such forceful terms), is often taken to explain the problems in Foucault's historical interpretations. At its most simple, the story goes that Foucault's (gay) dandyism has forced him to read the Greeks as (gay) dandies.[21]

Probably the best reply to this type of criticism is to argue that neither Foucault's contemporary ethics, nor his account of ancient Greek ethics, is significantly influenced by aestheticism. There are, however, several possible ways in which one could make this point. The way Halperin chooses is to argue that both Foucault and the ancients had an *impersonal* notion of the self: a notion which radically differentiates their positions from that of both aestheticism and our modern conceptions of personal identity. One interesting feature of Halperin's presentation of this argument is that he mobilizes Hadot's reputation to support Foucault, while ignoring Hadot's own criticisms of Foucault's reading.[22] While Hadot argues that Foucault imports a *fin de siècle* aestheticist self into his picture of Stoicism, thus misunderstanding the Stoic conception of self, Halperin assumes that Foucault's account in fact agrees with Hadot's reading. Halperin seems to think that by referring to the influence which Hadot's 'magisterial' work had on Foucault he has thereby answered Foucault's critics. While he maintains, quite rightly, that for Foucault the self is not a 'substance' but a 'form' (ECS, 121[718]),[23] he appeals to Hadot to show that for the Stoics too the self is impersonal; the soul is a 'fragment of divine reason'[24] – a conception which is very far from the modern idea of personal identity. Hadot, therefore, has shown us what the Stoics really thought (a pedant and a purist, no doubt) and Halperin has shown us what Foucault really thought. What emerges, to our immense relief, is that these two accounts – Foucault's and the Stoics', Hadot's and Halperin's – conveniently coincide. There is no need to worry about Foucault's historical scholarship because his version agrees with that of the authority in the field; likewise, there is no need to worry about Foucault's aestheticist tendencies because he is really a latter-day Stoic. Just as Gide in Greece would have been an 'austere philosopher' and Seneca in San Francisco would have been a 'gay leatherman – and a butch bottom, at that' so Foucault today is, we are led to believe, a 'Queer Stoic'.[25] Seneca is Foucault, Foucault is Seneca.

The difficulty with this argument is, as I have suggested, a question of the defensibility of an historical interpretation – a question to which Foucault would not be indifferent. It is so clear that Seneca is *not* Foucault and Foucault is *not* Seneca that even Halperin is unable to consistently maintain his argument. Having argued that the self is impersonal for the Greeks, he immediately characterizes their work on the self as a 'vehicle of *personal* autonomy'.[26] Similarly, having pointed out that in discussions of 'the self', in both the Greek texts and Foucault's, the word in question is a mere reflexive pronoun (*heautou* and *soi*),[27] he immediately has to recognize that the Greeks did in fact substantivate this 'self' as the soul (*psuche*). While this soul is indeed an 'impersonal' portion of the divine within us, it is undeniably *our* portion. As Epictetus taught, it has been entrusted to us by Zeus; it is our 'care' and our responsibility. It is *the* self which is within *us*. The point here, however, is not to offer an alternative, 'complete' account of either the Stoic conception of self, or Foucault's: it is simply to suggest that maintaining Foucault's sainthood by erasing the difference between Stoic philosophy and queer theory is, from the point of view of historical interpretation, bizarre. And when this strategy culminates in the argument that Stoic practices of the self 'marginalized' and 'queered' their practitioners,[28] we can be forgiven for hearing, above the sound of leathermen belting up, the stoical laugh of the *senator* Seneca and the *Roman Emperor* Marcus Aurelius.

If Seneca and Marcus Aurelius were not 'queer' in Halperin's sense, then neither was Foucault a queer Stoic. In his discussion of Foucault's aestheticism, Halperin warns against treating this aspect of his ethics 'reductively'[29] – it cannot be simply reduced to or equated with a Baudelairean or Wildean dandyism. Halperin's own treatment of Foucault, however, itself engages in just this form of reductivism. One of the unfortunate effects of constructing Foucault as the patron saint of gay activism,[30] is that he is presented as being both principally inspired by, and principally of use to, the 'queer community'. Foucault, we are told, saw the 'evolution of openly lesbian and gay worlds' as a '*unique* historic opportunity' to revive the ancient aesthetics of existence; and, what is more, an opportunity which, rather than being elitist, would be the 'common property of an entire sub-culture'.[31] This claim of historical uniqueness, however, sits rather uncomfortably with Foucault's involvement in a whole range of political struggles; struggles around psychiatry, the prison and 'traditional morality and hierarchy', which he saw as undermining 'the very bedrock of existence', and transforming those aspects of our lives which are 'most familiar, most solid and most intimately related to our bodies and to our everyday behaviour' (TL, 80[163]). In making this argument, I do not wish to deny the importance of a gay ascesis for Foucault's intellectual life, but simply to point out that he would never define his work exclusively in these terms; there is no such thing for Foucault as a 'unique' historical opportunity. Foucault had too much respect for the 'efficacy of dispersed and discontinuous offensives' (TL, 80[162]) to believe in a 'great soul of revolt'; for him, there are 'many different kinds of revolution, roughly speaking as many kinds as there are possible subversive recodifications of power relations' (TP, 123). The other side of this 'queering' of Foucaldian theory is the presentation of queer politics as the true manifestation of Foucault's approach: Halperin claims that 'certain forms of AIDS activism' are the 'most original, intelligent and creative political embodiment' of Foucault's thought.[32] Indeed, he goes so far as to contrast this use of Foucault with the (only other?) approach to his work – that of 'non-gay-identified critics and philosophers' for whom Foucault represents an end to their 'epistemological and political privileges'.[33] Foucault is a saint, therefore, who provides a model for a political movement; and this movement responds by being the true, unique embodiment of the saint's example. The point that must be made, however, is that while Foucault was, of course, greatly influenced by his experience as a gay man, and while he did see enormous potential in the gay community's reworking of sexual and interpersonal relationships, this connection is neither exclusive nor necessary. It would be a mistake, therefore, to think either that Foucault's thought is entirely determined by his gayness, or that the effect of this thought can be limited to its echoes in contemporary queer theory. This is just the sort of pinning down that Foucault tried, in both his life and his work, to avoid.

What Halperin's hagiography does, and what all hagiographies do, is not to represent an exemplary life, but to construct it. While Goldhill probes Foucault's virginity, Halperin 'exposes his ass';[34] and it is precisely his virginal innocence which allows him to be transformed into the theorist of fist-fucking, and the saint of queer activism. Even though Goldhill and Halperin adopt contrary approaches to Foucault's work, then, their readings are unusually complementary. Goldhill puts aside the political effects of Foucault's work and produces a virgin, Halperin puts aside the question of Foucault's 'accuracy' and produces a saint. Not that there is anything wrong with either approach *per se*. Foucault is important both to classical studies and queer theory; and writers in each field must criticize and appropriate Foucault as their field demands. My point is simply that, as strategies for reading Foucault's histories, each approach has significant drawbacks. In the first place, what has been called 'the Foucault effect' cannot be limited to Foucault's canonization and, secondly, the relation between Foucault's histories and his politico-ethical engagements deserves a reading which is both more open to its political effects and less reverential towards its historical dimensions. Perhaps Saint Foucault is in need of a devil's advocate.

THE TRUTH ABOUT HISTORY

Foucault, like Nietzsche, was a thinker who refused to be confined by disciplinary boundaries; like Nietzsche's, his work is a philosophico-historical intervention in the politics, culture and ethics of its time; and, again like Nietzsche, his writing is as much literary as academic and its effects are as much rhetorical as reasoned. The combination of detailed historical documentation with elegant and convincing prose can produce the effect (in Michel de Certeau's words) of a 'ballet dancer disguised as a librarian'.[35] But the disguise, so some historians would say, is rather thin.[36] and Foucault, far from being a ballet dancer, may also be seen as a 'barbarian horseman' riding with open reins over the multiplicity of historical facts.[37] Both characterizations are perhaps true: Foucault, one could say, is an elegant and accomplished marauder in the field of history. He takes what he wants and leaves behind what does not interest him; he drives the facts before him and bends them to his will. But the account he makes of this process is at once graceful, beguiling and, most importantly, *effective*. Effective, that is, in the sense that Nietzsche's genealogies are effective histories – *wirkliche Historie*.

Even though Foucault knows, for example, that *Madness and Civilization* is, from an historical point of view, 'partial and exaggerated'; and he admits that he may have 'ignored certain elements which would have contradicted me' (FE [805]), what matters to him is that this book affected the way people saw madness. And this is the effect from which the book has gained a status of truth today. Similarly, Foucault points out that during several prison riots in France in the mid-1970s inmates were reading *Discipline and Punish* and passages were being shouted from cell to cell. This effect, he claims – albeit 'pretentiously' – provides proof of the truth, of the 'political, tangible truth' of his book (FE [805]). Foucault clearly does not conceive of the writing of history as the faithful recording of the past; for him the past is not so much another country as another tool – a tool with which to intervene in the present for the sake of a future.

But is this sufficient to free him from the constraints of historical methodology? Is it not important that some things really happened, and some did not? Does the fact that Foucault will confine himself neither to the standards of history nor philosophy mean that his scholarship is entirely without standards? No: the fictioning of history does not necessarily mean the distortion of the past, nor does the cultivation of inter-disciplinarity – what Foucault calls 'de-disciplinizing' the disciplines (PN [19]) – mean the rejection of truth in scholarship. Indeed these questions themselves are based on the dubious assumption that fiction, as a contrary of truth, is equivalent to falsehood. For Foucault, on the contrary, each new interpretation of the past is also answerable to the facts, to what really happened. Foucault is not an historical dilettante: he is as familiar as his critics are with *'la poussière des faits'* (the dust of facts).[38] As we saw in the introduction to this chapter, he continuously appeals to the documentary, factual basis of his historical narratives. But are we not justified in suspecting that this is simply a game – a game of truth? What are we to think when we find that there are gaps, or even distortions in these narratives? What is the double game that Foucault seems to be playing here? How can he disregard *historical* truth in such a cavalier fashion, and justify this in terms of a *present* truth? What are these different forms of truth? Is one to be ignored and one to be pursued?

An answer to these questions lies partly in Foucault's understanding of 'genealogy' as opposed to 'traditional history'. In his 1971 discussion of Nietzsche's genealogical method (NGH), Foucault foreshadows all the concerns which animate his subsequent work. Genealogy is here differentiated from traditional history not by any disregard for historical accuracy but by its opposition to historical 'constants'. It is opposed to the assumption that there is anything in humanity which can escape the contingency of events (NGH, 153[147]). In *Discipline and Punish*, for example, Foucault demonstrates the 'inconstancy' of the human body. He shows how the spread of the techniques of surveillance, discipline and 'dressage', during the eighteenth and nineteenth centuries, produced a human body which was possessed of very different capacities and powers to the body which had preceded it. In the eighteenth century, for example, the soldier's body ceased to be a product of nature: the soldier was no longer a natural phenomenon possessing certain bodily characteristics of strength and agility. Rather, he was something which could be made: any non-military body could now be transformed, through the use of exercise and training, into an obedient and docile machine.[39] What is most significant about this transformation of the human body and of the 'political technology' which makes it possible, however, is that it in turn produces, as its effect and its instrument, a form of subjectivity which 'imprisons' the body. In Foucault's formulation, the disciplinary aspect of this mode of subjectivity is one element of the form of modern subjectivity which we looked at in Chapter

1. The modern 'soul', Foucault argues, the soul which is the object of scientific discourses and techniques such as criminology, psychology and pedagogy, this soul is the 'prison of the body' (*DP*, 30[34]). If the disciplinary seizure of the body, coupled with the discipline's knowledge of the soul, have produced the modern modes of individuality, then to write a history of these procedures is to write a genealogy of morality – an account of the transformations in the 'moral technologies' of modernity.[40] And it is a history, or a genealogy, requiring a specific methodology and approach.

One crucial feature of this approach relates to the status of the objects it chooses. Foucault does not write histories of periods, of individuals, or of institutions.[41] Strictly speaking he does not even write histories of madness, medicine, or the body. Instead, the objects of his analysis are, in the most general terms, ways of dividing the true from the false – it being understood that these are intimately related to practices which have 'real effects' on individuals. We could say that all Foucault's histories are histories of truth or, which is the same thing, histories of power/knowledge relations. For Foucault, truth has become the central problem in history: 'what is history, once there is produced within it the incessant division of the true and the false?' (QM, 11 [29–30]). But the history of truth which Foucault writes neither searches for truth's origin nor its ground of possibility; it is a history which is neither reverential in a Heideggerian sense, nor critical in a Kantian sense. It aims, instead, to understand how our forms of subjectivity have come to be constituted through 'games of truth' (*UP*, 6[12]) – or, through 'the political history of "veridictions"' (CCF, 81). This is a history which, consequently, takes as its primary object the function of truth-producing discourses in the practices of the government of self and others. Its question is: 'How do we connect the way we divide the true from the false to the way we govern ourselves and others?' (QM, 11[30]).

The first methodological problem facing such a history is that it will never be immediately apparent where its boundaries of relevance are to be set. To write a history of our contemporary relations of self to self, for example, is to broach an archive which in principle knows no bounds. There is no self-evident period in which these relations were developed: as Foucault's own trajectory shows, if we follow one particular line of development their emergence can be traced back to Classical Athens. In writing such a history, then, it should be clear that the ideal of exhaustivity cannot be applied: the point is not to give a complete picture of this development, it is rather to analyse some aspects of the practices and discourses by which it is driven. On these grounds it will be possible to say that of course it does not really matter how many Greeks actually practised the ancient techniques of the self, just as it does not really matter whether the multiple projects for prison reform in the nineteenth century were ever actually implemented. Rather, what is important is to understand the 'rationality' of these discourses, the way that they interacted with real contemporary practices, and consequently, the forms of power/knowledge relations which they instituted. A study of the relations between what Foucault calls the 'technology of power' and the 'genealogy of knowledges (*saviors*)', that is, a study of the very means for the production of truth itself, demands a different relation to and understanding of historical veracity (PN [18–19]).

Truth, Foucault argues, is neither outside power, nor is it lacking in power: it is neither the 'reward of free spirits', nor the 'child of protracted solitude'. Truth is 'a thing of this world: it is produced only by virtue of multiple forms of constraint' (TP, 131). In his inaugural lecture at the Collège de France in 1970 (OD), Foucault makes an early attempt to sketch these forms of constraint by which truth is produced. Here he treats the injunction to separate the true from the false as merely one among many of the ways in which discourse is ordered in Western societies. However, it is a form of constraint which, since fifth-century Greece, has gradually come to dominate; and it is this phenomenon which Foucault says he wishes to study in the following years. He outlines a history which will try to analyse the way in which 'we' came to 'choose truth' and the forces which continue to hold us to that choice. This 'morphology' of our 'will to know' (OD, 71[65]) will satisfy a need which continues to be resisted today: the need to continuously interrogate our will to truth (OD, 66[53]). If this will requires constant scrutiny it is because its relation to desire and power must conceal itself behind the facade of the true discourses in which it manifests. The true discourse 'cannot recognise the will to truth which pervades it', just as the will to truth is such that 'the truth it wants cannot fail to mask it' (OD, 56[22]). This mutual masking conceals the 'true' nature of the will to truth: 'a prodigious machinery designed to exclude' (ibid.). As late as 1984 this question, which had animated much of Foucault's work, was still being asked: 'How did it come about that all of Western culture began to revolve around this obligation of truth which has taken a lot of different forms? Things being as they are, nothing so far has shown that it is possible to define a strategy outside of this concern' (ECS, 126[723–4]).

In subsequent years, this insight, that the production of truth and of true discourses is made possible by relations between bodies of knowledge and individual and institutional practices, becomes central to Foucault's concerns. Already in his inaugural lecture Foucault had made the point that discourse is not simply the medium into which struggles and systems of domination are translated: it is also, and perhaps most importantly, that for which and by which one struggles – it is 'the power which one tries to seize' (OD, 53[12]). In later interviews this is presented in terms of 'regimes', 'politics' and 'political economies' of truth. Each society, Foucault argues, has its own 'regime of truth', its own ' "general politics" of truth': that is, it has its systems of distribution – of modes of discourse within the society, of true and false statements within a discourse and of speaking subjects who are sanctioned to participate in particular discourses (TP, 131). In 'societies like ours' this regime has five distinguishing characteristics: truth is centred on the form of scientific discourse; it is subject to economic and political incitement; it is widely diffused and consumed; it is subject to the (always provisional) control of institutions such as the university and the media; and it is what is at stake in a whole series of 'ideological' struggles (TP, 131–2). The task of the genealogist, and more generally of the intellectual, is to recognize that this does not call for a battle 'on behalf of truth': truth does not need to be, and cannot be, 'saved' from the pernicious effects of power. Instead, their task is first to analyse (historically and genealogically) 'the ensemble of rules according to which the true and the false are separated and specific effects of power attached to the true' (TP, 132). And second, in the present, to attempt to detach 'the power of truth from the forms of hegemony, social, economic and cultural, within which it operates at the present time' (TP, 133). A genealogical history, then, is not so much a search for the truth of the past, as an attempt to modify the truth of the present.

This gives rise to a second methodological 'problem': that to write such a history is necessarily to participate in its object of study, since any engagement in the production of a discourse of truth is also an intervention in the way that one governs oneself (and others). The 'truth' of such a discourse cannot be judged solely by its degree of correspondence with other histories: it must also be judged by its subjective effect on its author and its audience. It follows that a history such as Foucault's account of ancient ethical practices must be judged not only in terms of historiographical accuracy, but also in terms of the contribution it makes to the re-interpretation and re-constitution of ethical subjectivities today. The truth of such a re-interpretation comes from its effects as much as from its 'scientific' grounding. If, as Nietzsche holds, the development of humanity is a 'series of interpretations' (NGH, 152[146]), then the legitimate task of the genealogist is not only to record this history but to offer a new interpretation, one which will disassociate and dissolve the coagulated truths of the past. If truth is 'a thing of this world' (TP, 131), then it is subject to change, and if it is subject to change it demands constant re-interpretation. Such a reinterpretation, as we have seen, cannot be subjected to an ideal of exhaustivity or of impartiality: each present re-interpretation is answerable above all to the present in and for which it is produced. For this reason 'the task of telling the truth is an endless labour' (CT, 267[678]) – it is a labour which must be constantly renewed. And it is a labour whose aim is, ultimately, to help us to 'distance ourselves from ourselves' (*se déprendre de soi-même*).

In the 'long baking process of history' (NGH, 144[139]) many errors have become irrefutable truths. However the problem – for Foucault as much as for Nietzsche – lies not in their being errors, but in their being irrefutable. If truths are metaphors,[42] then irrefutable truths are those metaphors which have become hardened and congealed. The hardening of a metaphor, however, 'guarantees absolutely nothing concerning its necessity',[43] and since 'the drive toward the formation of metaphors is the fundamental human drive',[44] then the opposition to irrefutable truths becomes a primary function of critique. Effective history, therefore, is without 'constants' (NGH, 153[147]) in the sense that, for it, nothing in humanity is beyond contingency and also in the sense that, for it, truths must never become irrefutable. This is especially true of those truths which bind us to ourselves, and the whole point of genealogical history, for Foucault, is to contribute to the dissolution of these bonds. Genealogy is committed, not to understanding an identity which persists across time, but to 'cutting' the ties which bind us to that identity.[45] Its purpose is not to discover the roots or the origins of our identity, it is to 'commit itself to its dissipation' (NGH, 162[154]). And in order to do this, it must re-appropriate and re-interpret the appropriations and interpretations of the past.

While it might be the case, then, that from a certain point of view these historical accounts are 'fictions', what is important is that at the level of a present concern they are 'true'. 'I am well aware,' Foucault says, 'that I have never written anything but fictions' (P/K, 193[DE III, 236]). But a fiction is not merely a false or inaccurate telling of events; a fiction is a production, a creation, a transformation of reality; fiction is as much verb as noun. 'One 'fictions' history on the basis of a political reality that makes it true, one 'fictions' a politics not yet in existence on the basis of a historical truth' (ibid.). The first part of this statement elucidates Foucault's motivation in undertaking historical research in any particular field. There is always a 'political reality' which calls for the fictioning of a history. The political climate of the 1970s, for example, 'demanded' a history of the techniques of incarceration and normalization, just as it demanded a history of sexuality. These histories, *Discipline and Punish* and *The History of Sexuality*, volume I, are frequently cavalier in their generalizations and occasionally unreliable in their treatment of historical documentation; but the essential point for Foucault is that they contribute to a contemporary political situation. They do not contribute, however, by simply being pressed into the service of a pre-existing political agenda. Rather, as the second part of the statement shows, Foucault's intention is that they should produce, that they should fiction, a *new* politics. They aim to 'provoke an interference between our reality and what we know of our past history' – to produce an interference which, at its best, will produce 'real effects on our present history', effects which, rather than bolstering old positions, will defamiliarize and disaggregate, thus opening up a possible future. The relations which hold, in Foucault's practice of history, between the past and the present, truth and fiction are highly complex: a political reality gives rise to an historical fiction, which fictions a new politics that retroactively underwrites the truth of the history. It is, therefore, only in their future that Foucault's histories can become 'true'.

Our problem is to know how to balance these two demands: the demand that a history be true 'in terms of academic truth' and also true in the sense that it produces an experience which permits 'a transformation of the relation which we have to ourselves and the world' (EMF, 45–6). If Foucault's role as intellectual is to pose questions, not only 'effectively', but also 'truly' and with 'the greatest possible rigour' (EMF, 77), then who will decide when this level of rigour has been reached? And how effective will the questioning remain if this rigour is cast into doubt?

LEARNING FROM THE PAST

Over the last four chapters we have explored the specific features of Foucault's account of ancient ethics – that is, the defining characteristics which distinguish his interpretation from much of 'mainstream' classical scholarship. And we have also investigated the extent to which Foucault's more daring pronouncements on the nature of ancient ethics might contradict his own historical research. We have found that Foucault's account is certainly more 'aestheticist' than most, but that this emphasis is justified, to a great extent, by some of the defining features of ancient ethical discourse. Nevertheless, we have also seen that there are occasions when Foucault may overstate the case for an aesthetic interpretation of this ethics – especially in the more informal context of his late interviews. We have also looked, in particular, at two very different recent works on Foucault's history of ancient sexuality and argued that both reading strategies tend to ignore an important aspect of Foucault's concerns; that is, they fail to adequately take into account both Foucault's concern for truth and his concern for the present. But what have we learnt about Foucault's approach to contemporary ethics by following him on this 'journey to Greece'?

We have gained an insight into the importance of the interplay between historical fact and ethico-political project in Foucault's work. Foucault's histories are never purely a matter of history, just as his ethical and political engagements in the present are never focused exclusively on that present. Rather, a present situation motivates a particular historical research, which in turn modifies one's attitude to the present. Foucault, for example, works out and modifies his conception of power *through* the research he undertakes in *The History of Sexuality*, volume I:

> ... it is a question of forming a different grid of historical decipherment by starting from a different theory of power; and, at the same time, of advancing little by little towards a different conception of power through a closer examination of an entire historical material (*VS*, 90–1[120]).

The historical material, therefore, is not a passive object of study; it provides an opportunity to modify one's theoretical tools and to transform one's attitude towards the present. It would then clearly be an undervaluation of Foucault's work to read his histories simply against the criteria of academic historiography; just as it would be an undervaluation – or perhaps an overvaluation – to suppose that his histories can entirely escape these demands, or to suppose that 'sympathetic' readers must defend them in every detail of their interpretations. In other words, it is impossible to disentangle Foucault the 'historian' – the scholar who jokingly said he would 'cover [him]self with ashes' because he did not know the date of introduction of the baby's feeding bottle (CF, 228[329]) – from Foucault the 'intellectual' – whose aim was to help us to change the way that we think, act and relate to ourselves and others. There is no infallible scale on which a balance between these two equally legitimate demands can be measured. For those who value historical accuracy as an end in itself, no doubt Foucault does appear to be an uncouth 'barbarian'. And for those who wish to uncritically follow in Foucault's path, no doubt the demand for accuracy appears to be unnecessarily restrictive. From the point of view of my argument, however, the issue is not how much 'civilisation' should we impose on a 'barbaric' Foucault; but how much does this exploration of the particularities of volumes II and III of *The History of Sexuality* tell us about Foucault's vision of a contemporary ethics? Are we now in a position to say more about his understanding of the role the 'aesthetic' could play in ethics? Can we be more precise now about the kind of inspiration he drew from Greco-Roman examples?

In answer to the first of these questions we can say that for Foucault ethics once was and could again be an aesthetics in the sense that its *mode* of application could be technical and ascetic – that is, it could be aesthetic in an ethico-poetical sense. While Foucault's use of the aesthetic metaphor also plays on the idea of an aesthetic end for ethics, especially in his interpretation of the Classical Greek ethical model, it is clear that his most considered accounts are careful to distinguish between the mode and the end of ethics. In the next chapter we will see that this is also the case in regard to his preliminary suggestions about the shape of a contemporary practice of ethics.

In answer to the second question we can say that Greco-Roman reflections upon ethics are important for Foucault because they show not only a crucial stage in the emergence of Western technologies of the individual, but also because they provide an example of a culture which – for all its elitism, sexism and xenophobia – conceived of ethics in a way that placed the singular individual at the centre of an attempt to cultivate forms of liberty. The fact that Greek society was structured around fixed hierarchies and orders of domination does not, for Foucault, detract from the value of this particular aspect of its culture. If anything, it has the value of making us more aware both of what there is to gain and of what there is to lose in any attempt to arrive at new practices of liberty.

PART TWO

CHAPTER 6

Refusing the Self

We, however, *want to become those we are* – human beings who are new, unique, incomparable, who give themselves laws, who create themselves.

Friedrich Nietzsche[1]

Maybe the target nowadays is not to discover what we are but to refuse what we are ... We have to promote new forms of subjectivity through the refusal of this kind of individuality which has been imposed on us for several centuries.

Michel Foucault (SP, 785)

[The subject] is not a substance; it is a form ...

Michel Foucault (ECS, 121[718])

In Part One, I argued that Foucault's ethical project was to find ways of escaping from modernity's dominant forms of ethical subjectivity. In order to measure the extent to which an aesthetics of existence could respond to this demand, we made a long detour in through Foucault's interpretation of what he saw as the ancient Greek and Roman elaboration of this practice. Now we are ready to take up the challenge of indicating how a contemporary elaboration of that practice might look. In the Introduction I indicated that one test, or experiment, we might conduct here is to see if we could generate a model of a Foucaldian ethics based on Foucault's own fourfold division of ethical practices. In other words, would it be possible to extract from Foucault's late writings and interviews a coherent account of how, today, one could approach the question of the well-lived life? Could we extract an account which would address the ethical substance of such a life, its mode of subjectivation, its particular tools and techniques, and its telos, or aim. It seems to me that it is now possible to begin to sketch such a model.

We saw in Chapter 1 that the first element of the ethics which emerges in Foucault's late work, the ethical substance, consists of the forms of subjectivity which are imposed on us, and which we impose on ourselves, through a range of power/knowledge/self practices. These modes of sub-jectivity can range from forms of sexual identity, whether marginal or dominant, to the ways in which we are brought to embrace the ideals of our socio-cultural milieux. They involve complete ways of life which determine our modes of being, thinking and doing, and insofar as these modes of subjectivity become problematized for us, insofar as they become untenable, they become the material, the substance, for an ethical intervention and transformation. In this chapter, I continue to explore Foucault's under-standing of the substance of ethics, by addressing the question of the self that Foucault calls on us to refuse, and subsequently to create as a work of art. This will require me to give an account of Foucault's conception of critique – a conception which both rests upon a particular concept of the subject and makes possible the practical refusal of that subject in political and ethical terms. And it will also require me to address the question of the material which could be said to be formed in the process of subjectivation. If the subject is a form, what is the matter that is so formed? If ethics is an aesthetics of the self, then what kind of self is it that can be taken as the object of an aesthetic work, of an ascetic intervention?

HOW ONE REFUSES WHAT ONE IS

The point at which the critical projects of Foucault and Nietzsche converge – and at which their divergence from a large part of modern philosophy is greatest – is in relation to the question of Man, or the question of the subject. When the genealogical method is applied to this entity, when the subject is treated as a phenomenon with a history in which the complex interplay between relations of truth, power and self is evident, then the subject loses its foundational status. As soon as the subject becomes a natural, as opposed to a metaphysical or a transcendental, phenomenon, it is not only given a history but – crucially for ethics and politics – it is given a *future*.

Nietzsche argues that when we say 'the lightning flashes' we in fact 'double the deed' – we posit the phenomenon of lightning as both doer and deed – we treat the lightning as a substance which acts.[2] In the same way, he argues, we double the deed in relation to human action: our 'popular morality' operates on the principle that behind the moral conduct of indivi-duals there is a 'neutral substratum' which is *free* to behave either well or badly. But this substratum, for Nietzsche, does not exist: it is simply a self-deception of 'the weak and oppressed of every kind' who need to interpret their weaknesses as results of their free-will, as attesting to the moral quality of their own character.[3] What Foucault shares with Nietzsche, is the general principle that *behind* the moral behaviour of the individual there is no substantial self, no centre of free will which grounds and makes possible moral (or any other) behaviour. 'I do indeed believe,' Foucault says, 'that there is no sovereign, founding subject, a universal form of subject to be found everywhere' (AE, 50[733]). We have already seen, however, that he does not share Nietzsche's interpretation of the role of slave morality in the institution of the illusion of a substantive self. The shift from pagan to Christian ethics cannot be a question of a struggle between noble and slave moralities, for Foucault, because he sees many of those features that Nietzsche attributes exclusively to the Christian slave revolt already developing within Classical and Hellenistic ethics. Along with Nietzsche, however, Foucault also denies that the subject exists as a transcendental condition of possibility of experience. Rather, what we call experience is, for Foucault, a rationalization of the contingent and provisional process by which a subjectivity takes shape through a particular organization of a self-consciousness.[4]

The subject is neither a given nor a necessary condition. It is an achievement which emerges in the interstices of the power/truth/self triangle: 'the self is nothing more than the correlate of technology built into our history' (HL).[5] Already in *Discipline and Punish*, Foucault had argued that the Man which humanism urges us to liberate is 'in himself the effect of a subjection much more profound than himself' (*DP*, 30[34]). By subjection, he later makes clear, he means the process by which individuals become subjects (*VS*, 60[81]) – the process of subjectivation. As Paul Veyne explains in a different context: '*What is made*, the object [in this case the 'subject'], is explained by what went into its *making* at each moment of history; we are wrong to imagine that the *making*, the practice, is explained on the basis of what is made.'[6] This process of making a subject produces a subject in two senses: firstly, in the sense of being 'subject to someone else by control and dependence' and, secondly, in the sense of being 'tied to his own identity by a conscience or self-knowledge' (SP, 781). Both senses of the term, however, 'suggest a form of power which subjugates and makes subject to' (ibid.); as do both senses of the French term Foucault uses – *assujettisse-ment*.[7] It is interesting to compare this gloss on the two meanings of subject with Althusser's classic formulation of the subject as a free subjected being. For Althusser, the condition of becoming a subject is one's 'free' acceptance of one's subjection – and our subjective freedom is therefore an illusion.[8] Similarly, in Foucault, the sense of the subject as a free centre of consciousness and willing is replaced with the idea of being forcibly tied to a particular, imposed identity. To this extent, for both of them, one is always less free than one imagines.[9]

What are the implications of claiming that the subject is not a substance but a form? What view is Foucault implicitly rejecting here and what view is he proposing in its place? In a discussion of his own intellectual development, Foucault explains his philosophical trajectory as an attempt to escape, to 'get out from', what he calls the philosophy of the subject.[10] By philosophy of the subject he means any philosophy which gives the individual subject a fundamental role in the constitution of meaning. It is a type of philosophy which, in one way or another, sees 'the foundation of all knowledge and the principle of all signification as stemming from the meaningful subject' (SS, 8–9). For Foucault, the problem with this philosophical perspective is, firstly, that it cannot adequately account for the history of knowledge and, secondly, that it cannot account for those non-subject-centred mechanisms for the production of meaning which structuralism uncovered in linguistic and social structures.[11] While acknowledging that the two dominant paths out of this philosophy were, on the one hand, logical positivism and, on the other hand, semiology (incorporating linguistics, psychoanalysis and anthropology), Foucault characterizes his own path as leading towards a Nietzsche-inspired 'genealogy of the modern subject' (SS, 9). It was the reading of Nietzsche, he says, which first taught him that 'there is a history of the subject just as there is a history of reason' (SPS, 23). When Foucault rejects the idea that the subject is a substance, then, he is rejecting a modern philosophical tradition – from Descartes and Kant to Husserl and Sartre – for which the individual subject is a constant, ahistorical ground and source of human knowledge, meaning and value.

Foucault's subject is not a substance, it is a 'form' which has a history and a future. If there are no historically constant forms of subjectivity, if there is no transcendental subject to ground individual subjects, then how does history give shape to actual forms of subjectivity? To answer this question we do not need a general theory of human subjectivity, nor do we need to uncover a set of unsurpassable universals of human experience. What we need is a genealogy, rather than a metaphysics, of the subject. And Foucault provides us with a genealogy which, at least initially, focuses on a precise historical period – between the mid-eighteenth and the mid-nineteenth centuries. For it is during this period that Foucault sees the birth, not only of the sciences of man, but also of that Man which is their object. For Foucault, this is a crucial period in the history of modern Western subjectivity, because it was then that the currently dominant modes of power/knowledge/self were formed. While Foucault reconsidered his somewhat ambitious claim, made in *The Order of Things*, that this Man faced imminent erasure (*OT*, 387[398]), he nevertheless continued to hold that such an event *was* possible. No matter in what terms one speaks about the birth or the death of man, for Foucault the essential point to recognize is that these are historical events. The modern subject has a history, and therefore may have an end:

> ... in the course of their history men have never stopped constructing themselves, that is to say continually displacing their subjectivity, constituting themselves in an infinite and multiple series of different subjectivities which will never come to an end and will never bring us face to face with something which would be Man ... In speaking of 'the death of man', in a confused and simplifying way, that was what I wanted to say ... (EMF, 123[75]).

With every new stage of his work – as the above passage shows – Foucault redefined what had gone before. Hence, at a certain time he insists that scientific rationalities really were not what interested him; at a later time he rejects the idea that power is the central focus of his work; and, during the final stage of his work, he insists that neither knowledge nor power, but rather – depending on the interview – either truth or subjectivity are what he has *always* been interested in. What becomes increasingly apparent, however, is that three fields, or three axes, are being defined here which are all of equal importance in investigating the historical formation of subjectivities. In Foucault's work from the late 1970s, it is clear that any adequate account of the forms of human subjectivity has to position itself in relation to the power/knowledge/self triangle. It has to deal with the way that an individual is formed (and forms itself) by being subjected to (and subjecting itself to) a true discourse which entails effects of power (and a form of power which mobilizes effects of truth). But, how then is the subject formed?

The subject is not a substance, it is a form which is constituted through practices that are always specific to particular social and historical contexts. In *Discipline and Punish*, Foucault presents a picture in which bodies in modern societies are seized by concrete apparatuses of power/knowledge. The prison with its regulated time and space, the school with its hierarchically ordered pedagogy, the factory with its constant surveillance and measurement of activity, are practices that wring from individuals, or instil within them, the soul, subject, or self which guarantees their continued subjection. Slightly later, in *The History of Sexuality*, volume I, Foucault focuses on the modern emergence of sexuality, and here one gets a sense that this subjection is perhaps less violent, less directly corporeal than previously presented. The *scientia sexualis* is perhaps less violent than the arts of discipline. The example of Herculine Barbin,[12] which I discussed in Chapter 1, illustrates this difference in physicality. While Herculine is indeed subjected to a series of intrusive medical examinations (including a post mortem), the social, legal and religious apparatuses that regulate her sexuality do not operate primarily *through* her body. While prison inmates are normalized by means of a series of physical restraints placed on their movements, Herculine is abandoned by the disciplinary apparatus as soon as her body is found to be male. Later again, in volumes II and III of *The History of Sexuality*, the process of subjectivation becomes even less corporeal – indeed, despite the fact that the ostensible subject matter is sexual practice, one could be excused for thinking that bodies hardly enter into these two volumes. Instead, the process of subjectivation occurs in what, for want of a better phrase, one could call the psychological realm of the individual's relation to self. This is not only a form of subjection which is less physical, it is also one for which there is no clearly discernible external source. It is a subjection which is apparently self-imposed – at the individual's choice and instigation.

This does not mean that Foucault is abandoning an earlier emphasis on the physicality of subject-formation, nor does it mean that he is turning to some sort of subject-centred psychologism: rather, it indicates a progressive movement through the three axes which we have already identified. This movement involves neither the supercession nor the sublation of earlier moments, but rather an unequal emphasis depending on the historical epoch, or phenomenon being investigated. In an early work such as *Madness and Civilization*, Foucault examines the web of discursive practices which constitute the kinds of subject which, in the modern West, we have come to understand as mad. In *Discipline and Punish* he gives an account of the emergence of the delinquent as a form of subjectivity and, beyond this, investigates some key elements in the production, through the humanistic disciplines, of the modern subject. *The History of Sexuality*, volume I, sketches the emergence of the set of discursive practices which have formed 'us' as subjects of sexuality. It shows how, within the complex interplay between power formations and bodies of knowledge, certain forms of subjectivity and experience are constituted. Finally, the second and third volumes of *The History of Sexuality* treat the constitution of subjectivities in the light of the self-reflective practices in which individuals engage. These volumes prioritize the third point in the triangle (self) in their account of the modes and techniques of self-formation. Knowledge, power, self (or alternatively truth, coercion, subjectivity) are the three aspects under which Foucault considers the historically emergent modes of subject-formation. What he provides us with, in all of this work, is an account of the means by which forms of madness, criminality and sexuality were imposed upon certain individuals. And he also assesses the price individuals pay for accepting and telling this type of truth about themselves. 'This is my question: at what price can subjects speak the truth about themselves?' (SPS, 30). And the answer, or at least part of the answer, is: at the price of being (self-)constituted as a particular kind of subject, at the price of being tied (by oneself and others) to a particular identity.

Foucault's opposition to these modern practices of subject formation is both theoretically and practically motivated. He is hostile, firstly, to the philosophical *theory* that behind or beyond these historical phenomena there might be a transcendental substratum; because there is a close connection between the modern philosophy of the subject and the modern subjection of the individual. But he is also opposed to the actual *practice* of subject formation as it operates in modern societies. Because, in Foucault's estimation, the price we pay for these forms is too high. But how are we to combat these forms? How do we refuse to pay this price? How do we refuse what we are?

At a certain stage of his work, Foucault presents the subjection that is inherent in subjectivation in predominantly negative terms – it is born out of 'punishment, supervision and constraint' (*DP*, 29[34]). The individual, he argues, is not only an 'effect of power', it is also 'its vehicle' (TL, 98[180]). The individual, the subject, is not the elementary material upon which power is exercised – it is not opposed to power as freedom is to repression. Rather, it is a necessary link and 'point of articulation' ('*un relais*') which facilitates certain operations of power. Foucault also supplements this account with the view that this subjection is not only produced by *positive* as opposed to repressive means, but that it can give rise to new subjective potentialities, potentialities which may eventually be redirected *against* the very conditions which made them possible.[13] This view emerges in one of its earliest forms in 'What is Critique?', where Foucault undertakes an investigation into the emergence in modernity of what he calls the 'critical attitude' (QC, 382[36]).

This investigation leads Foucault to the hypothesis that the process which he described as 'the "governmentalization" of the state' (OG, 103) – a process beginning in the sixteenth century – cannot be separated from contemporaneous attempts to criticize and combat particular modes of government.'[14] If, on the one hand, the fifteenth and sixteenth centuries saw a 'veritable explosion in the arts of governing', an explosion whose guiding question was 'how to govern?', this period also saw the birth of a critical attitude whose guiding question was 'how not to be governed?', or more precisely, 'how not to be governed like that, at that price, in that way?' In other words, in response to the cultivation of the arts of governing in the fifteenth and sixteenth centuries, there emerged the counter-cultivation of the arts of not being governed – of not being governed '*like that*, by that, in the name of these principles, in view of such objectives and by the means of such methods, not like that, not for that, not by them' (QC, 384[38]).

It is through the growth of this attitude, as a necessary 'partner and adversary' of governmentalization (ibid.), that Foucault threads the commonality of an attitude which stretches from Martin Luther through the Enlightenment and Kant to twentieth-century critical theory and the French reception of Nietzsche's philosophy. If, on the one hand, govern-mentalization is a procedure which links power, truth and subjectivity in a particular way – it is a question of 'subjugating (*assujettir*) individuals ... by mechanisms of power that appeal to a truth' (QC, 386[39]) – then the critical attitude is a movement in which the subject claims the right 'to question truth on its effects of power and to question power on its discourses of truth' (ibid.). Its function is 'desubjectivation (*désassujettisse-ment*) within the game of what one could call, in a word, the politics of truth' (ibid.). But, to recall the Nietzschean echo mentioned above, this work of desubjectivation can only be carried out on the basis of, and using the tools provided by, the process of subjectivation itself. In a sense, government imposes freedom on the subject, it installs freedom as a central characteristic of modern subjectivity and, having done so, we should not be surprised if that installation leads to unexpected and undesired conse-quences – consequences such as the cultivation of the arts of 'voluntary inservitude' and 'reflective indocility' (ibid.). Far from being a neutral observer of these consequences – someone who would coolly and objectively describe their course – Foucault is actively committed to their advancement. No diagnosis of the present, he points out, can simply consist in a 'charac-terization of what we are' (SPS, 36). If 'what we are' is contingent and uncertain, if our forms of subjectivity are shot through with 'lines of fragi-lity', then our description must be made in accordance with 'these kinds of virtual fracture' (ibid.). Because it is these lines, these fractures, which help us to 'open up the space of freedom ... of possible transformation' (ibid.).

An important methodological tool in opening up this space is what Foucault calls – apologizing for the 'horror' of the word – '*événementialisa-tion*' (QC, 393[47]).[15] This tool emerges from an approach to history which insists that the apparent limits and universal necessities of our historical moment are merely *events* which are 'fragile' and 'impermanent' and have no validity or necessity beyond the fact of their occurrence (QC, 398[53]). It holds out the possibility that these singularities can be turned around, 'inverted' and 'stripped' of their coercive effects (ibid.). What eventalization makes possible and encourages, then, is precisely the voluntary insubordination of one's decision not to be governed. The 'theoretico-political' function of eventalization is both to undermine acceptance of established historical narratives and to contribute to the 'multiplication' of the kinds of historical explanation that are accepted.[16] It aims, firstly, to make it more difficult to mobilize historical constants and universal anthropological assumptions in the writing of history; it aims to uncover what Foucault calls *singularities*, where one had only seen instances of a universal (QM, 6[23]). Secondly, it proceeds towards a multiplication of the causes of a given event or occurence; rather than explaining a multiplicity of phenomena in terms of one cause or origin (the procedure of a form of history which Foucault rejects), it analyses a singularity in terms of a multiplicity of causes. If we take the prison, for example, as an historical singularity, this mode of analysis will lead to a proliferation of causes: one will be led to consider not only the techniques and discourses which are internal to the prison institution, but also the techniques and discourses of school discipline, of institutional architecture, of military training and of industrial organization (QM, 7[24]). But the patterns which are formed between these disparate practices and discourses, the strategic relations which join and separate them, are never more than one possible mode of organizing the field. It was not, for instance, necessary or inevitable that the prison, as disciplinary institution, would become the one, obvious apparatus of punishment in the nineteenth century. The fact that it did so is the particular contingent outcome of a multiplicity of strategic relations. This is a view of history which could be described as 'kaleidoscopic'. The pattern that exists at any given time is largely the outcome of temporary, contingent, fragile alliances and oppositions; and the next pattern is, by definition, totally unpredictable. But it is, nevertheless, a *pattern;* and as such it can be analysed and understood – although not 'explained' (in the sense of being traced back to a necessary origin or cause). What eventalized history amounts to is a form of history which, despite its inability to assign causal explanations and to deduce historical necessities, is a more effective embodiment of the critical attitude. It is more effective because its recognition of the contingency of any given pattern opens up the space in which modifications and transformations can be carried out.

The second key feature of a description which would promote such an opening is what Foucault calls 'problematization'. Problematization (or problemization[17]) is a term Foucault introduces in the early 1980s – apparently to refer both to an historical phenomenon which is to be analysed and to one aspect of the method of analysis itself. As a historical phenomenon, problematization is that movement by which thought detaches itself from what one does, 'establishes it as an object and reflects on it as a problem' (PPP, 388[597]). It is that process by which, for example, the practice of the love of boys by adult male citizens in Classical Greece becomes subject to a whole series of literary, philosophical and moral reflections. This process is itself by no means inevitable: it will only occur in relation to a domain of action which has been called into question or undermined in its familiar acceptance by the surrounding social and political context. And it is a process which does not lead to a single solution or way of dealing with the problem. Rather, it leads to a variety of potentially conflicting responses and proposed solutions.

From Foucault's point of view, what is interesting is to discern the way these responses all relate to a particular form of problematization; to discern, that is, 'what has made possible the transformations of the difficulties and obstacles of a practice into a general problem for which one proposes diverse practical solutions' (PPP, 389[598]). On this basis, he suggests, one could for example consider the diverse philosophical schools of the Hellenistic period as embodying different responses to 'the difficulties of traditional sexual ethics' (ibid.). Or, one could consider the multiple proposals for penal codes and systems of punishment at the end of the eighteenth century as varying responses to the shifting socio-economic and political context of illicit behaviour. Such an approach differs from either a history of ideas or a history of behaviours, because its focus is the work of thought upon itself. It maintains a focus both on the forms of problematizaton and on the practices on which these forms are based. In a sense, it situates itself between the history of ideas and the history of behaviours: its object of study is the field of continuous exchange between these two domains.

This is not an historical process, however, which is simply to be described and analysed; rather, it is a work of thought which, through an historical investigation, is to be taken up again and re-mobilized. Its critical aspect resides in the opportunity it gives one to open up the modes of problematization which still define the field of possible solutions today. In other words, it equips one to redefine the field of possible practices today by uncovering the process through which the dominant solutions emerged. In the field of ethics, for example, it leads to the suspicion that the modern solutions to the question 'how are we to live' do not exhaust the field of possibilities, just as in the field of sexuality it leads to the suspicion that the modes of sexuality which have been imposed since the middle of the nineteenth century are not the only possible ways of organizing a body's capacity for pleasure. Problematization not only entails an attitude towards the past, then, it also entails an attitude towards the present; an attitude of 'perpetual re-problematization'.[18] And it is an attitude which is based not only on the observation that this present, any present, is a fragile and contingent arrangement of possibilities, but also on the critical attitude that what is to be combated are all those who would attempt to deny this contingency and to preserve its accidental forms.[19] 'The work of thought,' Foucault suggests (echoing Nietzsche's hostility towards 'old habits'), 'is not to denounce the evil which, supposedly, secretly inhabits everything that exists; but to see in advance the danger which threatens in everything that is habitual, and to render problematic everything that is solid'.[20] Problematization is, therefore, both the subject matter of Foucault's history *and* the contemporary project of Foucault's critique.

WHAT ONE IS

If 'what one is' is a form, a contingent mode of organization, then one would be justified in asking: 'a form of what?'; 'an organization of what?' Does this formal conceptualization of the subject not also imply a substratum, a basic material *from which* a subject is formed? And if so, how can Foucault answer this question without appealing to something like a transcendental ground of subjectivity? When Althusser, whose account of the subject we have already referred to, is faced with this question he admits that the theoretical distinction between 'individuals' and 'subjects' (individuals are interpellated into subjects) is an artificial one. There is no such thing as a before the subject, since concretely existing human individuals have 'always-already' been subjects.[21] One might be tempted to take the same approach in relation to Foucault; that is, to argue that since we are always-already embodiments of particular modes of subjectivity there is no need, and indeed it is impossible, to question what we would be outside these modes. Because even though no one particular mode is unsurpassable, it is certainly not the case that we could hope to dispense with *all* such forms; there is no hint in Foucault that subjectivity itself is discardable – it is merely modifiable. Therefore, one might argue, it is a question which one is justified in avoiding. And yet, there is a sense in which this question is of crucial importance for Foucault's project, in that it helps to either expand or contract the limits of possibility of subjective transformation. What exactly is it that we as human beings can and cannot discard? Are there any limits to the undefined work of freedom?

Against all the critics for whom Foucault's late work constitutes a capitulation in the face of the moral superiority of humanism,[22] Gilles Deleuze offers a timely antidote.[23] Against the lack of imagination which would reduce Foucault's care of the self to a newly enlightened admiration for Man, he proposes a reading of the Foucaldian subject which does not betray Foucault's persistent nominalism. Foucault's subject, in Deleuze's Nietzschean reading, is merely the effect of a force which is folded back upon itself. The human animal is an initially (or, potentially) chaotic complex of forces, powers or capacities; and, on Deleuze's reading of Foucault, the Greek human animal was perhaps the first to achieve a bending back of these forces upon themselves. The Greek male citizen was, perhaps, the first human to create a form of interiority which we designate with the term subject. This 'perhaps' is important, as it is not clear if Deleuze is claiming that *no* fold of interiority had been achieved by earlier (or other) cultures, although he does entertain the possibility that what he calls 'the Orient' knew no processes of subjectivation.[24] However, whether or not this process of subjectivation is unique to the Greeks – a claim it would be difficult to justify – the Greeks may be said to give it a unique form. Because what they discovered, according to Deleuze, is that the bending back of a force upon itself, the folding of a force, can 'only' be achieved by 'strategy': that is, it can only be achieved on the basis of the agonistic relation between citizens. The government of the self can only (at least for the Greeks) be established on the basis of a government of others.[25] It follows, for Deleuze, that the most general formula of this relation to oneself is 'the affect of self by self, or folded force'[26] – an affect which always occurs in the context of a particular set of external power/knowledge relations.

On the basis of this understanding of the process of subjectivation, we can say that for Foucault the matter of that process, the material which in some sense can be said to be prior to the subject, is the brute, disorganized and relatively chaotic set of capacities, powers and forces which a human animal possesses. This bare minimum of human being, or what Patton has called this 'thin' concept of the human being, is distinguishable from the originary subject of either transcendental idealism or phenomenology because it, in effect, is *not* the (or even 'a') subject. If we recall the claim Foucault makes in *The History of Sexuality*, volume I – that 'sex' is nothing more than an 'ideal point' which is necessary to and conjured by the discourse of sexuality[27] – then we have a way of understanding the fictive status of the subject which has been theorized in modern philosophical discourse. One could argue that this subject is, like sex, nothing more than a 'fictitious unity' which combines the experiences of consciousness and self-consciousness into an ideal point which functions both as anchor and mask for the processes of subject-formation. What Foucault's analysis does, in its persistent nominalism, is to reverse the standard modern picture of this process. It argues that, far from the concrete, individual subject being an effect, or result, of a transcendental subject, it is the transcendental subject which is a mere after-effect, a holographic projection, of the historically, materially grounded work of subjectivation.

It follows that the question 'what comes before the subject?' can be answered for Foucault without appealing to some ahistorical universal form or ground of subjectivity – and also without simply making the (necessary) point that this 'before' can never be located in history. For Foucault, the material of the work of subjectivation is merely the (always mutating) set of brute capacities and forces of the human animal. At any particular point in history, however, what one has to deal with are not these 'brute facts', but the historically modified set of characteristics and capacities which subjectivation offers at that time. Any new subjective capacity, then – such as, for example, the capacity for introspection – becomes material which can be taken up, modified and put to different uses at a later time. It is this kind of possibility which Nietzsche, as we have seen, recognizes in a phenomenon such as asceticism: asceticism may indeed spring from *reactive* forces, but this does not prevent it from playing a part in later *active* modifications of subjectivities. Similarly, in Foucault's view, the fact that a practice such as, for example, '*l'écriture de sai*' is now a part of the cultural arsenal of Western subjectivity, opens up a completely non-predetermined future for its subjective effects.

One of the barriers to accepting this argument that the processes of subjectivation are prior to the subject, the soul, or the authentic self, is that in the idea of a relation of self to self, or of an art of the self, there appears to be a hidden assumption that 'the self' precedes this relation or art. In much of Foucault's discussion, whether of the ancient techniques of the self, or of the contemporary need for a new relation to the self, the reader is faced with a continuous temptation to give this self an ontological precedence. The preceding discussion, however, coupled with a consideration of the problems which arise from working between four languages (Greek, Latin, French and English) can help to remove this potential for misunderstanding. One source of this possible misunderstanding is the fact that while the Greek, Latin and French phrases *epimeleia heautou, cura sui* and *sauci de soi* avoid any implication of a substantial 'self', the English phrase 'care of the self' does not. In both the Greek and the Latin case the term which is translated as 'the self' is merely a reflexive pronoun which does no more than imply the kind of 'fold' or 'bending back' of which Deleuze speaks. These terms in no way fix or pre-judge the nature of the *source* of that force. In the case of the French phrase *souci de soi*, however, the structure

does seem to suggest something more than a mere reflexive pronoun –
especially when considered in the light of the English translation 'care of
the self'. This translation is, however, a misleading one: the French equivalent of 'care of the self' (with definite article) would be *sauci du* (de + le)
soi, not, as Foucault always gives, *sauci de sai*. A more correct rendition of
Foucault's phrase would, then, be 'care of self' – or even, in order to maintain a closer alliance to the Greek and Latin versions, 'self-care'. The point
is, that if we read volume III of *The History of Sexuality* as *The Care of
Self* (rather than *The Care of the Self*), and if we take Foucault to be
writing a history of reflexive practices, rather than practices which target a
substantial entity called 'the self', then we can more easily avoid the illusion
that Foucault's late work consists of a return to the subject, a return to a
'definite' self.

What fascinates Foucault in Classical Greek thought is that there the
practices of self-care, self-formation and auto-poesis appear not to be
thought in terms of a pre-given self, or subject, which must be either
deciphered or validated. Rather, the self in this form of thought is neither a
pre-given, nor an aim; in fact it could be said that it hardly exists, or that it
exists only in the embryonic form of its future becoming. And if, today, it
is the case that the self is no longer given to us – that identity, whether
cultural, political or sexual, is a hard-won effect rather than a pre-given
reality – then the playful creation and recreation of the self is no longer
either an impossibility or a luxury reserved for Wildean dilettantes and
dandies. It is an ethical imperative, perhaps the only imperative we continue
to recognize. The self, understood as the more or less homogenous coming
together of our modes of subjectivity, has become the material, the
substance of our ethical reflection and practice. It is the 'ethical substance'
of the model Foucault proposes.

CHAPTER 7

Creating a Self Oneself

In man *creature* and *creator* are united: in man there is material, fragment, excess, clay, dirt, nonsense, chaos; but in man there is also creator, form-giver, hammer hardness, spectator divinity, and seventh day ...

Friedrich Nietzsche[1]

The idea of the *bios* as a material for an aesthetic piece of art is something which fascinates me.

Michel Foucault (OGE, 348)

But couldn't everyone's life become a work of art? Why should the lamp or the house be an art object, but not our life?

Michel Foucault (OGE, 350)

If it is now time to abandon the relation to self which has characterized modern morality, then maybe the alternative which will replace this model is the kind of relation that an artist maintains with their work: perhaps we must now develop an aesthetics of existence and 'create ourselves as a work of art' (OGE, 351). This vision of the ethical life is one in which the individual recognizes, firstly, that their forms of life and modes of subjectivity are historically and culturally determined and, secondly, that there is no truth to be discovered (either in the self or the world) which is capable of grounding or directing the way that we live. The subject is not a substance, it is a 'form' which is capable of *trans*formation (ECS, 121[718–19]); and one of the possible ways of undertaking such a transformation is through the exercise, upon oneself, of certain arts of existence or practices of the self. Thus one can become not only the architect of one's life but also the artist of one's self.

In what sense can one's life or one's self become a work of art? Is Foucault proposing that in the absence of universal grounds of ethical action we should simply concentrate on giving our lives and our selves the most beautiful form possible? And if so, then how would he go about grounding the criteria by which the beauty of a life would be judged? In the first section of this chapter I argue that to follow such a line of questioning would be to misunderstand the sense in which Foucault mobilizes the concept of an art of the self, or an aesthetics of existence. It would be to mistakenly suppose, firstly, that Foucault wants us to relate to our selves as art objects – in the sense in which that category operates in modern aesthetics. And, secondly, it would be to suppose that beauty, the beauty of the finished work, is the central focus of his concern.

THE SELF AS A WORK OF ART?

'But couldn't everyone's life become a work of art?' (OGE, 350). With these words Foucault enters into a debate which has endured in Western philosophies of art and ethics since at least the end of the eighteenth century. It is a debate in which what is at stake is the continued separation of art and life, or the maintenance of an autonomous aesthetic sphere. This separation, which is one of the characteristic achievements of modernity, received its first enunciation in Kant's critical philosophy. For Kant, the beautiful exists independently of all considerations of either science or ethics: it is neither an object of our knowledge, nor can it give us knowledge; it is neither subject to our ethical judgements, nor can it influence our actions. This philosophical development was, of course, closely paralleled by the social development, from the same time, of art as a realm which is (or ideally should be) independent of all religious, political and economic influence. However, at both the theoretical and the institutional level, the ideal of autonomy has, since its inception, been constantly subject to a counter-discourse. To take one example only, early twentieth-century avant-garde movements, such as Dada and Surrealism, tried to overcome the very distinctions between art and life, aesthetics and ethics, firstly by undermining the traditional categories of art, and secondly by attempting to develop new forms of life based on artistic practice.[2] Foucault's statement here would seem to be aligned with this particular attack upon the modern phenomenon of the autonomization of the aesthetic sphere. In fact, it is striking that the view he espouses echoes precisely that put forward by the early twentieth-century avant-garde; both positions involve a call for the rejection of the restrictions inherent in the category *objet d'art*, a questioning of the specifically modern notion of the artist, and an attempt to reintegrate the practice of art into life.

The concept of an aesthetic ethics tends to provoke hostile reactions, and not just because ancient Greek and Roman societies are perceived as offering dubious models for modern societies. In fact the most alarming images we have of the dangers of ethical aestheticism are much more modern, and much more frightening – they are images of the Nazi and Fascist states of the 1930s and 1940s. These fears are founded on the perhaps justifiable suspicion that a personal ethics which abandons both Aristotelian virtue and Kantian duty in favour of the idea of the self as a work of art can very easily slip into, or at least collude with, a politics which treats the masses as a raw material to be moulded by the will of their masters. While the suggestion that Foucault's ethics might inadvertently be in alliance with such a politics may seem to be unfair to Foucault, this has not stopped some critics from making such a connection. One distinctive feature that Foucault shares with the avant-garde discourses of the twentieth century is that his work too has been judged to be a dangerous and foolish 'experiment' which may lead to barbarism and 'terroristic practices'.[3] In the words of Richard Wolin, Foucault's 'aesthetic decisionism' constitutes a form of immoralism which tends towards a 'politics of nihilistic catastrophe'.[4] A It was Walter Benjamin, however, in 'The Work of Art in the Age of Mechanical Reproduction',[5] who first postulated a connection between aestheticization and fascism, and this is the account I will use as a basis for differentiating Foucault's aestheticism from the implications of such a politics.

In his essay, Benjamin offers an analysis of the work of art which is based upon the idea that art, in the age of its mechanical reproducibility, is in the process of losing its traditional dependence upon the effect of 'aura'. Aura, for Benjamin, is that effect which results initially from the art work's origin in the sacred and the ritual. Today however this effect, which Benjamin describes as a simultaneous distancing and presencing ('the unique phenomenon of a distance, however close it may be' (p. 224)), is shattered by a reproduction which 'pr[ies] an object from its shell' (p. 225) and, literally, brings it halfway to meet the viewer. For Benjamin, the most important result of this destruction is the fact that it changes the function of art in society. If, in the age of its mechanical reproducibility, the work of art is freed from its 'parasitical dependence on ritual' (p. 226), and therefore can no longer be judged on the criterion of authenticity, then what Benjamin calls its 'total function' is reversed (p. 226). Under these circumstances, Benjamin says, 'instead of being based on ritual, it begins to be based on another practice – politics' (p. 226).

It was an integral part of Benjamin's understanding of history, that every epoch which experiences what he calls a 'shattering of tradition' (p. 223), would also experience a contrary movement towards a renewal of tradition.

Such a conflict can be understood as the result of the ambiguous nature of any moment of origin. The positive significance of film, for example, is offset by its 'destructive, cathartic aspect', its 'liquidation of the traditional value of the cultural heritage' (p. 223). To our present destruction of tradition then, there are two possible responses; either we choose to respond ritually by aestheticizing politics, or we respond politically by politicizing art.[6] Notwithstanding Benjamin's much remarked ambivalence towards the loss of aura, there is no doubt that, in the terms of this opposition, he is very strongly on the side of the politicization, rather than the ritualization, of art. And, it is equally clear that, in his view, the primary contemporary force which favours ritualization is fascism. However, we should also bear in mind that this opposition – 'aestheticized politics' against 'politicized art' – is to an extent false. In fact, it is the tendency to ritualization, or the production of 'aura', to which Benjamin is opposed, and such production can of course occur in politics just as easily as in art. By 'politicized art' then, Benjamin would mean an art which resists ritualization and the imposition of aura, *not* an art which is pressed into the service of a political regime. Similarly, by 'aestheticized politics', he would mean a politics – such as fascism – which functions precisely through the ritualization of political life, whether that be through the use of artistic means (Benjamin's example would be propaganda films), or for example, the promotion of a Führer cult. The choice with which we are confronted would, therefore, be between ritualizing *both* politics and art (fascism), or de-ritualizing them both (communism).[7]

Benjamin elaborates this point by showing how fascism organizes the newly formed masses while simultaneously maintaining existing property structures. It achieves this by giving its subjects merely 'a chance to express themselves' (p. 243). In newsreel footage of parades and rallies, for example, the masses are brought 'face to face with themselves' (p. 253) and they are given the opportunity to *portray* themselves. What this means for Benjamin, is that the principle of aesthetic expression and the beautiful illusion (the *schöner Schein*) takes precedence over the principle of political rights. Hence, Bertolt Brecht's satirical characterization of Hitler as 'the house-painter' and the 'redecorator' who is whitewashing the falling house of the Weimar Republic. Fascism 'violates' the masses in the same way that it violates the apparatus of film in order to make it produce 'ritual values' (p. 243). It proceeds by a successive aestheticization (and hence ritualization) of political life; it institutes the Führer cult, it glorifies war, it confers upon the people, the blood, the soil the magical qualities of the auratic cult object.

More than this, however, through its presentation of the masses *to* the masses, it mobilizes a certain change in human perception which Benjamin sees as being an integral product of modernity. Building upon Marx's analysis of alienated labour, Benjamin points to the much more general phenomenon of alienated sense perception which characterizes the modern era. As he suggests in one of his essays on Baudelaire,[8] the modern individual is subjected to a series of shocks to the sensory system which have the effect of provoking a state of anaesthesia, and it is this state which makes possible the attitude towards the world which Benjamin summarizes in the slogan '*Fiat ars – pereat mundus*' ('Make art – let the world perish') (p. 244). Fascism, by harnessing this potential, can render humanity capable of experiencing its own destruction as 'an aesthetic pleasure of the first order' (p. 244). As Howard Caygill puts it, the people 'participate avidly in their own history while spectating it as someone else's history; they participate in political action and view it from a distance; they participate in their own destruction and enjoy the spectacle'.[9]

If Benjamin is correct in his analysis of the political grounds of fascism, it nevertheless remains possible to wonder whether there is not something in the particular aesthetic involved in fascism's aestheticization of politics which is equally determinant in the ultimate forms which that politics takes. In other words, rather than attributing fascist politics to aestheticization *tout court*, should we not examine the precise nature of the aesthetic model which fascism invokes? Without entering into a detailed study of the aesthetics of fascism, I think that an instructive comparison can be made between the aesthetic principles of a figure such as Marinetti and the aesthetic principles which are implicit in Foucault's ethics. Making such a comparison has the virtue of disallowing the immediate and unreflective rejection of a project such as Foucault's, and thus delegitimizes what we could call the commentary by condemnation which is often practised by his critics.

While recognizing that the relationship between Italian Futurism and Italian Fascism remains an issue of heated debate, I will follow not only Benjamin's lead, but also that of Andrew Hewitt, in my assumption that Italian Futurism was 'radically and fundamentally fascistic'.[10] My concern, however, is less with Futurism's connections with Mussolini or the Italian Fascist Party, than with its echoing of a certain form of thought. One of the most telling presentations of this thought remains Marinetti's writings themselves; in particular, his *War, the World's only Hygiene*.[11] This work attacks traditional aesthetics and proposes to replace it with 'the wholly mastered, definitive Futurist aesthetic of great locomotives, twisting tunnels, armoured cars, torpedo boats, monoplanes and racing cars' (p. 81). Speaking, in much the same terms as Benjamin, of our 'world of ceaseless shocks' (p. 91), Marinetti predicts and welcomes the future antidote to this problem – the development of the long dreamt-of metallized body. In the future, Marinetti says, our flesh will force itself to 'resemble the surround-ing steel' (p. 105) of our environment. The 'young modern male' (p. 92) will extricate himself from the twin lures of woman and beauty and will turn instead to a new ideal of 'mechanized love'. This development is already foreshadowed, Marinetti believes, in the mechanic's love for the beautiful machinery that 'glow[s] with pleasure beneath his ardent caress' (p. 90).

In every sense of the word, we can say that this metallized body is a fantastic body, and of course he who fantasizes it fails to recognize his fantasm. As Marinetti insists, 'this is no fantasy, but almost a reality that in a few years we will easily be able to control' (p. 90). What Marinetti is imagining and identifying with here could be expressed as the ideal of the complete, wholly formed body; an identification which, according to Lacan,[12] leads to the formation of an armoured identity and seems to guarantee mastery and control – the masculine virtues that Marinetti values above all the virtues of woman and beauty. It is not by chance that Lacan, speaking at the end of the Second World War, draws a connection between the 'captation' of the subject by this image of a unified, sovereign body and 'the madness that deafens the world with its sound and fury'.[13] This capta-tion, he says, gives us the most general formula, not only of individual madness, but also of what we could call social madness. In other words, Lacan saw only too well the lengths to which human subjects will go in order to establish and maintain the illusion of a unified and invincible social body.

This theme of completeness, hardness and virility is one which recurs all the way from Marinetti's first manifesto of 1909, up to the greatly expanded, but essentially similar, rhetoric of German and Italian fascism. Ernst Jünger, for instance, writing in the 1930s, has this to say about the beauty of machines:

> Today we are writing poems of steel, and we are fighting for power in battles that unfold with the precision of machines. There is a beauty in it which we can already sense: in these battles on land, on sea and in the air in which the hot will of our blood controls itself and finds expression in the mastery of the technical miracle machines of power.[14]

Whether in Italian or German fascism then, what is in question is the assumption of an image which is defined by its *uniformity* (literally, as Benjamin says, 'the uniform represents their highest end'[15]), its *permanence* (we think of the Thousand Year Reich) and its *clarity* (as Hitler says, 'to be German is to be clear'[16]). In both cases, it is an image which in-forms a Party and a people. Hence, for Mussolini, fascism was more than just a lawgiver and a founder of institutions; 'it does not merely aim at *remoulding the forms* of life', he says, 'but also their content, man, his character, and his faith'.[17] Similarly, for the Nazis the entire nation in all its manifestations was to be remade by the artist statesman in the image of an idealized purity and strength of race. Hence, for instance, the ease with which the leader could be identified with the nation, and the insistence of the slogan, 'Hitler is Germany, Germany is Hitler'.

If there is something characteristic about the fascist aestheticization of politics then, it must be sought in this insistence upon the ideal of a non-fractured subject which finds itself reassuringly reflected in a non-fractured, uniform public space. When thought in these terms, it becomes possible to understand and explain the fascist theme of the politician as the plastic artist who moulds the people to his will, and gives them a harmonious and beautiful form. In the Lacanian schema, his is none other than the child's desire to fashion his/her own body in the form of the image which presents itself in the mirror. Similarly, Marinetti's twin themes of the metallized body and the beauty of war, find their source in the ineradicable tension between the image of the fully-formed body and the aggressivity which is unleashed by its continually threatened disintegration. Again, we can draw a parallel here between Marinetti's vision of the human body with its 'surprising' new organs,[18] and Lacan's reference to the grotesque visions of the fifteenth-century painter Hieronymus Bosch.[19]

In response to concerns that Foucault's project runs parallel to this fascist form of aestheticization, we need to consider whether the aesthetic sensibility of his project mirrors that of, for example, Marinetti. Is Foucault motivated by a vision of a hard, unified, resistant self; or a vision of a self which is fluid, open and, to play on Marinetti's fears, 'soft'? In more general terms, is Foucault's notion of the self as a 'work' of art to be understood as *œuvre* or as *travail*? Does the concept of 'work' function in Foucault's project (as it does in Marinetti's) as a finished product; or does it function as a process – as a labour which does not necessarily have an end (either in the sense of a goal or a completion)?

While it is true that Foucault uses the conventional French expression *œuvre d'art*, it is also the case that he constantly emphasizes those aspects of the work on the self which resonate with Nietzsche's call for 'long practice and daily work'.[20] This distinction between work as product (*œuvre*) and work as process (*travail*) mirrors the distinction I have made between the aesthetic as relating to *beauty* and as relating to *techniques* of transformation.

In the Introduction, I pointed out that in his use of the term aesthetic Foucault oscillates between indicating a technique (a *techne tou biou*) and indicating a work of beauty – an 'aesthetic piece of art' (OGE, 348). While drawing on the ancient tradition of the techniques of the self he makes use of the modern conception of the work of art as an object of beauty. As I suggested at the end of Chapter 4, Foucault uses 'beauty' to advance his cause – the end of morality. He appears to be as attracted as Nietzsche was to the Classical ideal of the complete, harmonious, beautiful individual. But he also, again like Nietzsche, distrusts both the processes and the results of this harmonizing, unifying drive. This means that we must hold in view, at the same time, his attraction to the project of creating oneself as a unified whole and his equally important hostility towards efforts and techniques which would circumscribe fixed, immutable limits around one's subjectivity – even if these limits are self-imposed. To a large extent this play between the two senses of an 'art' of the self is made possible by combining the ancient notion of art as *techne*, a making of almost any kind, with the more limited modern notion of art as the making of beautiful objects. Foucault exploits the conceptual and semantic potential of these two frameworks by trying to revive the older one in the context of the newer one and by applying both in the field of ethics. What he does not do, however, is mobilize this conception in the interests of a defence of unity and harmony at the expense of fluidity and discord.

Paul Veyne reminds us that for the Greeks 'an artist was first of all an artisan, and a work of art a work'.[21] This conception of the aesthetic is one which is markedly different from the idea of artistic production which is still largely dominant today and which grew out of German Idealism and Romanticism. According to this more recent model, the artist is first of all, as Kant says, endowed with genius and the work of art is primarily 'artistic'. Whether or not Foucault was always conscious of this distinction is still open to question. Andrew Thacker, for example, is right to point out that Foucault's use of the term aesthetic displays a certain 'semantic slipperiness',[22] although it may be a little unfair on Foucault to say, as Thacker does, that he confuses the Greek and the Kantian senses of the term. Admittedly, it is true that Foucault often employs the central concepts of Kantian aesthetics. In many cases, he would seem to be speaking of a creative process which finds its telos in an object of beauty. In addition, the social distribution, or rather lack of distribution, of these practices in Greek society would also seem to suggest the idea that only a small number of people were capable of creativity; in other words, that society can quite unproblematically be divided into those who can 'create' and those who can only 'make'. At other times, however, Foucault seems to be well aware of the importance of differentiating his position from the Kantian model. There is, for example, the statement quoted as an epigraph to this chapter, in which he questions the legitimacy of that other fundamental principle of nineteenth-century aesthetics – the principle that the aesthetic sphere is autonomous from all those spheres of life in which what Kant calls 'interest' predominates: 'Why should the lamp or the house be an art object, but not our life?'

To this rhetorical question, a commentator such as Richard Wolin would reply that this cannot happen because it is a fundamental and unalterable feature of modernity that the aesthetic has become separated from the other spheres of life. Indeed, he argues that it is this very autonomy which guarantees the critical power of art. However, Foucault is less interested in the critical power of art, than in the 'artistic' or 'plastic' power of critique. For Foucault, not only do no special advantages accrue from the autonomy of the aesthetic, but this autonomy unnecessarily restricts our possibilities for self-constitution. Hence, not only is Foucault aware of the specific nature of aesthetics after Kant, he is obviously hostile to it. It is a curious fact that among those who address this issue as it develops in Foucault's late work, there are many who exhibit what seems to be an extreme anxiety at the thought that the aesthetic is going to be allowed to leak out of its hermetically sealed container to contaminate science and politics. The aesthetic, we are told, is blind to other values, and if it becomes the sole principle of our action, we will become insensitive, undemocratic manipulators of other persons. This distrust of the aesthetic is illustrated when Richard Wolin complains of Foucault that, 'it is not enough [for him] that *objects* are artistic'.[23] One gets the unmistakeable impression that for Wolin even that is almost too much. One of the presuppositions on which such arguments are founded, is that there are only two ways of thinking about the relationship between aesthetics and politics. According to the first, of which the Greek model is a good example, there is a coalescence of aesthetics and ethics, with the result that every aesthetic judgment – that something is beautiful, or harmonious – necessarily implies an ethical judgment – that that thing is good, or praiseworthy. According to this model, there is no doubt that if one's life and one's behaviour have a beautiful form, then they will also be good. According to the second model – the Kantian one – the aesthetic sphere is, on the contrary, separate from the cognitive and the practical. Therefore, according to such a model, there could be no guarantee that an action, or a life, once judged to be beautiful would also be good. If these are the only models available to us, then it becomes easy to argue that Foucault's project fails, on the grounds that neither of these models are capable of adequately founding a contemporary political practice. In the case of the former, it is vain to suppose that one could return to the world of the Greeks in which the life spheres have not yet separated; while, in the case of the latter, perhaps one would know if an action was beautiful, but one would have no way of judging if it was good.

Another striking feature of such arguments is their apparent willingness to accept the inevitability of what is called the present arrangement of the cognitive, moral and aesthetic realms. Even though this arrangement is not seen as being ideal, we are told that it does have the advantage of affording art and imagination a comfortable niche from which they can fulfil their role of social critic and utopic visionary. More importantly, it is an arrangement which, it seems, we tamper with at our peril. To attempt its reconfiguration, as we have seen above, is to risk anything from the accusation that one has engaged in nonsense experiments, to being responsible for the unleashing of barbarism, fascism and terroristic practices. From such a point of view, Foucault naturally becomes the purveyor of a dangerous (and foolish) pan-aestheticism – a creed whose anti-Enlightenment nihilism allies him with the forces of a new reactionary conservatism.[24] However, the crucial problem with this argument, at least from a Foucaldian perspective, is its assumption that what it calls 'aesthetic autonomy' is a *necessary* feature of modernity. Any possibility that things could ever be differently arranged is relegated, along with the entire aesthetic sphere, to some impossible, utopic future. This relegation is made on the basis that it is impossible to rearrange one element of the 'life spheres' withotit changing them all in their entirety. As Habermas argues, the concentration of one's efforts upon a single cultural sphere will lead only to what he calls a 'false negation of culture'.[25] Hence, all attempts by, for instance, the avant-garde in the practice of art, or the so-called New Conservatives such as Foucault and Derrida, to reconfigure social practices and discourses is branded as false negation, false sublation, or simply as barbarization.

Needless to say, such an attitude towards the so-called necessities of our contemporary social reality is one which Foucault would totally reject. In Foucault's view, society is not a uniform, stable, monolithic structure which can only be changed completely, or else not at all. Rather, he would argue that our contemporary social reality is continually prone to shocks and seismic tremors, and that its history is a discontinuous series of unforeseen and unforeseeable events. Thus, he argues that we must get away from the idea that a total programme is required in order to bring about any transformation. To borrow Paul Veyne's formulation, Foucault does not have to wait for the revolution, because for him 'the self is the new strategic possibility'.[26] For Foucault, to attempt to bring about a change in our political and ethical subjectivity is not to attempt a total reconfiguration of the cognitive, the practical and the aesthetic spheres. This is not to deny, however, that such a project may, and indeed will, bring about a change in this configuration. It is simply to say that the task of beginning this transformation is not one which should be put off to some never-to-be-seen tomorrow.

Returning now to the central focus of this section, if we want to successfully demonstrate the extent to which Foucault's ethical project differs from Benjamin's 'aestheticization of politics', we must be able to give a more precise account of Foucault's understanding of the aesthetic. In Chapter 2, I suggested the possibility that Foucault's use of the term aesthetic may neither be ancient nor modern, neither Platonic nor Romantic. And in Chapter 5, I argued that for Foucault ethics could be aesthetic by virtue of its technical, ascetic *modes*, rather than by virtue of any striving after unity, harmony, or purity per se. For Foucault, the ethical practice which is called for by our contemporary situation is aesthetic quite simply by virtue of the fact that it involves, as do all artistic practices, the giving of form. To speak of the individual as the artist of his/her own life, is to suggest that the constitution of the individual as an ethical subject is (or could be) a question of giving one's life a certain style, rather than a question of following a code, or seeking the truth of one's subjectivity. But this style should not be understood as a superficial posturing, as a purely theatrical dandyism. It should, rather, be understood as the result of a fundamental re-constitution of the subject in and through certain techniques of life. What this would suggest, is that for Foucault the most important aspect of Greek ethics was not its ideal and goal of the beautiful life, but the way in which it posed the fundamental question 'how are we to live?' This it did on the basis of the understanding that, in trying to answer this question, even the most rudimentary terms of reference could not be accepted as given. For Foucault, its most important insight was the idea that ethical practice was primarily a matter of giving a form to one's life through the use of certain techniques. And, furthermore, it recognized that one would have to invent for oneself the principles and rules according to which these techniques would be developed and this form would be given.

While this model is suggested to Foucault by his reading of Greek thought, it does not follow that for him the aesthetic is the realm, as it was for the Greeks, of a beauty which would automatically coincide with the good. Similarly, the fact that he continues to speak of ethics in terms of the production of one's life as a work of art, does not mean that he understands the aesthetic in the Kantian sense, as a realm in which an inspired genius creates objects intended for disinterested contemplation. Rather, for Foucault the aesthetic is a realm in which we work to develop techniques which will allow us to give a form to our lives, our behaviour and our relationships with others. As such, it is a work for which no eternal principles of good taste can be deduced. We, like the artist, have no model to follow which will guarantee a good, or a beautiful, result. Indeed, it is characteristic that, in one case as in the other, there will never be any general agreement as to the way we should proceed. However, and here Foucault's aesthetics of existence differs from the work of the artist, it is a work which is not confined to those who are artistically gifted. Rather, it presents itself as a necessity to anyone who recognizes the contemporary crisis in ethics. It is in the light of such a recognition that Foucault is attempting a new configuration of the aesthetic and the political; one based upon a thought which, by forcing the limits of what presents itself as its historical necessity, attempts to think differently. It is a thought which, by putting into practice a new form of aestheticized politics, attempts to avoid not only totalitarian narcissism, but also the narcissism of mindless radicalism.

In the most general terms, I think two main differences can now be distinguished between Foucault's aestheticism and that which is attributed to fascism. First of all, there is the difference relating to what we could call the form of the aesthetic in question. In the case of Foucault, this would be an aesthetic based upon the acceptance of fragmentation, plurality and instability, whereas in the case of fascism, it would be an aesthetic of uniformity, identity and permanence. Foucault's opposition to all totalizing forms of discourse would, on its own, prevent him from adopting the ideal of a closed, self-sufficient whole, regardless of the harmony and beauty such a unity might possess. In addition to this, his concept of the subject as a precarious, ever-changing, substance-less form which is the site of endless conflict, differentiates him, at a fundamental level, from the fascist goal of the stable, armoured individual who embodies the eternal (or at least 'thousand year') truth of his/her race. For Foucault, there is no true, no pure form of the subject, and its constitution has more to do with the precarious 'daily work' of which Nietzsche speaks, than with the inspired, spontaneous creation of genius.

The second difference operates on the level of the telos of the aesthetic intervention. In Foucault's case, this should be conceived of as a non-auratic, non-autonomous object, whereas in the case of fascism, the object to be created is ritualized and distanced. In the terms of Benjamin's argument, the work of self-constitution in Foucault is not a work which culminates in an auratic object; it is not a production to which could be applied what Benjamin calls the 'out-moded concepts' of creativity, genius, eternal value and mystery.[27] Consequently, it is not a production which leads to a 'processing of data in a Fascist sense' (ibid.). While one could argue that, for the Greeks, this work *did* lead to an object which shared certain characteristics with the ritualized work of art (for example, one's life could be endowed with a certain aura which would cause people to remember it after one's death), for Foucault the contemporary reactivation of this model of ethics would forgo any such auratic effect. The critical task, and therefore the artistic task, according to Foucault, requires a constant work on, and surpassing of, the limits of our subjectivity. Hence, he characterizes his own 'philosophical ethos' as a 'historico-practical test of the limits that we may go beyond, and thus as work carried out by ourselves upon ourselves as free beings' (WE, 47). Rather than being a question of forming an object then, which by definition would resist change, it is a question of continually breaking the limits of the rigid, object-like forms of subjectivity which are given to us by our culture – even when these forms are self-imposed. The result of such a work, if one can call it a result, is an ephemeral, never to be completed work-in-progress; one which will always resist both ritualization and the imposition of aura.

For Foucault, the antidote to the dangers of a crypto-fascist aestheticism is an aestheticism in which the notion of the aesthetic indicates a range of techniques for the transformation of the self; techniques which would continuously undermine the drive towards an imposed unity. An aesthetic ethics would primarily consist of a particular relation to self, an attitude towards the self which would demand a particular engagement with the self as work-in-progress rather than as object of beauty. But it would also be open to the possibility of using some notion of beauty as a guideline in this work. It is a notion of the aesthetic and of art which is as far from that of Marinetti and Junger as is Bertolt Brecht's in the following lines:

> Canalising a river
> Grafting a fruit tree
> Educating a person
> Transforming a state
> These are instances of fruitful criticism
> And at the same time
> Instances of art.[28]

AUTOPOESIS

When Foucault makes a distinction between the four aspects that constitute any system of ethics, he characterizes the second one as the mode of subjection. This is the way the subject brings him/herself into relation with the ethical model in question. If the first aspect, the ethical substance, answers the question '*what* part of myself should I address?', the second aspect answers the question '*why* should I cultivate certain behaviours or attitudes?' While different ethical systems may share an element of code, such as 'practise conjugal fidelity', they will answer this question differently. A Christian, for example, may practise fidelity because it is divinely ordained as a condition of the institution of marriage, while a Stoic may practise it because it will give their life a form that is consonant with the order of the universe. The mode of subjection of a particular ethics, therefore, embodies the kind of attitude towards the self which that ethics demands. The Christian is called upon to relate to him/herself as a being who bends to the will of God; the Stoic relates to him/herself as a being who uses reason in order to align their personal form of life with the cosmic form of life. What, then, is the attitude towards the self, the form of relating to the self, that Foucault's proposed ethics would demand? Why, according to Foucault, should we engage in the task of self-transformation?

The answer to this question, one which has been slowly emerging in the course of this thesis, is that the attitude to self required by Foucault's ethics is akin to the attitude that an artist takes towards their material. The artistic metaphor which is usually used here is that of the plastic artist, in particular the sculptor. Epictetus and Plotinus, for example, speak of the self as a statue which must be worked, while Seneca makes a comparison between the self as a work and one's furniture as works. And Foucault, as we have seen, complains that today only the house or the lamp can be art objects, but not our lives. Following this same metaphor, I have suggested that the form of self-relation demanded by Foucault's ethics is analogous to that between a sculptor and their material. I will now pursue the idea of an aesthetic attitude towards the self, however, through a consideration of a different art form – literature. My reasons for making this choice are, firstly, because it will show that Foucault's use of the aesthetic metaphor does not rely exclusively on the plastic arts, and secondly, because one of the best examples of an attempt to effect the kind of ethics Foucault proposes was, arguably, carried out through the medium of literature. That is, the act of self-creation that Nietzsche embodies in the work *Ecce Homo*.[29]

Nietzsche wrote *Ecce Homo* in 1888, the last year of his productive life, and in it he offers a final answer to a question which was at the centre of his attempt to formulate an ethics that would replace traditional moralities. The question, already posed in 'On the Uses and Disadvantages of History for Life' and in *The Gay Science* (Sections 270 and 335), was 'how does one become who one is?'[30] Used as a subtitle for *Ecce Homo*, the statement (here it is not a question) 'How One Becomes What One Is' suggests not only that Nietzsche can now tell us how this is done, but that he will tell us how he has done it in his life. The book then takes on an autobiographical significance. However it is not autobiographical in the sense of being a 'confession of the self'; it does not follow an Augustinian model, or even a Rousseauian one. Rather than recounting a life, it deliberately creates a life through the reinterpretation of the literary products of that life. In the Foreword, Nietzsche tells us that at the end of this year (1888), a year in which he had begun the *Revaluation of All Values*, collected the *Songs of Zarathustra* and completed *Twilight of the Idols*, he feels an 'indispensable' 'duty' to say who he is, and most of all to say who he is not. And, in a way that echoes Walt Whitman's 'Song of Myself',[31] he ends the Foreword, 'And so I tell myself my life.' But this telling himself is neither a simple telling, nor is it to himself: it is a public act that creates in a literary text the character who had produced a series of literary texts. Nietzsche becomes who he is by creating in literature the author of his texts.

In *Human, All Too Human*, Nietzsche gives what could be seen as a pessimistic assessment of the chances of succeeding in any such attempt at self-creation:

> *The unalterable character*. – That the character is unalterable is not in the strict sense true; this favourite proposition means rather no more than that, during the brief lifetime of a man, the effective motives are unable to scratch deeply enough to erase the imprinted script of many millennia. If one imagines a man of eighty-thousand years, however, one would have in him a character totally alterable: so that an abundance of different individuals would evolve out of him one after the other. The brevity of human life misleads us to many erroneous assertions regarding the qualities of man (*Human, All Too Human*, I, 41).

However, one could say that in response to this apparent pessimism, in *Ecce Homo* Nietzsche not only affirms the possibility of self-creation within an individual life, but that he demonstrates how this can be done through the medium of writing.

This interpretation of *Ecce Homo*, as the act of creating a life through literature, has been most forcefully and elegantly argued by Alexander Nehamas in his *Nietzsche: Life as Literature*.[32] Nehamas confronts the many paradoxes that are inherent in Nietzsche's injunction that we must 'become who we are'. How can we become that which we already are? Why does Nietzsche want our 'becoming' to solidify into 'being'? Does he imply that we already have a definite, natural essence? How, Nehamas asks, can a self that must be created and that does not yet exist, be that which an individual already is?[33] Nehamas resolves these questions by arguing that, for Nietzsche, to 'become who one is' is to integrate and unify all those traits, habits and experiences that make up one's character. However, there is no 'state of being unified' that replaces an earlier 'state of becoming'; rather, unity is a continual process – a process not of improvement and perfection, but of integration and stylization. This is a process in which the individual gradually 'owns' (and 'disowns', by modifiying) more and more of their characteristics and their experiences. To become who one is, to create the self, is therefore to develop the ability to 'accept responsibility for everything that we have done and to admit ... that everything that we have done actually constitutes who each one of us is'.[34] Hence Nietzsche praises Goethe, who created himself by taking 'as much as possible' upon himself, by embracing a 'joyful and trusting fatalism', by recognizing that 'in the totality everything is redeemed and affirmed'.[35] This trusting fatalism, this 'will to self-responsibility'[36] is the same *amor fati* that Nietzsche affirms in *Ecce Homo* as his 'formula for greatness in a human being' ('Why I am so clever', 10).

It is in the book *Ecce Homo* (literally, 'behold the man') that, according to Nehamas, we first behold Nietzsche the complete, unified, integrated character. Unified and integrated, that is, in the sense that all his contradictions and paradoxes are allowed to stand. His entire literary and philosophical development, from his earliest to his latest publications, is put to use in order to present a unity of character and task that only emerged slowly as his *œuvre* grew. In this narrative, the turning point occurs in 1876, after his break with Wagner, when he begins to write *Human, All Too Human*. It was then, he says, that he realized that both his attraction to Wagner and his professorship of philology at Basel had been nothing more than distractions from his true 'task'; 'I realised it was high time for me to think back to *myself*' ('Human, All Too Human', 3). This recovery of himself, this return to his 'deepest self', was facilitated by an illness that forced him to change his habits, to abandon 'selflessness', and even to cease reading – 'for years at a time I read nothing – the *greatest* favour I have ever done myself!' (ibid., 4). But the realization that he had for so long failed to recognize his task (ultimately, the 'revaluation of all values') does not make him repudiate what had preceded it. He can even claim Wagner as 'the great benefactor' of his life; 'I am strong enough,' he claims, 'to turn even the most questionable and perilous things to my own advantage and thus to become stronger' ('Why I am so clever', 6). In the same way, his years as a philological scholar, his capacity 'to have been many things and in many places' has enabled him 'to become *one person* ... to attain *one thing*' ('The Untimely Essays', 3). In *Human, All Too Human*, he finally liberates himself, he says, from 'that in my nature which *did not belong to me*' ('Human, All Too Human', 1). However, this becoming one person, this act of self-stylization, is something that happens only in and through the writing of *Ecce Homo* itself. If, as Nehamas argues,[37] to 'become what one is' is not to reach a specific new state, but to both identify oneself with all one's actions and experiences and to fit all this into 'a coherent whole', then it is in *Ecce Homo* that Nietzsche finally achieves and justifies the 'one style' that he thought was the mark of human greatness. It is in a work of litera-ture that his life, as biography, becomes what it is.[38]

How does this discussion of Nietzsche's autobiographical self-creation relate to Foucault's attempt to formulate an ethics of autopoesis? I should emphazise firstly, that I am not suggesting here that Foucault shares either Nietzsche's prioritization of *unity* of style, or his insistence that one must 'become who one is'; although there are, of course, a great many parallels and echoes between these two paths of thought.[39] Rather, the point of discussing Nietzsche is to show *one* way in which an individual can adopt an 'aesthetic attitude' towards both themselves and their life. If we follow Nehamas's reading then, Nietzsche adopts just such an attitude in *Ecce Homo*; he takes his life, his habits, his experiences and his literary and scholarly output as material to be formed, shaped and infused with meaning. In the literary text, he constitutes an 'I' who is both a self-description and a self-creation. Whether or not Nehamas is correct in suggesting that this *literary* self-creation is the culmination of Nietzsche's ethics of the self, it still offers a model which can help to concretize Foucault's formulation of an aesthetic ethics.

Nehamas's interpretation of the injunction 'Become who you are' can, for example, help to clarify the relation between 'work' as *œuvre* and as *travail* in the notion of self-creation that emerges in Foucault's work. Nietzsche's conception of the ideal life, according to Nehamas, necessarily involves a commitment both to the idea that a life is a work (*œuvre*) which must be formed by 'one style', and the recognition that the process of creating this work can never be completed; that the process is only ever complete at the moment of death – if even then. If Foucault's appeal to the idea of the self as a work of art is also read in this way, then a large part of the concerns about 'crypto-fascism' discussed in the previous section would disappear.[40] More importantly, however, the Nietzschean model offers a way of thinking about the relation to self that constitutes the second element of Foucault's ethics; it gives us a model for understanding its mode of subjection.

This is an aesthetic attitude which does not require a contemplative gaze. Its aim is not (primarily) to produce an object that is pleasing to look at; although, as Nietzsche, Foucault and some Classical Athenians acknowledge, this sometimes occurs. It is, rather, the attitude that sculptors take towards their material, that narrators take towards their narrative, that authors can take towards their work. If we view art from the point of view of its creators and producers, rather than from the point of view of its audiences and consumers, and if we expand our concept of art to include every act of creating, every act of *poesis*,[41] then the adoption of such an attitude towards the self becomes possible. Foucault's 'aesthetics of existence' would then be aesthetic not because it calls on us to make ourselves beautiful, but because it calls on us to relate to ourselves and our lives as to a material that can be formed and transformed. In the ethics that Foucault is formulating, the mode of subjection, that is the answer to the question 'why should I live my life in one particular way, as opposed to any other?', is: because myself and my life have no shape, no purpose, no justification, outside of the form which I give to them. It is, therefore, imperative (non-categorically imperative) that I think about that form, develop the techniques that will help me to transform it, and that I reflect upon the ends, the teloi, to which I will direct it. If this still sounds like crypto-fascism to some readers, then, as Foucault has said in a different context, '*nous ne sommes pas, c'est manifeste, de la même planéte*' (*UP*, 7[13]).

CHAPTER 8

The Practice of Philosophy

But the genuine philosopher ... lives 'unphilosophically' and 'unwisely', above all *imprudently*, and feels the burden and the duty of a hundred attempts [*Versuchen*/experiments] and temptations of life – he risks *himself* constantly ...

Friedrich Nietzsche[1]

I am an experimenter and not a theoretician ... in the sense that I write in order to change myself and in order to no longer think the same thing as before.

Michel Foucault (EMF, [42])[2]

In sum it is a question of searching for another kind of critical philosophy. Not a critical philosophy that seeks to determine the conditions and the limits of our possible knowledge of the object, but a critical philosophy that seeks the conditions and the indefinite possibilities of transforming the subject, of transforming ourselves.

Michel Foucault (HL)

In the previous two chapters I presented the first two aspects of the ethics that Foucault sketches: its ethical substance and its mode of subjection. The third element, its ascesis or technique, however, is perhaps more difficult to identify. What conceptual and practical tools for self-transformation would a Foucaldian ethics call for? We could follow James Bernauer in characterizing the technique of Foucault's ethics as the genealogical method itself; or, following Paul Rabinow, we could give it a broader definition in terms of critical activity in general.[3] One of the dangers of attempting any precise characterization of a key element in an ethics which was never systematized by its author, however, is that we will either limit the possible ways of thinking about that ethics, or we will elevate more or less contingent elements to the status of essential principles. We need to remember, therefore, that it is not necessary to fix, or enumerate, the set of techniques

which Foucault would have considered capable of contributing to an ethics
of self-transformation. While Foucault found the genealogical method to be
particularly fruitful in his engagement with the subjective limits of our
present, there is no reason to suppose that this method is an essential
feature of any such engagement. Similarly, while Foucault valued the
contribution which sado-masochistic sexual practices could make to a reconstitution of individuals as subjects of desire and pleasure, there is no reason
to suppose that sado-masochism is an essential feature of his model of
ethics.[4] What is essential in Foucault's vision of ethics, however, is a certain
attitude towards the self; an attitude which facilitates continuous critical
self-transformation and which may manifest in practices as diverse as S/M
or genealogical critique.

In this chapter, I focus on another practice that was central to Foucault's
attempts to formulate a contemporary ethics – that is, philosophy itself. In his
late work, Foucault came to increasingly value philosophical practice as a
technique that was capable of contributing to the task of self-transformation.
In his engagement with ancient philosophy, he encountered a tradition
(roughly, the Socratic tradition) that not only cultivated practices for self-
transformation, but also developed some of the conceptual tools that initially
define the critical tradition in Western thought. Through the notion and
practice of *parrhesia* (freedom of speech, truth-telling), for example, this
tradition offers a way of conceptualizing the relations between truth and
subjectivity that is radically different from the models prevailing in modern
philosophy. The central argument of this chapter then, is that some time in
the late 1970s Foucault came to a conception of philosophy which allowed
him to see it as a very useful tool for the transformation of the self – as a
practice which could contribute to the third aspect of a new ethics. Like
genealogy or S/M, however, it is a tool which, although it was crucial for
his own practice of ethics, and may be for ours, does not thereby acquire
exclusivity or precedence over other ethical techniques.

PHILOSOPHY AS A WAY OF LIFE

It may at first seem curious, in a discussion of Foucault, to attribute such
importance to philosophy. Influential though Foucault's thought has been
in the last two or three decades, it has not necessarily been so among those
who, strictly speaking, call themselves philosophers. Foucault's influence
would seem to have been felt much more strongly in the fields of social and
political theory, in history, literary theory, sociology and classical studies.
This fact is not surprising when we consider that Foucault himself, at least

up until the end of the 1970s, consistently refused to identify himself as a philosopher, or to identify his work as belonging in or contributing to, the field of philosophy. In an interview from 1978 he states bluntly, 'I do not consider myself a philosopher' (EMF, 27[42]). He goes on, 'What I am doing is neither a way of doing philosophy nor a way of suggesting to others not to do it' (ibid.). Not only is he not a philosopher, then, but his work does not in any way even intersect with the field of philosophy. He goes on to insist that the authors who had most influence on him as a student were the *'non-philosophes'* Bataille, Nietzsche, Blanchot and Klossowski. It was these authors, he explains, rather than the representatives of what he calls the 'great philosophical machineries of Hegelianism and phenomenology' (EMF, 30[43]), that had most influence on him, because they were interested not in the construction of a system, but in a 'personal experience' (ibid.). Their work aimed to 'tear the subject away from itself', to ensure that the subject would 'no longer be itself', that the subject would be brought to its 'annihilation, or dissolution' (ibid.). And, it is this kind of book, what he calls an 'experience-book' (*'un livre-expérience'*) as opposed to a 'truth-book' or a 'demonstration-book' (EMF, 42[47]), that he always tries to write. He sees his own books as 'direct experiences which aim to tear me away from myself, to prevent me from being myself'; they are part of an attempt at 'de-subjectivation' (ibid.).

In order to fully appreciate this idea of the 'experience-book' we must bear in mind the several meanings of the word experience (*expérience*) in French. Because *expérience* does not only mean 'experience' in the common, although in no way unproblematic, English sense; it also carries the meaning of 'experiment'. Hence, *un livre-expérience* is a book which not only conveys the experience of the author, or changes the experience of the reader, it is also a book which constitutes both an experiment which the author carries out on him- or herself and an experiment in which the reader too can participate – thus participating in the subjective transformation which the book makes possible. Foucault wants to write books which will lead to a transformation in his own form of subjectivity and which will also facilitate a similar transformation on the part of his readers. 'I am an experimenter,' he says, 'in the sense that I write in order to change myself and in order to no longer think the same thing as before' (EMF, 27[42]). Given that this was his motivation for intellectual endeavour, it is perhaps not surprising that Foucault found few, or perhaps no, precursors among professional philosophers. Instead he turned to literary theorists, social theorists and to that most 'anti-philosophical' of thinkers, Nietzsche.

Six years later, however, in the introduction to *The Use of Pleasure*, Foucault seems to have changed his mind about the possibility of philosophy participating in such a project of subjective transformation. One of the clearest ideas which emerges from both volumes II and III of *The History of Sexuality*, is that philosophy once was, and could again be, a critical, reflective practice whose aim is to transform and de-subjectivize the individual. In the introduction to volume II, in the section entitled 'Modifications', Foucault tries to justify the long wait – a period of eight years – between the publication of the first and second volumes, by appealing ultimately to the standards which a 'philosophical' investigation imposes. His initial project, he explains, was reformulated and modified many times during this eight year period – but, what else is 'philosophical activity', he asks, if not this 'critical work of thought upon itself' (*UP*, 9[14])? His unwillingness to reproduce accepted forms of thought, in turn, is justified by an appeal to the nature of 'philosophical discourse' (*UP*, 9[15]). The task of philosophy, he says, is not to lay down the law for others, it is to 'explore that which, in its own thought, can be changed' (ibid.). Its task is to 'know to what extent the work of thinking its own history can free thought from what it thinks silently and permit it to think otherwise (*penser autrement*)' (ibid.). It is clear that by 1984 Foucault sees his work as belonging very much in the field of philosophy, and that he sees his own activity as contributing explicitly to that discourse. So, the question we need to ask is, how can we reconcile this view of philosophy as a critical work of thought upon itself, with Foucault's earlier view of, let us say, 'non-philosophical critique' as a work which transforms subjectivity and ways of life? How can we show that this 'adoption' of philosophy is part of a continuation of, rather than a break from, his earlier views?

The first way that we might try to answer this question would be to point out that, for Foucault, to change one's way of thinking is, inevitably, to change not only one's way of being, but also one's way of life; since there is no social practice which is not also a practice of thought and, similarly, there is no mode of thought which does not support and make possible a way of life. However, if we want to understand Foucault's position here in a little more depth, we need to do more than make this simple point; we need also to consider, in the first place, the way in which he uses the idea of the philosophical 'essay' to illustrate his understanding of philosophy and, secondly, the extent to which his reading of Classical and Hellenistic philosophy informed this understanding.

The continuity between the more or less 'anti-philosophical' stance of the 1970s, and the avowedly 'philosophical' one of the 1980s, should become more clear if, in our reading of Foucault's account of the philosophical essay, we bear in mind the multiple meanings of the term *essai*. An essay is a written account of a topic which canvasses and pushes to the limit possible arguments. In the sense in which Montaigne used the term, it implies a test and an effort of thought – in short, it comes from the verb *essayer*, to try, to attempt, to 'weigh up' or test. However, when Foucault says that the essay is 'the living body of philosophy' (ibid.), he does not simply mean that philosophy is, as he has already said, a work in which thought tests its own limits. Rather, it is also an *essai* in the sense of an experiment: and here we must remember that the term *essai*, like the term *expérience*, has the connotation of scientific experiment. An essay is a test, an attempt, an experiment: a technique which forces the subject to a limit and, in this process, transforms and modifies it. It is, Foucault says, an '"ascesis", an exercise of the self', a 'test (*épreuve*) which modifies the self' (*UP*, 9[15]). Indeed, for Montaigne too, the *essai* had this connotation of a work carried out on the self. His book of essays, a portrait of his own 'conditions and humours', his 'imperfections' and 'natural forme',[5] is a portrait whose ultimate function is as a tool in the living of his own life:

> Have you knowne how to compose your conduct? you have done more than he who hath composed bookes. Have you knowne how to take rest? you have done more than he who hath taken Empires and Citties. The glorious masterpiece of man is to live properly (Bk. III, Ch. 13, p. 156).

If we were to take Foucault's *History of Sexuality* as such an *essai*, as such a *livre-expérience*, we would read it as a philosophical exercise which, although it was 'long and hesitant' and often needed to be 'restarted and corrected' (*UP*, 9[15]), finally led Foucault (and potentially the reader) to 'think otherwise'. However, it is not only a question of changing the way one thinks; for what value could such a change have, Foucault asks, if it did not lead also to a shift, an *égarement,* a wandering, a getting lost on the part of the subject itself? 'After all, what would be the value of the passion for knowledge if it resulted only in a certain knowledgeableness and not, in one way or another and to the extent possible, in the knower's straying afield of himself (*l'égarement de celui qui connaît*)' (ibid.) It is this getting lost which, against all the inertia of habit and prejudice, forces a change in modes of behaviour. It is a question, then, of an exercise which is certainly one of thought upon thought, but is also one which implicates the subject of knowledge, and leads to a modification in his or her way of being and acting in the world.

It is clear then, that some time around the early 1980s, Foucault began to attribute to philosophy all of the characteristics which, hitherto, he had reserved for the *non-philosophes* of cultural, social and literary theory. And the reason, I would suggest, is that at this time he re-encountered a philosophical tradition with which he could identify his ethics of self-transformation – the ancient tradition of philosophy as a 'way of life', or a 'spiritual exercise'.[6] From Socrates in the fifth century BC, to Marcus Aurelius in the second century AD this tradition constitutes philosophy as a practice of the self, as a way of life which places truth and the relation of the self to truth at the centre of its concerns. What Foucault sees in this tradition is the emergence of the central themes and techniques of the Western critical attitude. And the practices it cultivated, especially in the era of late Roman Stoicism, were part of an 'aesthetics of the self' – for in cultivating such an attitude,

> ... one does not have to take up a position or role towards oneself as that of a judge pronouncing a verdict. One can comport oneself in the role of a technician, of a craftsman, of an artist, who – from time to time – stops working, examines what he is doing, reminds himself of the rules of his art, and compares these rules with what he has achieved thus far (DT, 112).

And it was a practice of the self which, as the Cynics in particular showed, did not have to be without social and political import. Foucault follows Pierre Hadot in regarding this tradition, which stretches from Socrates's 'the unexamined life is not worth living',[7] through Diogenes of Sinope's efforts to 'deface the currency',[8] to the Stoic cultivation of the *technai tou biou* as 'spiritual' insofar as it involves the subject of philosophy in an experimental self-transformation.

> By spirituality, I understand ... that which precisely refers to a subject acceding to a certain mode of being and to the transformations which the subject must make of himself in order to accede to this mode of being (ECS, 125[722]).

This is a form of philosophy which demands that the individual, to borrow Nietzsche's phrase, 'risk *himself* constantly'.[9] In this tradition, to 'do' philosophy is not to engage in a purely intellectual pursuit; it involves much more than a search for objective knowledge which has no implications for the subject's own mode of existence. In the Socratic *elenchus*, for example, this requirement comes in the form of Socrates's insistence that his respondents should say only what they themselves believe.[10] If they do not comply with this demand then there is no chance that their encounter with Socrates will lead them to an examination of themselves; that is, to the care of themselves. In the Cynic movement, as in Stoicism, there is a similar assumption that what is at stake is the way of life, the mode of being, of the individual. And while Stoicism certainly had a much greater theoretical apparatus than Cynicism (one ancient commentator characterized Cynicism as 'a shortcut to virtue'[11]), we have already seen that its primary goal was nonetheless to *live* in accordance with virtue.

But it was not simply the critical experimental nature of this practice of philosophy which interested Foucault. It was also the way that it conceptualized the relation between the subject and truth. In a course he gave at the Collège de France in 1982 (CCF, 82), Foucault draws a distinction between two different ways in which it is possible to understand the relation between truth and subjectivity; or, between truth and the subject who has access to or gives witness to that truth. Firstly, in antiquity the subject must implicate himself (and, in antiquity, it invariably was a 'he') in the pursuit of truth: there can be no access to truth, no right to speak the truth, unless the subject has engaged in a certain work on the self, an elaboration of the self, an ascesis. The subject of truth, in effect, is responding to the oracular and Socratic imperative 'Care for thy self.' Truth, here, is not gained by simply investigating the world around us; rather, it follows upon a 'conversion', and is attained through the practice of 'spiritual exercises'. By implication, any truth, once attained, will have a reciprocal effect on the subject: 'during antiquity, the philosophical question of truth and the practice of spirituality had not been separated'.

The situation after the 'Cartesian moment', however, is the reverse: now knowledge, and its imperative 'know thyself' (*gnothi seauton*), takes precedence over techniques. The subject can gain access to truth by a simple 'act of knowledge'. It is no longer necessary for the thinker to bring his or her own subjectivity into question; in fact all such 'spiritual' practices are 'disqualified' from the philosophical field at the very beginning of modern philosophy. According to this contrast, in antiquity philosophy was understood as responding to the oracular imperative of 'care for the self'; philosophy was a technique, a practice, which implicated and transformed the subject, and which was made possible by a 'conversion'. On the other hand, in modernity, philosophy has been understood as responding to the demand for knowledge; it has been seen as a means of attaining certainty, as an 'analytics of truth'. What Foucault regrets in this shift is that after the Cartesian moment 'truth is no longer capable of transfiguring and saving the subject'.[12] His problem, then, is to try, in some sense, to 'reclaim' this pre-modern tradition in order to go beyond, or to circumvent, the great modern philosophical machineries.[13]

In the Socratic tradition, which stretches from Socrates in the fifth century BC, through the Cynics in the late Classical era, to the Stoics of the Roman Empire, Foucault finds a way of practising philosophy that seems to echo his own dissatisfaction with the philosophical system-builders (whether they be Plato, Aristotle, Hegel or Husserl). This is a conception of philosophy that, if revived, could contribute to the task of working out new ways of living and thinking. However, it is also a conception of philosophy that makes an essential link between this work on the self and a concomitant critical engagement with the society in which one lives. And it is this combination of self-criticism with cultural and political critique that ultimately qualifies this notion of philosophy to be a central technique in Foucault's ethics.

SPIRITUALITY AND CRITIQUE

One of the central features of the Socratic tradition, and the one that makes it susceptible to appropriation by a thinker such as Foucault, is that it is, in an almost modern sense, a *critical* tradition. Kimon Lycos, for example, argues that the Socratic technique, which involves the provocation and inducement of a reflection about what it is to live well, amounts to a 'new form of the activity of cultural critique'.[14] And, alluding to Plato's simile of the cave (*Republic*, 514a–521b), he suggests that Socrates's task is to 'turn around the souls' of his interlocutors, so that they will be led to reflect upon and reconsider the power of justice in social life.[15] This critical task is, moreover, a lifelong one, since a reflective practice of justice 'involves a constant *revision* of how one thinks of the ideal or the standard itself in the light of new aspects of human living that may emerge'.[16] The act of turning around the soul, then, as well as the reflective process which it leads to, requires a constant re-enactment; and it is this re-enactment which Socrates engages in through his encounters with the citizens of Athens.

For Plato, to 'turn the soul around' is to effect a conversion (*Republic*, 518d), to bring about a shift in perception and understanding, and consequently a change in one's way of life. In his discussion of this concept of conversion in Classical and Hellenistic Greece, Pierre Hadot argues that the idea of conversion (*conversio* in Latin and either *epistrophe* or *metanoia* in Greek) has profoundly marked Western consciousness.[17] If we bear in mind the two etymological senses of conversion – that is, either a 'return to an origin' (*epistrophe*), or a 'rebirth' (*metanoia*) – then we could, Hadot argues, frame the whole course of Western history as a continuously renewed effort to perfect the techniques of conversion – whether in the former sense of a 'conversion-return', or in the latter sense of a 'conversion-mutation'.[18] Hadot cites a passage from the *Republic*, for example, in which education is characterized as just such a conversion: 'the organ by which [man] learns is like an eye which cannot be turned from darkness to light unless the whole body is turned' (*Republic*, 518c). And this 'turning around of the mind itself might', Socrates suggests, 'be made a subject of professional skill [*techne*]' (518d). What ancient philosophy sets out to achieve, according to Hadot, is then the return to an original nature (*epistrophe*) through a profound rupture with the common modes of life. And it is in the history of these techniques of 'conversion-mutation' – what Hadot calls the history of 'spiritual exercises' – that we must situate philosophy, or at least philosophy as it has at times been practised – and certainly philosophy as Foucault finally came to conceive it.[19]

An illustration of the critical potential of such a conversion is the stance taken by the Cynics in relation to social conventions and norms. As Diogenes Laertius reports, Diogenes of Sinope possessed that harmony of word and deed which Plato had praised in Socrates.[20] Having recounted the story of Diogenes's scandalous behaviour in public (not only did he masturbate in the *agora*, he even ate there!), and of his reported saying that 'the most beautiful thing in the world' is 'freedom of speech (*parrhesia*)', Diogenes Laertius concludes:

> This was the gist of his conversation; and it was plain that he acted accordingly, adulterating currency in every truth, allowing convention no such authority as he allowed to natural right, and asserting that the manner of life he lived was the same as that of Heracles [Hercules] when he preferred liberty to everything (*Lives*, VI, 71).

Diogenes 'adulterated currency in every truth' by challenging social conventions and by challenging and unsettling the 'currency' of language.[21] He combined the flouting of social conventions, in favour of that which is 'natural', with what we could call a critique of the moral vocabulary of his contemporaries. For example, he called into question accepted notions of what it is to be a master: when he was being sold as a slave, according to Diogenes Laertius, he asked the herald to announce 'Does anyone want to buy a master for himself?'[22] Similarly, in his celebrated (and perhaps apocryphal) encounters with Alexander the Great he compared Alexander to a fearful slave who had to carry arms at all times – even when he was asleep. In contrast, Diogenes was able to speak to Alexander fearlessly and with outrageous insolence, because he, Diogenes, was master of himself.[23]

An important feature of this tradition, and one which makes it most 'useful' for us today, is the notion and practice of *parrhesia*.[24] *Parrhesia* is generally translated as either the right of 'freedom of speech', or as the act of 'speaking frankly'; Foucault often speaks of it as truth-telling (*le dire vrai*), although it literally means 'to say everything'. Foucault identifies the emergence of *parrhesia* in the plays of Euripides and traces its 'descent' through Plato's early Socratic dialogues to the philosophical practice of the Cynics. One anecdote among many will give some idea of its ancient currency. Lucian, a Roman author writing in the second century AD, tells a story about a Cynic who, while mounted on a stone, insulted a passing proconsul by calling him a 'catamite' (a catamite being a boy kept by a man for his own sexual gratification). When the proconsul wanted the Cynic to be beaten or sent into exile, however, an onlooker intervened, requesting clemency on the grounds that the Cynic was merely practising traditional *parrhesia*.[25]

In its 'original', political sense *parrhesia* denotes a particular relation both between the speaker and what he says,[26] and between the speaker and the person (or group) to whom he is speaking. The former is a relation in which, firstly, the speaker says exactly what he believes: he is completely frank in conveying his own opinion. Secondly, what he says is *true*; and the truth of what he says is not guaranteed through any conception of evidence or proof, but rather through the *moral* qualities of the speaker. In a sense, the truth of what is said is guaranteed by the verbal activity of *parrhesia* itself, or by the particular relation which obtains between the speaker and what he says. And this relation is obvious from the speaker's courage in speaking the truth. This courage is an essential feature of *parrhesia* because what the parrhesiast says is always, in some way, dangerous for himself. In the case of messengers or advisers addressing a king or ruler this danger is obvious; in the case of a citizen addressing the Assembly it arises from the possible loss of reputation and influence which one risks by displeasing one's fellow citizens; in the case of friendship it arises from the risk of angering or losing one's friend;[27] finally, in the most extreme cases it involves risking one's life. This is the situation of Socrates, for example, in his trial: 'I am fairly certain that this plain speaking (*parrhesia*) of mine is the cause of my unpopularity; and this really goes to prove that my statements are true' (*Apology*, 24a).

The conceptualization and practice of *parrhesia*, which emerges in the fifth century BC, had been made possible by the radical shift in the Greek relation to speech and truth.[28] Foucault sees a representation of this shift in the basic structure of Euripides's *Ion*, a play which he characterizes as 'primarily a story of the movement of truth-telling from Delphi to Athens' (DT, 20). In its structure the play closely parallels, and yet reverses, the story of Oedipus. In Sophocles's *King Oedipus*, the god Phoebus Apollo has revealed the truth through his oracle, but human attempts to evade this prophecy lead to the tragedy of Oedipus's fate. Here it is the god who has spoken the truth, and by the time Oedipus and Jocasta are commited to uncovering it, the prophecy has already been fulfilled. In *Ion*, on the other hand, the same god (Apollo) rapes a young woman and continuously refuses to either admit his misdeed or reveal the truth of his son's identity. His attempts to deceive, in the face of the woman's search for truth, can only be overcome by recourse to *human* truth-telling. And it is here, in the 'shift of the place of truth's discourse' (DT, 19), from Delphi (the site of Apollo's oracle) to Athens, that Foucault sees a representation of a fundamental modification in the Greek relation to truth and true speech.

When *parrhesia* emerges in the plays of Euripides it refers primarily to a political practice – to what Foucault calls the 'parrhesiastic contract'.[29] This 'contract' is effected in a relation between two people which is characterized by an extreme power differential. It involves a speaker who has the courage to speak a truth to a person (a King or a ruler) who they have good reason to fear and who may or may not decide to hear the speaker's truth without exacting retribution. In *The Bacchae* for instance, the messenger who brings news of the women's 'strange and terrible doings' requires a specific assurance from Pentheus, the King, that he will not be punished for speaking freely – and Pentheus agrees, thus entering into the contract.[30] This example illustrates two of the key features of such a contract: firstly, the 'parrhesiast' (the truth-teller) takes a risk in telling the truth; and secondly, the willingness of a King or ruler to enter into such a contract is a mark of their *arete* (excellence/virtue) as a ruler.

Parrhesia, however, is not only something that occurs in such situations of inequality; it is also, and more problematically, a central feature of Athenian citizenship. Along with *isonomia* (equal participation in exercise of power) and *isegoria* (equal right of speech), it is one of the basic rights of every Athenian citizen: the right to speak frankly to their fellow citizens on any matter of civic importance. In another play, Euripides portrays loss of this right, loss of *parrhesia*, as the chief hardship endured by the exile; because of course *parrhesia* only exists in Athens, and is the exclusive right of its well-born citizens.[31] This right is both a guarantee against the excesses of an intemperate ruler (because it gives what Foucault calls 'the right of criticism', (DT, 13), and a means by which the well-born can participate in the exercise of power – in its absence, one is reduced to 'a slave's life'. Understood in these senses, *parrhesia* is a positive characteristic, both of the political constitution of the city and the ethical constitution of its citizens. Its negative side emerges, however, when the right is freely granted to all in a democratic polis. Between the mid-fourth and mid-fifth centuries BC, the tension between these two aspects – especially as manifested in debates about democracy – gave rise to what Foucault calls a 'crisis of *parrhesia*': a crisis which manifests in a 'new problematization of the relations between verbal activity, education, freedom, power and the existing political institutions' (DT, 47). The 'democratization' of speech which occurred during the fifth century BC led to concerns that if everybody has the right to, literally, 'say everything' then a great deal of what is said will be at best worthless or at worst dangerous to the city. The discovery of this paradox – that *parrhesia* may itself be dangerous for the polis, that freedom of speech and democracy may be antithethical – is a discovery which led the Greeks into a 'long impassioned debate' about the relations between democracy, *logos*, freedom and truth (DT, 49). For some, the problem was that when those of vicious character are allowed a role in public deliberations, bad decisions will be taken by the city. For Isocrates, for example, the flatterers and demagogues are the only 'parrhesiasts' to whom the Assembly will listen. While for Plato the problem with *parrhesia* is more that it offers each man the opportunity to choose his own way of life – thus undermining the unity of the city.[32] While certain forms of *parrhesia* were being condemned for their political effects, however, there was a parallel development, around the figure of Socrates, of the theme of its ethical significance: that is, its importance for individual character. It is Socrates who, through Plato's dialogues, is at the centre of the turning point between political and ethical *parrhesia*.

In the figure of Socrates (in Plato's early dialogues and in the later Stoic and Cynic traditions) we have a model of the true ethical parrhesiast. Socrates is a man, a *mousikos aner*, who speaks the same truth as he lives; who has the same courage in speech as in battle; and who is unafraid to make the most powerful men in the city 'give an account of themselves'.[33] Unlike the political *parrhesia* of Euripides's plays, however, this ethical *parrhesia* is more a question of individual character than of political, institutional guarantee. Indeed, if engaging in the political life of the city is corrupting (as Socrates claims in the *Apology*[34]), then ethical *parrhesia* must be practised *in spite of* political institutions and guarantees. The new features which this Socratic, ethical *parrhesia* introduces with respect to political *parrhesia* are: firstly, it takes place not between a speaker and a large group, but between two individuals face to face; secondly, it raises the question of how to harmonize one's speech with one's way of life, one's *logos* with one's *bios*; thirdly, according to Foucault, it raises four questions about truth-telling as an activity – who is able to tell the truth? about what? with what consequences? with what relation to power? (DT, 114). These questions, which emerge from Socrates's encounter with the Sophists, put *parrhesia* at the centre of a particular form of philosophical reflection from the end of the fifth century BC.

It is in the 'Socratic tradition' that Foucault finds a model of the relation between truth and subjectivity in which the truth of the subject is not guaranteed by appeal to a science of the subject – such as the modern 'science of sexuality', for example. In this tradition, the truth of the subject is, rather, grounded by the subject him/herself through the relation which they constitute between their speech (*logos*) and their life (*bios*). Socrates becomes, for this tradition, an exemplar insofar as his speech always harmonizes with his actions; and the Cynic lives a life which, in its scandalous non-conformism attests to his or her philosophical principles. What this model offers, then, is a conception of truth in which truth is neither a correspondence between words and things, nor a question of internal, logical consistency; rather it is a question of what we could call a subjective consistency, or a correspondence between discourse and action. Truth, here, emerges from a certain relation with the self; it becomes a question of 'transfiguring and saving the subject' (CCF, 82). The ethical implications of this model are that the individual does not need a science of the self in order to pursue conformity with a moral truth. Rather, it is their critical engagement, both with themselves and their society, that gives them the resources to begin to address the question of the well-lived life.

In claiming this Socratic tradition for contemporary critique, Foucault carries out a manoeuvre that links the '*exercices spirituels*' of ancient philosophy with his own concern to formulate a contemporary ethics of self-transformation. In 'What is Critique?', as we saw in Chapter 6, Foucault characterizes critique as 'the art of not being governed so much' (QC, [38]). And if government, in his sense of the term, is an array of techniques and mechanisms which subjectivize individuals through mechanisms of power that lay claim to a certain truth value, then critique tries to desubjectivize individuals through the transformation of a certain politics of truth. Both government and its contrary critique operate in the field formed by the relations between power, truth and the subject; and critique, in opposition to government, cultivates an 'art of voluntary inservitude', or 'reflective indocility' (QC, 386[39]). In the same lecture, Foucault identifies one of the origins of this phenomenon in the Christian tradition of Biblical interpretation. In an age when governmentality was primarily a spiritual art, or rather an ecclesiastical art, critique was essentially Biblical. From John Wyclif in the fourteenth century to Pierre Bayle in the seventeenth century, critique was the practice of interrogating Scripture as to its truth and the Church as to its embodiment of that truth. Expanding on this point, Foucault suggests that 'one of the first great forms of revolt in the West was mysticism' (QC, [59]).[35] The individual and collective phenomena of religious revolt in the Middle Ages were, in a sense, one of the only available vehicles of resistance to both religious and secular government. Indeed the fact that they function as such a vehicle is crucial to Foucault's point:

> When one sees that these experiences, these movements of spirituality very often served as clothing, as vocabulary, but even more as ways of being and as supports to the hopes of struggles which one can call economic, political, which in Marxist terms one could call class struggles, [when one sees this] I think one has there something which is fundamental (QC, [59]).

If we put this together with Foucault's attempt to provide an historical link between contemporary critique and the critical practices of the Socratic tradition in antiquity, then we are presented with a genealogy of the critical attitude whose connecting thread is some notion of spirituality. From ancient philosophical ascesis, to the techniques of Medieval mystics; and from the Scriptural criticism of the Reformation to the refusal of government today, Foucault draws together the most disparate social and political phenomena under the unifying rubric of spirituality. And the culmination of this process is the seemingly incongruous appeal for a contemporary political spirituality':

> Isn't the most general political problem the problem of truth? How do we connect the way we divide the true from the false to the way we govern ourselves and others? The will to found each in a completely new way, to found each by the other (to discover a different division through a different manner of governing, and to govern on the basis of a different division), that is 'the spirituality of politics' (*la spiritualité politique*) (QM, 11[30]).

The 'return' to Greek philosophy allows Foucault to understand the modern critical project in terms of a long philosophical tradition in which critical reflection not only constitutes a certain relation between subjectivity and truth, but also – as Socrates held – makes an essential contribution to the ethical task of 'living well'. In the most general terms, I think we can say that philosophy, for Foucault, is a critical, reflective practice which, by calling into question our present modes of subjectivity and their relation to truth, our present modes of thinking and doing, is capable of transforming the way that we relate to ourselves and others, and thus of changing the way that we live. Despite the fact that Foucault's formulation of this conception – in terms of 'de-subjectivation' and the 'annihilation' of the self – may seem to some to be 'un-Greek' or even 'un-philosophical', it has the invaluable virtue of making possible, even of making necessary, a profound reappraisal of what it is that we do when we do philosophy. In Foucault's ethics, one of the most important things that we do, or should do, when we do philosophy is to prise open the relations of truth–power–subjectivity which make us the kind of individuals that we are. And while this 'conversion' can still draw on the techniques of the return to nature of Stoicism and the Cynics, it could be more properly characterized as a continuous 'mutation'. A mutation whose only telos is the field of possibilities, the field of freedom, which is opened up through de-subjectivation. This is the practice of philosophy that can make an essential contribution to the third aspect of Foucault's ethics.

CHAPTER 9

The Art of Freedom

In Paris [J. M.] Synge once said to me, 'We should unite stoicism, asceticism and ecstasy. Two of them have often come together, but the three never.'

W. B. Yeats[1]

... the moral problem ... is the practice of liberty. How can one practise freedom?

Michel Foucault (ECS, 115[711])

In Foucault's ethics, philosophy, or at least that mode of philosophy which is typified by the spiritual exercises of the Socratic tradition and the experimentalism of Nietzsche, can be an important technique for self-transformation. In the face of, and in opposition to, the forms of subjectivity to which we find ourselves fixed, critical philosophy is a tool which can help us to untie the knots of our identity. It cannot, of course, untie these knots in any absolute or final sense; rather what it assists in is the task of retying them differently. If, following Foucault's fourfold division of ethics, we say that these knots are the ethical substance of ethics, that the aesthetic is the attitude we adopt towards them, and that philosophy is one of the ethical techniques for their transformation, then we are still faced with the question of the telos of this work which is carried out on the self. In this final chapter, I argue that for Foucault the telos, the aim of this work, is freedom. I have already noted the difficulty involved in making this kind of precise characterization of an ethics which was never systematically presented by its author. And we may also note the necessarily incomplete and contingent character of any such attempt. In arguing that Foucault's ethics requires some notion of freedom as its telos, I am pushing to its limit the interpretations that, for example, Bernauer and Rabinow have made (discussed in Chapter 8). Bernauer characterizes the telos of this ethics as 'a permanent provocation to the forces that war against our creativity',[2] while Rabinow characterizes it as 'disassembling the self'.[3] My suggestion is that these interpretations only make sense if Foucault is seen as embracing some notion of freedom as both the condition of possibility and the aim of such practices of the self.

It is not difficult to imagine Foucault echoing J. M. Synge's reported wish to unite 'stoicism, asceticism and ecstasy'; and one could surmise that he would conceptualize this unification as the deliberate work of giving form to freedom. Freedom would operate as both the ontological condition of this ethical work, and as its ultimate aim: that is, to maintain the openness and malleability that made the form-giving possible in the first place. The questions this raises, however, are whether Foucault's philosophical position allows him to make such a claim on freedom as the ontological condition of ethics; and whether he can then give a satisfactory account of the relationship between the ethical work of self-transformation and the task of opening up spaces of freedom.

SPACES OF FREEDOM

One of the commonly received opinions about Foucault is that his critical project is purely negative, that his genealogical unmasking has, and can have, no positive moment. This view comes largely from critics such as Habermas and Fraser for whom Foucault's project suffers from the lack of a 'blueprint' or proposed alternative to current social relations.[4] From this point of view, Foucault's historical analyses can only take on their real value if they are placed in the context of a theory which, unlike Foucault's, can lay claim to 'some positive, concrete, palpable alternative social vision'.[5] In the absence of any such positive vision Foucault risks falling into political quietism: this, according to Michael Walzer, is the 'catastrophic weakness' of Foucault's political theory'.[6] The problem, in Fraser's words, is that he cannot answer the question 'Why is struggle preferable to submission? Why ought domination to be resisted?'[7] What seems to annoy these critics so much, is that even though Foucault was 'good' in practice (he always engaged in the 'right' political struggles and he produced 'empirical insights' which are useful to these struggles), he was so very 'naughty' in theory (he denied both the liberal-humanist and the Marxist bases for normative political theory).[8] Fraser's response to this dichotomy is to try to tolerate the 'naughty' Foucault, in the same way that one forgives the unreliability and 'outrageousness of a lover, while remaining loyal to someone else (perhaps Habermas?) who would supply the solid virtues of a 'husband'.[9]

In response to such criticisms, one could argue that Foucault does not need to justify struggle over submission, because his histories are simple descriptions which, while they make clear the conditions of possibility of resistance, do not themselves promote such resistance. This argument has been developed most effectively by Paul Patton who argues that, in relation to Foucault's project, 'it is not a question of advocating such resistance, of praising autonomy or blaming domination as respective exemplars of a good and evil for all, but *simply of understanding why such resistance occurs*'.[10] He thus responds to the charge of crypto-normativity (or 'a-normativity') by arguing that Foucault is simply describing how it is that resistance comes about – and if these descriptions are then used by people who struggle it is not up to Foucault to provide them with a normative justification. Another possible way of responding to such criticisms is to argue that while Foucault does not appeal to anything these critics would recognize as a normative ground, he nevertheless goes beyond providing a neutral account of the nature of power and resistance. I would suggest that the risk of minimizing Foucault's *positive* critical impetus is an unnecessarily high price to pay for answering his critics. Would it not be possible to allow Foucault to be both 'non-normative', 'non-universalist', 'non-foundation-alist' and also committed to a 'social vision' which embraces certain values? On this interpretation, Foucault would be offering us a description certainly, but one which, as Thomas Flynn has argued, operates as a 'propaedeutic' to a politics of '*suggestion* and *exemplification*'.[11] Isn't it time to take up the challenge Foucault gave himself in 'What is Enlightenment?' – 'We must obviously give a more positive content to [our] philosophical ethos' (WE, 45).

The major barrier to carrying out such a task – and the second reason why Foucault is generally received as a negative or sceptical critic – is the fact that he himself continuously denied having any positive plan, blueprint, or vision. From his early characterization of his own work as doing no more than equipping a 'tool box', to his later rejection of a politics of imperatives, Foucault always seemed to be in hiding.[12] He always seemed to be at pains to say that his own personal commitment to a particular cause – whether it was the situation of prisoners, the imposition of martial law in Poland, or the plight of the Vietnamese 'boat people' – was a separate issue from the status of his historico-critical discourse. He insisted that his critical discourse commanded neither him nor anybody else to engage in such a struggle, but it could help an individual who already had such a commit-ment to better undertake the struggle. Philosophy is never more ridiculous and dangerous, he argued, than when it tries 'to dictate to others (*faire la loi aux autres*), to tell them where their truth is and how to find it' (*UP*, 9[15]). However, as is usual with Foucault, the question is not quite so simple. In a course at the Collège de France in 1978 (*DG*), he admits that there is no discourse, or even analysis, which is not in some way 'traversed or supported by something like an imperative discourse (*discours à l'impér-atif*)'. In the case of his discourse, however, this must not consist of saying '"love this, hate that", "this is good, that is bad", "be for this, suspect that"'; instead, what he favours is something he calls a 'very light discourse' (*un discours bien léger*), one which can only operate within a particular 'field of forces', one which can make no claim to universality, one which is not categorical but conditional.

> Hence, the imperative which supports the theoretical analysis which we are trying to do here – since we do have one, an imperative – is one which I would just like to be conditional, something like this: 'if you want to struggle, here are some key points, here are some lines of force, here are some knots and some blockages' ... I would like these imperatives to be nothing more than tactical hints ... so that one can carry out an analysis which is effective in tactical terms (*DG*).[13]

Foucault assumes that the commitment to resistance is already present, and it is only on the basis of such a pre-existing commitment that he can then tell people what they 'should' do.

Foucault's critics have always regarded this refusal to even consider a normative basis for resistance as a significant weakness, especially when considered in conjunction With his insistence that power relations are ubiquitous in human society. Foucault, it is thought, offers no hope of a society in which power would not operate. For this reason, Charles Taylor argues that one of the central weaknesses of Foucault's critical project is that for him there can be 'no escape from power into freedom'.[14] In answer to these criticisms, Foucault insisted that the fact that 'power is everywhere' does not mean that nothing is possible – it means, rather, that everything is possible: 'if there are relations of power throughout every social field,' he argues, 'it is because there is freedom everywhere' (ECS 123[720]). This redefinition of power, however, carried with it the danger of removing the possibility of specifying those situations in which there is no freedom. In rejecting the view that power is an evil which is opposed to freedom, it carried the danger of implying that there is actually no such evil, that the removal of freedom is an impossibility. This problem was compounded by Foucault's perceived inability to differentiate between power relations and states of domination. If power relations are inevitable, and they cannot be distinguished from relations of domination, then Foucault would seem to be giving, at the very least, a general justification for forms of domination. As a result of these concerns, Foucault was forced, in the late 1970s, to clarify a distinction which had only ever been implicit in his work – the distinction between power and domination. He began to argue that power, or power relations, are always characterized by a more or less open play of 'strategic games between liberties' (ECS, 130[728]), while states of domination are characterized by a shrinking space for freedom of action.[15] On the one hand, a power relation can only exist in a situation in which a subjective choice is possible: 'there cannot be relations of power unless the subjects are free' (ECS, 123[720]). On the other hand, relations of domination (what we 'ordinarily call power') are those in which the power relation is fixed to such a degree that the possibility for subjective choice is almost non-existent. The examples Foucault gives of such relations are the relations between men and women in Western European societies in the eighteenth and nineteenth centuries and the relations between colonizers and colonized in many societies of the same time. So when Foucault argues that all social relations are relations of *power*, he is not suggesting that *domination* is inevitable. He is rather suggesting that domination is the perversion of power; it represents the violent closure of social and political relations.

This distinction is interesting from our perspective because it appeals to freedom as a condition of possibility of a certain kind of social relation: freedom is a prerequisite for what we could call politics. Even more important for our concerns, however, is Foucault's further claim that freedom, or at least a minimal space of freedom, is also a condition of possibility of ethics; indeed, it is its 'ontological condition' (ECS, 115[712]). He states explicitly that in the opposition between power and domination, an opposition in which power relations will always have a tendency to become relations of domination, it is the 'task' of critical philosophy to sound a warning.[16] Critical philosophy 'is precisely the challenging of all phenomena of domination at whatever level or under whatever form they present themselves' (ECS, 131[729]). The problem, the political problem, is to work out forms of social relation which minimize the effects of domination. If we understand social relations as relations of power, as relations in which individuals try to conduct and determine the actions of others, then the task is to work out ways which would 'allow these games of power to be played with a minimum of domination' (ECS, 129[727]). And it is this task – the minimization of domination – which connects the fields of ethics and politics; it is their 'point of articulation' (ECS, 130[727]). The political task of working out these forms, the 'rules of law [and] the techniques of management', cannot be dissociated from the ethical task of formulating an ethos, a particular mode of self-relation and a practice of the self, which would contribute to an opening up, rather than a closing down, of the space of freedom.

The suggestion that freedom is the telos of Foucault's ethics may seem at first sight to raise almost as many problems as it resolves. The first such problem is the possibility of misunderstanding. To say that freedom is the telos of ethics might be taken to imply that the aim of ethics is to achieve an individual or collective freedom which is grounded in a universal human nature, or in some inviolable human right. When the French National Assembly promulgated 'The Declaration of the Rights of Man and the Citizen' in August 1789, it based its account of those rights on the assertion that 'Men are born and remain free...';[17] echoing the earlier observation of Rousseau that 'Man is born free; and everywhere he is in chains.'[18] To say that Foucault has returned to an Enlightenment concern with freedom might seem to suggest that he came to embrace an eighteenth-century notion of universal 'Man' – a creature endowed with inalienable rights and duties. It may also seem to suggest a late rapprochement between Foucault and the discourse of humanism which he repudiated for so long; a return, perhaps, to a transcendental subject which guarantees not only an episte-mology but also a deontology. We have already seen how Foucault's late return to the subject can be interpreted in ways analogous to this and, in Chapter 6, I argued that such interpretations are based on a misunder-standing. If, however, in answer to the suggestion that Foucault returns in his late work to a conception of the subject, we point out that for him 'the subject', as historically determined, is understood nominalistically, then a similar argument can be made regarding his conception of freedom.

Freedom, for Foucault, is not a universal historical constant; it is neither a Rousseauian point of origin, nor a Marcusian point of culmination. It is an historically conditioned possibility which arises only in the context of given power relations; it does not oppose these power relations, either ontologically or morally. On the contrary, just as there could be no social relations without relations of power, so there could be no freedom without these same relations. Freedom, therefore, is not a state for which we strive, it is a condition of our striving; and as such it can also function as a yardstick for that striving. Freedom is not a substance. It is as relational as power, as historically pliable as subjectivity. It is neither an ideal state towards which one strives by overcoming the finitude and limitations of one's individual existence, nor is it an essential feature of a transcendentally grounded human nature. Rather, like power (which exists only in a relation between forces), freedom exists only in the concrete capacity of individuals to refuse, to say 'No'. To say 'No', for example, to being governed in a certain way, or to governing oneself in a certain way. It is this capacity to refuse, a capacity which only exists to a very limited degree in states of domination, that makes possible the creative work of both ethics and politics. Rajchman distinguishes this Foucaldian notion of freedom, which is practical' and 'nominalist', from a view which would see freedom as an 'ideal' waiting to be realized (Hegel and Marx).[19] In Foucault's version of critique, freedom is rooted in our 'unwillingness to comply' rather than in an essential autonomy. This unwillingness is 'specific and unpredictable' and therefore could never be abstracted and instituted into a new form of life;[20] it cannot provide the blueprint Fraser demands. Instead, it grounds the continuing work of responding to and modifying the forms of government and self-government that shape the way we live.[21] When freedom is understood in this sense it emerges as both the condition of possibility and the task of ethical practice.

On the one hand, freedom is the ontological condition of ethics (just as it is the condition of politics); on the other hand, ethics is the form we give to our freedom – it is freedom's 'deliberate (*réfléchie*) form' (ECS, 115[712]). One of the criteria by which one might judge the desirability of any particular ethical (or political) system would be the extent to which its deliberate form manages to preserve a maximum of freedom and a minimum of domination – of both self and others. It is in this sense that, as Foucault suggests in a different context, 'perhaps one must not be for consensuality, but one must be against non-consensuality' (PE, 379). Non-consensuality, or domination, is to be avoided because it closes up the space of freedom; that 'space of concrete freedom ... of possible transformation' (SPS, 36) which is opened up by critical philosophy, by political struggle and by the ethical work on the self. Our freedom, as Rajchman argues, would therefore lie 'in our capacity to find alternatives to the particular forms of discourse that define us'.[22] Freedom is the contrary of neither power nor domination. It is merely an effect of our capacity to challenge the effects of both; it is not 'the end of domination', but a 'revolt within its practices'.[23]

While recognizing the practical and theoretical importance of Foucault's refusal of the role of *maître de vérité*, the role of architect for a social utopia, it is still legitimate to ask what positive contribution his critical philosophy makes to the effectiveness of such revolts against power. What positive content do his 'tactical hints' contain? What is the general direction in which his 'conditional imperative' points?

In the *Nichomachean Ethics*, Aristotle points out that the Greek term for 'character', *ethos*, is closely related to the term for custom or habit.[24] Thus, moral character is a product of the cultivation of the right habits, the right personal customs or attitudes. When Foucault speaks of a philosophical ethos, he too is making a connection between the ethics of the intellectual and a certain set of attitudes or habits. In other words, that ethic would not be defined, for Foucault, by a normatively grounded code of behaviour;

rather it would be characterized by a general attitude, outlook or approach. And while this ethos may not be codifiable, Foucault does give it a coherent formulation. Its first feature is that, as an attitude, it is closely related to that 'critical attitude' which Foucault sees as arising in response to the growing governmentalization of modern societies, and which he relates both to the sixteenth-century Reformation and the eighteenth-century Enlightenment. In Foucault's 'What is Enlightenment?' lecture, this attitude is exemplified, firstly in the question asked by Kant – 'What difference does today introduce with respect to yesterday?'[25] and secondly in the figure of Baudelaire, who seems to answer the question by saying 'this modernity does not "liberate man in his own being"; it compels him to face the task of producing himself'.[26] And for Baudelaire (as for Foucault), this compulsion is based on a valorization of the present – but a valorization of the present which is 'indissociable from a desperate eagerness to imagine it, to imagine it otherwise than it is, and to transform it not by destroying it but by grasping it in what it is' (WE, 41). We must re-imagine and transform our present: our selves, our modes of behaviour and our ways of thinking.

In this form of critique, the task of transforming ourselves has two moments: firstly, the analysis of our historically imposed limits – what Foucault calls the 'critical ontology of ourselves' (WE, 50) – and, secondly, the imaginative, creative attempt to surpass those limits which we judge to be no longer necessary – a 'historico-practical test of the limits that we may go beyond' (WE, 47). To elucidate the growing importance of some notion of freedom in Foucault's work, let us turn to some examples of the kinds of practical test he saw as exemplifying this critical work of self-transformation. In the early 1980s, he began, for example, to see the position of gay men in contemporary Western societies as a particularly fruitful locus for reflection on this question.[27] In a series of interviews he gave at this time to the French, American and Canadian gay press he discusses the potential the position offers for subjective and communal transformation. In his view, the key aspects of the position of gay men are, firstly, that they are significantly excluded from the dominant institutional modes of legitimating personal and sexual relations; and, secondly, that having to a large degree attained what we can call 'freedom of sexual choice', they are now faced with the question of how to 'use' this freedom. By virtue of its marginality *and* its relative freedom and openness, the position poses the question of how – outside the dominant institutional frameworks – it is possible to imagine and build new forms of affective relationships. To this extent, the position is analogous both to that of the Greek male citizen (who, in Foucault's picture, enjoyed relative freedom *without* a completely determining institutional structure) and to that of all those today for whom the 'traditional' moral systems (whether those of Christianity, humanism or Marxism) can no longer provide an acceptable practice of freedom. For this reason, the position of gay people in Western societies can be taken as emblematic of a contemporary crisis in the way that we practise our freedom. And Foucault's interest in it arises not only from the fact that it was a position which he himself occupied, but also from the fact that the 'solutions' being developed had a significance far beyond the gay community per se.

These 'solutions' can be divided into, firstly, those relating to the actual practice of sexual relations, and secondly, those relating to the attempt to develop new 'forms of life', new ways of 'being together', new modes of affective relations. In relation to the practice of sexuality, what Foucault sees as being particularly 'promising' in gay culture is the growth of the practice of sado-masochism (S/M) as a 'creative enterprise' to achieve the 'desexualisation of pleasure' (SPPI, 30). Since the first volume of *The History of Sexuality*, Foucault had formulated the need for a cultivation of pleasure which would circumvent the established modes of 'sexuality' in favour of 'bodies and pleasures' (*VS*, 157[208]); and now, in the 'laboratories of sexual experimentation' (the gay bath-houses) of New York and San Francisco (SCSA, 298), Foucault saw just such an attempt to loosen power's 'grip' on 'bodies and their materiality, their forces, energies, sensations, and pleasures' (*VS*, 155[205]). What is interesting about S/M, according to Foucault, is that – contrary to its popular image – it is not about the domination of one person by another. It consists, rather, of a relationship which, being both regulated and open, resembles a 'chess game' in which either person may 'win' but both parties enjoy the intensification of sexual relations which results from this 'perpetual tension', 'perpetual uncertainty' and 'perpetual novelty' (SCSA, 299). What S/M represents for Foucault, is a creative response to the space of freedom which opens up as soon as one rejects the modes of behaviour which the modern discourse of sexuality would impose: it is 'a kind of creation' which represents the cultivation of 'new possibilities of pleasure' (SPPI, 30).

S/M also represents a form of relation that Foucault continuously championed in his late work. That is, a relation which could combine regulation and structure with open fluidity and suppleness. Foucault's admiration for any form which successfully combines these features can be seen in his characterization of classical Greek ethics as an 'open demand' (*une exigence ouverte*) (*UP*, 92[106]) to subject oneself to certain 'general formal principles' (*UP*, 89[103]).[28] This was an ethics, according to Foucault, which could satisfy both the human longing for form and the need to be relatively free in relation to this form. This concern to steer a course between two extremes (the anarchistic refusal of all government versus the embracing of totalitarian forms of social organization[29]) can also be seen in Foucault's rejection of the possibility of a 'culture without constraints'. When asked if such a culture was possible, Foucault replied that the important question is not whether such a culture is possible (in his view it is not), but 'whether the system of constraints in which a society functions leaves individuals the liberty to transform the system' (SCSA, 294). If we reject even the theoretical possibility of abstracting human beings from the cultures in which they live, and if we recognize that all cultures are shot through with power relations (which are always, in some sense, constraining), then we arrive at a position in which freedom (as a universal) is not a state of being for which one strives, but freedom (as a context-specific possibility) is one element in an agonistic game between conflicting forces. The crucial test for any cultural system would then be the extent of the spaces of freedom (the possibilities of transformative action) which that system allowed. Hence, the whole problem – in sexual, affective and social relations – would be to find ways of combining form, structure and necessary constraint with openness and the potential for continual transformation. Foucault saw an example of this kind of development in S/M – and also in the ancient practice of *philia*, friendship.

In the context of his discussions of 'homosexual ascesis' (AMV, 206[165]), the ancient theme of *philia* emerges as a key reference point. If the central problem facing gay people today is, according to Foucault, 'how can we develop forms and styles of life which are specific to "us" (but not based on essentialist definitions of a gay identity) and which maintain the openness of the "virtualities" of our position?', then his suggestion is that 'friendship' may be a useful starting point (AMV, 207[166]). In Classical Greece, friendship (between men) was a very important social relation: one 'within which people had a certain freedom, a certain kind of choice (limited of course), as well as very intense emotional relations' (SPPI, 32–3). It therefore combined suppleness and constraint in a vehicle for emotional intensity; and even though Foucault recognizes that we cannot return to it, it is a model which he nevertheless finds '*passionant*'. Faced with a contemporary 'impoverishment of relational possibilities' (STSW, [311]), it becomes imperative for members of the gay community to develop a 'gay culture' which would 'invent modes of relationship, modes of existence, types of value and forms of exchange between individuals which would be really new, which would be neither homogenous with nor super-imposable on general cultural relations' (ibid.). These new forms of relations could be (and, in fact, would 'have to be') available not only to gay people, but also to non-gay-identified people who suffer, in the same way, from the 'impoverishment' of relational possibilities. As to the precise nature (whether legal or informal) of these new structures, Foucault of course refuses to elaborate – quite simply because it is not possible to either dictate or predict the outcome of such a creative enterprise.

Despite Foucault's unwillingness (and perhaps, inability) to specify details, the important point to note here is that Foucault's ethics, or ethos, does have a clearly specifiable *direction*. And that direction is clearly away from excessive constraint and towards the opening up of spaces of freedom – spaces in which multiple creative enterprises can be undertaken. In a discussion about the policing of homosexuality in France, for example, Foucault makes the following 'categorical' statement: 'here one must be intransigent, one cannot make a compromise between tolerance and intoler-ance, one can only be on the side of tolerance' (FNC, [337]). In another interview, Foucault makes a distinction between sexual acts (some of which – e.g. rape – must not be 'allowed') and sexual choice about which, on the contrary, 'one has to be absolutely intransigent': one must insist upon the freedom of sexual choice, and of the expression of that choice (SCSA, 289). In selecting these quotations I am not arguing that Foucault, in spite of his own best efforts, really does embrace categorical imperatives; I am not suggesting that he is a 'crypto-normativist' who finally shows his true colours. Rather, what I want to suggest is that in his late work Foucault came to give freedom (as both historical constant *and* ethical principle) such a fundamental role that his entire critical trajectory needs to be considered in its light.

It is, perhaps, surprising that when Foucault finally decided to 'come out' and 'own' the ethos which had driven all of his research, the key feature of that ethos would be a value which, in the eyes of many of his readers, he had consistently rejected for several decades. The notion of freedom, and especially of individual freedom, seemed to have been rejected by Foucault along with the humanist, or the liberal-individualist, notion of the subject. A whole body of criticism attacked his work from the 1970s as denying the possibility of autonomous human agency, and thus as denying the possibility of effective resistance to regimes of power. In Foucault, the story was told, the subject was powerless because power was all-powerful. Given this, how can Foucault now base his entire historico-philosophical project on an ethical commitment to 'autonomy', 'liberty' and 'freedom'?[30] The short answer would be to say that he can do so because those criticisms have already been effectively answered. Foucault never intended to present power as a force which incapacitates human actors; the subject, in his view, always was capable of resisting, of engaging in autonomous action, without appealing to a transcendental or constitutive freedom. While this response is certainly an effective defence of the Foucault of *Discipline and Punish* and

The History of Sexuality, volume I, I am not convinced that it adequately accounts for Foucault's later pre-occupation with the Enlightenment values of freedom and autonomy. Foucault's commitment to these values, in his late work, amounts to more than just a straightforward recognition of the fact of resistance and social change: indeed, in announcing this as the key term in his *ethos* he has already given it the status of ethical principle rather than historical constant.

WE OTHER LUMIÈRES

Geoffrey Harpham remarks that Foucault's final engagement with the Enlightenment is seen by many as 'one of the most remarkable and ... incomprehensible "turns" in recent intellectual history'.[31] One of the reasons this turn is so incomprehensible is precisely because it involves the championing of some notion of freedom. Foucault, the unmasker of the Enlightenment ideals of reason, humanity and autonomy, had suddenly become Foucault, the champion of 'freedom' as the condition of possibility of individual ethical practice. This transformation, from counter-Enlightenment bad boy to curious Kantian, can only be understood by examining how the appeal to freedom itself is inextricably linked to that 'remarkable turn'. In an article that functions almost as an obituary for Foucault, Habermas remarks that Foucault had suggested in 1983 that he, Habermas, Rorty, Taylor and others should come together for a colloquium (which never actually took place) on Kant's 1784 article 'An Answer to the Question: What is Enlightenment?'[32] Habermas expresses the disappointment he felt when he eventually read Foucault's 'What is Enlightenment?' lecture: it seems his hopes that the wayward child had returned to the fold had been premature.[33] If Foucault's 'turn' to the Enlightenment surprises people like Habermas, it is perhaps not so much because of the incongruity of Foucault taking a text such as Kant's seriously, but because they cannot quite understand the bizarre, apparently counter-Enlightenment use he makes of it.

Foucault engages with Kant in the same way that he engages with any other philosopher – as someone who may provoke a new way of thinking about a particular problem. In this case, the 'problem' is the question of the relationship between critique and modernity: how does the activity of thought, the work of thought upon thought, relate to the social, political and individual realities of modern Western society? The contribution Kant makes to thinking about this problem does not, for Foucault, consist of his suggestion that the thinker and the monarch should settle into a fully armed *détente* – in fact, Foucault is all but dismissive of much of the *content* of Kant's analysis.[34] Rather, from Foucault's point of view, Kant's contribution consists of his elaboration of a certain attitude towards the present. In Foucault's view, this is a new philosophical attitude, an attitude which interrogates the present as to its 'difference ... with respect to yesterday' (WE, 34). The specific features of Kant's answer to this question are not important to Foucault; his aim is not to 'reactivate' the concept of maturity, or to define the relative domains of the use of public and private reason. Instead, he takes the question as emblematic of one of the central features of modernity, and of modern critical reflection: an attitude towards the present which both valorizes it *and* tries to surpass and transform it.

> For the attitude of modernity, the high value of the present is indissociable from a desperate eagerness to imagine it, to imagine it otherwise than it is, and to transform it not by destroying it but by grasping it in what it is (WE, 41).

This gloss on Kant's approach prioritizes the *critical* impact of any questioning of the present. It is not, however, critical in the sense of Kant's three great critiques (the critiques of pure reason, practical reason and judgement). Instead, Foucault identifies a different critical tradition that emerges from Kant's work, one which pursues an 'ontology of the present' rather than an 'analytics of truth' (QL, 95[687]). For Foucault, the importance of Kant's text lies in its reflection 'on "today" as difference in history and as motive for a particular philosophical task' (WE, 38). By posing this question, Kant is giving voice, according to Foucault, to one of the key features of the attitude of modernity: the idea that the task of thought – in philosophy, literature and the arts – is to question, criticize and transform fundamental features of the reality one inhabits.[35]

The relationship between contemporary critical philosophy and the Enlightenment is, however, far from simple. According to Foucault, this relationship must be defined both negatively and positively. Negatively, contemporary critique, must refuse the 'blackmail' of the Enlightenment: while recognizing that this intellectual movement has 'to a certain extent' determined us, we do not have to take up a position as either 'for' or against' it. Secondly, it must reject the 'always too facile' equation which is often made between the Enlightenment and humanism. The phenomena of Enlightenment and humanism are far from being in alliance, in Foucault's view; rather, the Enlightenment attitude is in tension with – and a useful antidote to – the dangers of humanism.[36] The contemporary relationship to the Enlightenment can be defined positively in terms of the attempt to transform Kant's critique from a reflection on the necessary limits of knowledge into an analysis of the limits that we *can* transgress. Lewis Hinchman, for example, argues that while Foucault's appeal to the critical values of Enlightenment thought parallels that of Kant, Foucault reverses Kant's understanding of critical reflection upon limits.[37] For Foucault, this reflection is genealogical not transcendental: it does not progress from 'the form of what we are' to the limits of what is possible, but from the 'contingency that has made us' to the possibility of surpassing our limits (WE, 46). Secondly, this project attempts to carry this historical analysis over to a practical attitude: it involves the 'experimental' task of putting that analysis to the test of 'contemporary reality' in order to grasp both what can be changed and how it should be changed (WE, 46–7). This philosophical ethos consists of a particular attitude to the past (the source of our present modes of being, thinking and doing), a particular attitude to the present (a more or less contingent set of practices which are, perhaps, modifiable), and a particular attitude to the future (an open horizon of possibility which draws forward the 'undefined work of freedom'). Its positive content, to return to our earlier question, is its undeniable commitment to social and subjective change – and not just change for its own sake, or change for the sake of 'Life', or change according to one's fleeting desires, but change *away from* 'the intensification of power relations' (WE, 48) and *towards* freedom.

When Foucault situates his final conception of critique in this context it becomes possible to argue that, despite all previous appearances to the contrary, he is one of *les lumières*. This is not because he ascribes to any of the doctrinal elements of eighteenth-century philosophy, but rather because he seeks to reactivate the *attitude*, the *ethos* which, in his view, was the driving force behind the critical effect of this thought. He understands Enlightenment, and modernity, as an 'attitude' rather than as an historical period, because he sees it as defined more by the task which it sets itself, than by the historical and social conditions which made it possible.[38] This attitude, rather like the ancient attitude of care of the self, is capable of having an effect today; it can be 'reactivated', not copied or imitated but 'actualized', in the sense that contact with it today can produce something new, something which was not, strictly speaking, present in the original.[39] Adapting the metaphor used by Habermas (that Foucault admires Kant because he aimed an arrow at the heart of the present[40]), we could say that Foucault sees Kant as passing on a baton that must be carried forward into the future. In Foucault's view, Kant engaged upon a path of thought that has not yet been fully explored, and he sees himself as carrying on Kant's project. To this extent he is in agreement with Habermas, for whom the

Enlightenment is an 'unfinished project'.[41] The aspects of the project that Foucault wants to pursue, however, are not the same ones that Habermas champions. Where Habermas values the ideals of the public use of reason, and the pursuit of consensus (Kant's *communis sensus*), Foucault identifies a certain attitude towards the present and the valorization of autonomy as the Enlightenment's essential kernel.[42]

Foucault, we could say, is a *lumiére* because his project is to defend and expand the freedom of the individual. When he summarizes the features of the Enlightenment attitude which he wants to reactivate, his commitment to the expansion of autonomy is clear. When he argues that the ethos of the Enlightenment requires us to find 'the contemporary limits of the necessary' he does not consider the possibility that freedom and autonomy may be historically specific modes of subjectivity which we can now discard. Far from being expendable, he suggests, we must analyse (and reject) that which is no longer necessary for us to constitute ourselves 'as *autonomous* subjects' (WE, 43).[43] The ideal of autonomy itself is not to be discarded. When he insists that Enlightenment and humanism, far from being the same thing, are in fact 'in a state of tension', he suggests that the humanistic sciences of man can be effectively opposed by the Enlightenment principle of 'a critique and a permanent creation of ourselves in our autonomy' (WE, 44). Again, this autonomy itself is essential. Turning to the positive aspects of the attitude, Foucault characterizes it as a '*limit-attitude*': a critique which does not set limits, but which makes possible the transgression of 'whatever is singular, contingent, and the product of arbitrary constraints' (WE, 45). What this attitude does, in particular, is to give 'new impetus, as far and wide as possible, to the undefined work of freedom' (WE, 46). Again, this work of freedom is not conceived as a limit to be transgressed, it is rather what makes trangression possible. When he introduces the practical, experimental aspect of this work, Foucault characterizes the attitude as a 'historico-practical test of the limits that we may go beyond, and thus as work carried out by ourselves, on ourselves as *free* beings' (WE, 47).[44]

Finally, Foucault poses the question whether critique today requires 'faith in Enlightenment' (WE, 50). He professes uncertainty about this question; although whether his uncertainty arises from the idea of 'faith' or of 'enlightenment' is not clear. What he is certain of, however, is that his task, the critical task, still requires 'a patient labour giving form to our impatience for liberty' (ibid.). This labour, and this impatience, are the threads that connect Foucault to *les lumières*; and, crucially, they provide his ethics with the condition of its possibility, the field of its practice and the goal of its work.

THE AIM OF ETHICS

In Chapter 6, I argued that Foucault's response to the problem of 'How one refuses what one is' involved a conception of history as critique and of subjectivity as an historically malleable form. When we consider the question 'how does one become what one is not?', we arrive at an answer that cannot do without some notion of freedom – both as human capacity and as ethical aim. It is the introduction of just such a notion that most clearly distinguishes Foucault's late work from his middle period (*Discipline and Punish* and *The History of Sexuality*, volume I). If, during that period, freedom operated primarily as historical constant,[45] then in his late work it began to take on the additional role of ethical principle, or telos.

While it was Kant who first raised the question that expressed the attitude of Enlightenment, according to Foucault it was Baudelaire who gave it its distinctly modern form. In Baudelaire this attitude crytallizes around the problem of modernity, rather than the question of Enlightenment. However, it is an attitude that maintains the two essential features of the former: it is concerned with the present as both an actual state of affairs and as a task to be accomplished individually and collectively. Modernity, for Baudelaire, is 'an exercise in which extreme attention to what is real is confronted with the practice of a liberty that simultaneously respects this reality and violates it' (ibid.). For this reason, the individual in modernity is not the person who tries to discover him- or herself through, for example, the techniques of the hermeneutics of the self; rather, modern individuals try to 'invent' themselves (WE, 42). If Kant's Enlightenment forces us to take up the challenge of *Sapere aude!* (Dare to know!), then Baudelaire's modernity compels us to take up the challenge of creating ourselves. The significance of Foucault's discussion of Baudelaire in this context could easily be overlooked. He points out that for Baudelaire, this work on the self – 'this ironic heroization of the present, this transfiguring play of freedom with reality, this ascetic elaboration of the self' (WE, 42) – can only take place in the realm of art. Without elaborating on the significance of this assumption on the part of Baudelaire, and without returning to the apparent counter-example of the 'asceticism of the dandy' (WE, 41), Foucault simply moves on to the next part of his lecture. In the context of my argument here, however, this observation suggests something crucial: that the task Foucault sets himself, in the elaboration of his own ethical practice, is precisely to bring these ascetic practices out of the realm of art and into the field of politics and 'society itself' (WE, 42). His task is to make it possible, for example, for an individual to bring together *in their life* 'stoicism, asceticism and ecstasy'. It is in the context of this task that the critical questioning of the present, inaugurated by Kant and continued by Baudelaire, takes on the form of an art of freedom which has not yet had its full impact at the level of society, politics and ethics.

To create oneself through an art of freedom does not involve pursuing an inner truth or a personal authenticity, nor does it involve freely submitting to a self-imposed moral law: it is neither existentialist nor Kantian. Rather, it involves both the task of identifying those aspects of our lives where we are more free than we thought (more free, because historically contingent) and the task of creating new forms of life within those newly opened spaces of freedom. Freedom functions as both ontological condition – because without spaces of freedom the practice cannot occur – and as teleological aim of this art. As aim it is continuously renewed, because it is a goal which is never achieved. Since freedom is not a state, but a field of possibilities, there is a sense in which the labourer in this field can never rest. It is for this reason that the aim of Foucault's ethics can be characterized as an *art* of freedom: the task of giving form to one's liberty, of moulding and giving a style to one's life and one's relations with others, is a task, like that of the artist, which knows no completion. No doubt the Western art world since the eighteenth century has promoted the notion of the *chef d'œuvre*, of the work which is *achevée*, complete unto itself: but the concept of art which Foucault mobilizes comprises no such possibility. The *techne* of Socrates in the art of turning around the souls of others was never complete; the exercises cultivated by the Stoics in their care of themselves were never finished; and the ethical concern for the self to which both Nietzsche and Foucault appealed was an 'infinite labour'. If the aim of critical philosophy is to help us to untie the knots of our identity, then the aim of ethics is to work out ways of retying them in new and less constraining ways. The art of freedom, the aesthetics of existence, is the hard-won skill (*techne*) of analysing, untying and re-constituting the forms of individual and collective life which we inherit: it is the art of giving a style to the expanding space of liberty which, through critique, we can create in our contemporary reality.

Conclusion

... out of such long and dangerous exercises of self-mastery one emerges as a different person, with a few more question marks.

Friedrich Nietzsch[1]

He is a nomad, even in his work: do you believe that he has built his house? Not at all. 'That's not it', he said to me about his last volume, 'I've been mistaken. I have to re-cast everything. Go elsewhere. Do it otherwise.'

Hélène Cixous[2]

Solutions, by definition, are always a matter for tomorrow.

Pierre Vidal-Nacquet[3]

My principal aim in undertaking this study of Foucault has been to see whether his late work could provide an answer, or at least the outline of a provisional, contemporary answer, to the very ancient question, 'how is one to live?' This pursuit has led us from 'we other Victorians' to 'we other Greeks' and back again, perhaps most surprisingly, to 'we other *lumières*'.[4] In *The History of Sexuality*, volume I, Foucault investigated the institutional and discursive apparatuses which have fixed modern individuals to specific forms of sexual identity. The central argument of his diagnosis of our sexual malaise was that the sexual liberation movements of the 1960s and 1970s could not offer adequate solutions to this condition. Foucault's response to this failure was to pursue the more distant origins of the Western constitution of the desiring individual; through Medieval and late Hellenistic Christianity to the emergence of Western medical and philosophical discourse in Classical Athens. In his study of the Classical and Hellenistic relation to sexual pleasure Foucault 'discovered' a model of self-relation which he thought could be of great use to us today. It was a model which, at least in his interpretation, treated the self as an open possibility to be moulded and formed according to freely adopted principles. While, in certain essential features, 'we moderns' are fundamentally dissimilar from the (free, male) citizens of Classical Athens, like them we are searching for new models, new principles by which to guide our lives. Given the similarity of our positions, the Classical Greek response to the task of giving oneself an ethics can be an instructive example for us, 'we other Greeks', today. If we define this task in its most formal characteristics – as an acceptance of responsibility for the way one leads one's life – then we can also see it in relation to the central task of Enlightenment. The ancient Greeks were, essentially, attempting to emerge from what Kant called 'mankind's ... self-incurred immaturity'.[5] And since this task is one which must be continuously renewed, 'we other Greeks' are also 'we other lumières'.

The trajectory of Foucault's late work, from the nineteenth-century sciences of sexuality, through the ancient Greek arts of the self, and back to the eighteenth-century pursuit of freedom, has largely determined the structure of this work. I have followed Foucault on this path in order to understand his claim that only an aesthetics of existence can respond to the contemporary crisis of morality. In Part One, this required undertaking a critical reading of Foucault's history of Classical and Hellenistic practices of the self. In particular, I argued that Foucault's contemporary project – to assist in the demise of modern morality – had led him to exaggerate the aesthetic motivation behind ancient Greek ethics. I also argued, however, that this tendency to overestimate the aestheticism of Greek ethics did not crucially undermine either Foucault's history or his attempt to formulate a contemporary ethics. Since the historical and the ethical aspects of his work are inextricably linked, I argued, we cannot judge Foucault's research exclusively by the standards of academic historiography. The genealogical method must be judged by criteria that give equal weight to both historical detail and contemporary effect.

On the basis of this assessment of Foucault's interpretation of ancient Greek ethics, I was able in Part Two to draw a picture of what a Foucaldian aesthetics of existence would look like. I developed this model by following Foucault's fourfold analysis of the essential aspects of any ethical system. I argued that in Foucault's ethics, the ethical substance consists of the aspects of ourselves, our lives and our societies which have become intolerable to us; these are the forms that demand transformation. In order to engage in a work of transformation, however, we must adopt a particular attitude towards the work to be carried out – the second aspect of ethics, the mode of subjection. This is not a task that has been imposed either by a divinity or by a science of man; rather, it is a freely made decision to modify that which one's personal history and the history of one's society has given. The third stage in this ethical practice is the cultivation of tools or techniques that can assist one in the task of self-transformation. I argued that the 'experimental' philosophy that emerges from Nietzsche's work and draws its inspiration from the critical tradition in Western thought is a key technique of the self in Foucault's ethics. Philosophy, when understood in this sense, is a crucial, although by no means exclusive, tool for self-transformation. Finally, I argued that the aim of this work on the self is freedom. Even though Foucault occasionally suggests that beauty was the aim – at least in Classical Greece – I argued that his interventions in contemporary political and ethical debates clearly suggest that the only satisfactory characterization of the aim is some notion of freedom. I argued that Foucault's final return to a consideration of the legacy of the Enlightenment provided him with a way of speaking about freedom and autonomy that his earlier work lacked. It allowed him to conceive of freedom as both the ontological condition and the aim of ethics: an aim which, strictly speaking, can never be achieved, but which demands the patient and continuous practice of an art of living.

I would not like to suggest, however, that either this ethical model or the path Foucault followed in its formulation, are without conceptual and practical problems. I still think that Foucault's return, in search of an ethics, to the world of the male citizens of Classical Athens and Imperial Rome bears the hallmarks of a cultural valorization of which one must be suspicious. The identification of European elites with the masters of the ancient world, from the Renaissance humanists, through Lessing, Burckhardt and Nietzsche, to Jaeger and Foucault, is a phenomenon that deserves critique. I am also alert to the fear that Foucault's ethics is too individualist, that it fails to address one of the central questions of ethics, 'how should I relate to the other?' In framing this work around the question 'how is one to live?' (rather than the alternative formulation, 'how are *we* to live?'), I avoided directly confronting this fear. In Foucault's work, however, it is almost impossible to separate the problems and tasks of individuals from the problems and tasks of collectivities, the tasks of ethics from the tasks of politics. I hope that Foucault's recognition of the fundamental connection between the concerns of ethics and politics has been, if not explicitly shown, at least clearly implied in this work.

The final question I must address, is whether this view of ethics really is capable of responding to the collapse of traditional moralities in late modernity. Can, as Foucault claims, an aesthetics of existence fill the lacuna left by the contemporary challenges to code-based moralities? This is a question which, for a very specific reason, cannot be answered by this work. In his essay 'Schopenhauer as Educator', Nietzsche decries the fact that universities never teach philosophy – or, at least, never teach it in a way that would really 'prove something'. Rather than 'trying to see whether one can live in accordance with' a particular philosophy, they simply teach a 'critique of words by means of other words'.[6] In universities, according to Nietzsche, the teaching of philosophy is very far from the practice of philosophy as a way of life. If this is true in relation to university teaching, it is even more so in relation to the writing of philosophical monographs. Following Nietzsche, one would have to conclude that the only work which could 'really' show the value of Foucault's ethics would be one which was a testament to an individual's attempt to live in accordance with it; this work is obviously not of that type. What I hope this book *has* done, however, is, firstly, shown that a coherent ethics does emerge from Foucault's late work and, secondly, given some indication of the direction, the style and the shape of a life lived according to that ethics. Whether such a life would qualify as an acceptable model of the well-lived life, or whether the aesthetics of existence is capable of responding to the collapse of morality, is however, as Vidal-Nacquet might say, 'a matter for tomorrow'.

Notes

Introduction

1. Friedrich Nietzsche, *On the Genealogy of Morals*, trans. W. Kaufmann, New York: Vintage Books, 1969, Essay III, 27.
2. This diagnosis of the contemporary failure of morality is not restricted to Nietzschean philosophers. It has also been made by philosophers as Un-Nietzschean as Alasdair MacIntyre and Bernard Williams. See: Alasdair MacInryre, *After Virtue*, 2nd edn, London: Duckworth, 1985; and Bernard Williams, *Ethics and the Limits of Philosophy*, London: Fontana Press, 1993. See also Zygmunt Bauman's work on the postmodern demise of the various moral projects of modernity: *Postmodern Ethics*, Oxford: Blackwell, 1993 and *Life in Fragments: Essays in postmodern morality*, Oxford: Blackwell, 1995.
3. Thomas Mann, *Last Essays*, New York: Alfred Knopf, 1970, p. 172.
4. Friedrich Nietzsche, *The Gay Science*, trans. W. Kaufmann, New York: Vintage Books, 1974, Section 299.
5. Ibid., Section 290.
6. Translation modified, emphasis added.
7. See the modified French version of OGE (*DE* IV, 630); Foucault refers to Burckhardt's work here (and in *UP*, 11[17]). For Renaissance aestheticism, see also Michel Onfray, *La sculpture de soi: la morale esthétique*, Paris: Grasset, 1993.
8. See WE, 50: the critical task 'requires work on our limits, that is, a patient labour giving form to our impatience for liberty'.
9. Nietzsche, *The Gay Science*, Section 299.
10. Ibid., Preface 4.
11. Ibid., Section 290.
12. Nietzsche, *On the Genealogy of Morals*, Preface 2.
13. Thomas Mann, *Doctor Faustus* (orig. published 1947), Chapter 21, in *Thomas Mann*, various translators, New York: Secker and Warburg, 1979, p. 249.
14. In an interview, Foucault comments, 'The idea of the *bios* as a material for an aesthetic piece of art is something which fascinates me' (OGE, 348). However, in the version that he re-worked for French publication, this sentence has been removed. In its place, the revised version includes the following remark (my translation): 'That life, because of its mortality, has to be a work of art, is a remarkable theme' (*DE* IV, 615).

15. Foucault uses this term in relation to the changes in ethical subjectivity which occurred in the early Roman Empire (*CS*, 95[117]).

16. In the French version of this interview this comment disappears, being replaced by a comment about the complexity of the domain of the practice of the self and the necessity of recognizing in it a creative possibility: 'we must understand that the relation to the self is structured as a practice which can have its models, its conformities, its variants, but also its creations' (*DE* IV, 617). This is far from having the same force as the comment which was originally made in English.

17. Williams, *Ethics and the Limits of Philosophy*.

18. Nietzsche, *The Gay Science*, Section 335.

19. Hurley translates '*penser autrement*' as 'to think differently'; however, I prefer 'to think otherwise' as it conveys some of the sense, crucial for Foucault, that it is through the confrontation with an historical 'other' that we begin to recognize the contingency of our present.

20. '*un champ de forces réeles*,' in *DG*.

21. '*la lutte et la vérité*,' ibid.

22. As illustrated, for example, by the title of Foucault's Collège de France course of 1980–81, 'Subjectivité et vérité'.

23. See, for example: James Bernauer, *Michel Foucault's Force of Flight*, Atlantic Highlands, NJ: Humanities Press International, 1990; John Rajchman, *Michel Foucault: The freedom of philosophy*, New York: Columbia University Press, 1985; Thomas Flynn, 'Truth and Subjectivation in the Later Foucault', *The Journal of Philosophy*, 82, 10, Oct. 1985, pp. 531–40, and 'Foucault as Parrhesiast: His last course at the Collège de France (1984)', *Philosophy and Social Criticism*, 2–3, Summer 1987, pp. 213–29.

24. See, for example: Jurgen Habermas, *The Philosophical Discourse of Modernity*, Cambridge: Polity Press, 1992; Nancy Fraser, 'Foucault on Modern Power: Empirical insights and normative confusions', *Praxis International*, 1, 3, Oct 1981, pp. 272–87, and 'Foucault's Body Language: A post-humanist political rhetoric?', *Salmagundi*, no. 61, Fall 1983, pp. 55–70.

25. See Charles Taylor, 'Foucault on Freedom and Truth', *Political Theory*, 12, 2, 1984 (reprinted in David Boy (ed.), *Foucault: A critical reader*, Oxford: Blackwell, 1986); Paul Patton, 'Taylor and Foucault on Power and Freedom', *Political Studies*, no. 37, 1989, pp. 260–76; and Taylor's 'Reply' to Patton in the same issue. These are, however, discussed: see Chapter 6 for Patton and Deleuze and Chapter 9 for Habermas, Fraser, Taylor and Patton.

26. See, for example: the contributions to Barry Hindess and Mitchell Dean (eds), *Governing Australia*, Cambridge: Cambridge University Press, 1998; and Graham Burchell, Colin Gordon and Peter Miller (eds), *The Foucault Effect: Studies in governmentality*, Hemel Hempstead: Harvester Wheatsheaf, 1991.

27. Amy Richlin, 'Foucault's *History of Sexuality*: A useful theory for women?' in D. Larmour, P. Miller, C. Platter (eds), *Rethinking Sexuality: Foucault and Classical Antiquity*, Princeton: Princeton University Press, 1998, p. 148. See also, in the same collection, Page du Bois, 'The Subject in Antiquity after Foucault'. Like other aspects of Foucault's late work, this tendency has as yet received little attention from feminist philosophers. Important excep-

tions are; Lois McNay, *Foucault and Feminism: Power, gender and the self*, Cambridge: Polity Press, 1992 and her *Foucault: A critical introduction*, Cambridge: Polity Press, 1994. See also Catherine MacKinnon, 'Does Sexuality Have a History?' in Donna Stanton (ed.), *Discourses of Sexuality*, Ann Arbor: University of Michigan Press, 1992.

28. This failure and this crisis are not themselves the subject of this work. Rather, my background assumption is that such a crisis is ocurring; this is also Foucault's (and Nietzsche's) presupposition. I would argue that the contemporary resurgence of fundamentalist and extreme moral and political projects is evidence in favour of this assumption, rather than evidence against it. At the very least, it is evidence of an intense contemporary 'problematization' of morality – Foucault's notion of problematization is discussed in Chapter 6.

29. See the discussion in *UP*, 25–8[32–5] and OGE, 356–8.

30. The term 'bias' is not used here as a term of moral disapproval, but more in the French sense of the 'slant' or 'angle' (*biais*) of his approach. The sense in which Foucault's histories can be said to be distorted is dealt with in Chapter 5.

Chapter 1

1. Friedrich Nietzsche, *Human, All Too Human*, trans. R. J. Hollingdale, Cambridge: Cambridge University Press, 1996, Volume 2, Part 1, 218.

2. Friedrich Nietzsche, 'On the uses and disadvantages of history for life', in *Untimely Meditations*, trans. R. J. Hollingdale, Cambridge: Cambridge University Press, 1997.

3. This was the year Hegel gave the first course, at Jena, on which his *Lectures on the History of Philosophy* (trans. E. S. Haldane, London: Routledge and Kegan Paul, 1892) is based.

4. The year Heidegger's *An Introduction to Metaphysics* (trans. R. Mannheim, New York: Doubleday, 1961) was conceived.

5. Translation modified.

6. I owe the metaphor to an otherwise damning account of this journey: Maria Daraki, 'Michel Foucault's Journey to Greece', *Telos* 67, Spring 1986, pp. 87–110.

7. According to Halperin, the book is 'the single most important intellectual source of political inspiration for contemporary AIDS activists': see David Halperin, *Saint Foucault: Towards a gay hagiography*, New York: Oxford University Press, 1995, p. 15. See also Mark Blasius, 'An Ethos of Lesbian and Gay Existence', *Political Theory*, 20, 4, 1992, pp. 642–71.

8. The category of the 'intolerable' was important for Foucault in the early 1970s, especially in relation to his involvement in the Groupe d'Informations sur les Prisons. See, for example, the interview 'Je perçois l'intolérable' (*DE* II, 203–5) and the Preface to *Enquête des vingt prisons* (Paris: Champ Libre, 1971) reprinted in *DR* II, 195–7.

9. Bernauer, *Foucault's Force of Flight*, p. 6.

10. All of these comments are taken from a discussion, with a group of Lacanian

psychoanalysts, entitled 'Le jeu de Michel Foucault' (CF [2981). However, this passage is, inexplicably, absent from the English translation ('The Confession of the Flesh').

11. Foucault is arguing against the view that power operates essentially by prohibition, denial and repression.

12. This was the French title of an interview with Bernard Henri-Levy, published in English as 'Power and Sex' (PS).

13. Foucault uses the terms *'entêtement'* and *'obstinément'* in the French text of the 'Introduction' to the English edition of *HB* (*see DE* IV, 116): this text, which I will draw on here, contains some passages which are not present in the English version.

14. For Foucault's discussion of the role of the confessional art of *'discrétion* 'in the fact that Herculine was never 'discovered' by the women she lived with, see *DE* IV, 120.

15. By apparatus Foucault means 'a thoroughly heterogenous ensemble consisting of discourses, institutions, architectural forms, regulatory decisions, laws, administrative measures, scientific statements, philosophical, moral and philanthropic propositions – in short, the said as much as the unsaid ... The apparatus itself is the system of relations that can be established between these elements' (CF, 194[299]).

16. See CF, 209[312], where Foucault says that the original title of the 'History of Sexuality' project was to be 'Sex and Truth'.

17. Both italicized in the original, *VS*, 139[183].

18. Hubert Dreyfus and Paul Rabinow, *Michel Foucault: Beyond structuralism and hermeneutics*, Sussex: Harvester Press, 1982, p. 168.

19. It is actually possible to pinpoint the moment when Foucault's theorization of 'bio-power' is superceded by his interrogation of 'governmentality' – in January 1978. In his first lecture of that year at the Collège de France, Foucault introduces the year's theme as being the series of phenomena which he had called 'bio-power' (see the published tape recording, *DG*). However, in the fourth lecture of that year, he says that what he really wants to do in the course is 'a history of "governmentality" ' (OG, 102[655]). From that moment the term bio-power disappears from Foucault's vocabulary, since conceptually it is included in the concept of governmentality.

20. The phrase is used by Nietzsche: see Nietzsche, *The Gay Science*, Section 290; and 'On the uses and ...', p.77.

21. Rajchman, *The freedom of philosophy*, p. 32.

22. This finally became the almost complete, but never published, fourth volume *Les aveux de la chair* (The Confession of the Flesh).

23. It is important to note that Foucault later rejects this contrast, both in its detail (he no longer thinks that Roman culture had an erotic art) and because he later thinks that he should have contrasted 'our' science of sexuality with a practice from *within* 'our' culture – for example, the ancient Greeks (OGE, 347–8).

24. Foucault recognizes that his sources are primarily Catholic rather than Christian, but he asserts that the reformed pastoral comprises similar mechanisms for 'putting sex into discourse' (*VS*, 21 n. 4[30 n. 1]). And also: there is 'a certain parallelism in the Catholic and Protestant methods of

examination of conscience and pastoral direction' (*VS*, 116(153]). A discussion of the justifiability of these claims would go beyond the scope of the present argument.

25. These seminars, all presented in English, were subsequently published as: 'About the Beginning of the Hermeneutics of the Self' (BHS); 'Technologies of the Self' (TS); 'Sexuality and Solitude' (SS); and the unpublished, 'The Howison Lectures' (HL), a transcript of which is in circulation.

26. As represented by a passage from 'On Anger' in Seneca, *Moral Essays, Volume I*, trans. J. Basore, Loeb Classical Library, Harvard University Press, Cambridge, 1958, pp. 340–1. (This reference is provided by the editor of BHS.)

27. The texts Foucault cites in relation to this, and the following account are Tertullian's *On Repentance*, Jerome's *Epistles* and unnamed texts by John Chrysostom and John Cassian. The lack of precise referencing is, of course, a consequence of the nature of an oral presentation.

28. See BHS, HL, and SS.

29. The latter, of course, does not supplant the former: the whole point of Foucault's 'auto-critique' is that both aspects must be considered – taken together, in their intersections, they constitute the field of 'government' (see HL).

30. The text HL is an unauthorized seminar transcript and I have not, therefore, given page references.

31. Foucault published three versions of this introduction: the first, 'Preface to *The History of Sexuality*, Volume II' (PHS); the second, revised and greatly expanded, 'Usage des plaisirs et techniques de soi' (see *DE* IV, 539–60); and the third, almost identical to the second, in the book itself, *UP*, 3–32[9–39].

32. See *UP*, 4–6[10–12] and all of PHS.

33. These are the two examples Foucault cites (*UP*, 11[17]); but one could add to the list – for example, the seventeenth century '*honnête homme*' (see Donna Stanton, *The Aristocrat as Art*, New York: Columbia University Press, 1980).

34. Alluding to St Francis de Sales (author of *Introduction to the Devout Life*), Foucault describes Deleuze and Guattari's *Anti-Oedipus* as an 'Introduction to the Non-Fascist Life'. See his 'Preface' in Gilles Deleuze and Felix Guattari, *Anti-Oedipus; Capitalism and Schizophrenia*, Minneapolis: University of Minnesota Press, 1983.

Chapter 2

1. As we will see in Chapter 3, Western discourse about male–male sexual relations has always been highly conscious of the relative social status of the men in question. Wilde, the colonial interloper, was finally convicted for his affair with the son of the Marquess of Queensbury.

2. See, however, Arnold Davidson's discussion of the contribution the model has made to the study of the history of ethics in general: 'Ethics as Ascetics', in Gary Gutting (ed.), *The Cambridge Companion to Foucault*, Cambridge: Cambridge University Press, 1995.

3. For Foucault's account of this division, see *UP*, 25–8[32–5] and OGE, 356–8.

4. Curiously, the 'general' is omitted from the English translation.

5. See OGE, 341.

6. My emphasis.

7. Plato, *Alcibiades I*, trans. W. Lamb, Loeb Classical Library, *Plato*, Vol. VIII, London: William Heinemann, 1927. While Foucault notes the doubts about the authenticity of this dialogue, he rightly insists that such debates have no relevance to his reading of the text – a text which is undoubtedly a 'genuine' product of the early fourth century BC. Consequently, he maintains the (French) convention of attributing it to Plato.

8. Recordings of this Collège de France course, 'L'Herméneutique du sujet', henceforward, CCF, can be consulted at the Centre Michel Foucault, Paris, 82. See also the summary of the course in *RC*, 145–66. I will refer to both sources.

9. The translation of 1927 uses the expression 'to take pains over oneself' for *epimeleia heautou*. In this discussion, however, I will use the English equivalent of Foucault's French version, '*souci de soi*' – care of the self.

10. Or, according to the subtitle of the dialogue, the 'nature of man'.

11. See CCF, 81.

12. Against Foucault's reading, we should note here Socrates's comment that 'when I speak of the need of being educated I am not referring only to you, apart from myself; since my case is identical with yours except in one point' (that is, that Socrates's 'guardian', God, is better than Alcibiades's guardian, Pericles), (*Alcibiades*, 124c). The mature Socrates recognizes, then, that he too is in need of education.

13. The English translator gives 'cultivation' for '*culture*', but in most cases I prefer 'culture', since Foucault is generally speaking about a whole set of cultural practices, valorizations and modes of experience – which, of course, *include* 'cultivation', but cannot be subsumed under it. See *CS*, Part II, '*La culture de soi.*'

14. See, for example, *CS*, 50–67[65–84].

15. Foucault's partial recognition of this alternative version is present, for example, in his comment that Alcibiades practices the *souci de soi* in order to be capable of governing others ('*pour être capable de gouverner les autres*'). This comment appears in the modified French edition of OGE (see *DE IV*, 609–31).

16. Plutarch, *The Rise and Fall of Athens*, trans. I. Scott-Kilvert, London: Penguin Books, 1960, 'Alcibiades', 16.

17. SS, 184[215]: emphasis added, translation modified.

18. This is a rhetorical question that offers a way in to thinking about the issues; it is *not* a statement that in fact the 'political operator' is a more constant human type than the 'aesthete'. As we will see in the course of this book, Foucault can be read as arguing that, far from being an anachronism, the aesthete is one, recent manifestation of a much longer tradition of ethical self-formation; a tradition which emerges in Classical Athens.

19. Seneca, *Letters To Lucilius*, Letter 5 in Moses Hadas (ed. and trans.), *The Stoic Philosophy of Seneca*, New York: Anchor Books, 1958.

20. Richard Ellmann, *Oscar Wilde*, Harmondsworth: Penguin Books, 1988, pp. 43–4.

21. In defence of Foucault, it should be noted that nearly all of the most striking examples of an 'aestheticist' interpretation of the ancients occur in interviews rather than in texts. This is relevant for two reasons: firstly, they are more relaxed, informal exchanges from which scholarly exactitude can be largely absent. Secondly, as Hubert Dreyfus has pointed out to me, Foucault treated interviews as a very important part in the production of what has been called the 'Foucault effect'; therefore, he may be expected to have used formulations and arguments which were more striking than accurate, in order to produce an effect on his interlocuters (and eventual readers). Nevertheless, as we have already seen, the 'aestheticist' theme is also present – albeit in a more muted form – in Foucault's written texts.

22. For general discussion of the craft analogy, see for example: Richard Parry, *Plato's Craft of Justice*, Albany: SUNY, 1996; David Roochnik, 'Socrates' Use of the Techne-Analogy', in H. Benson (ed.), *Essays on the Philosophy of Socrates*, New York: Oxford University Press, 1992; Terence Irwin, *Plato's Moral Theory*, Oxford: Clarendon Press, 1977.

23. Aristotle, *Ethics*, trans. J. A. K. Thomson, Harmondsworth: Penguin Books, 1976: Book One, 1101a.

24. Ibid., 1106b. However, as Julia Annas points out, Aristotle makes an important distinction between craft as *poesis* and virtue as *praxis* – they are not, ultimately, assimilable. See Julia Annas, *The Morality of Happiness*, Oxford: Oxford University Press, 1994, pp. 66ff.

25. Epictetus, *The Discourses*, I, xv, 2, trans. W. A. Oldfather, London: Loeb Classical Library, 1925.

26. Ibid., II, vii, 30–1.

27. Seneca, *Letters to Lucilius*, Letter 90.

28. Ibid., Letter 34, also cited in *CS*, 53[69].

29. See, for example, Sextus Empiricus, *Outlines of Pyrrhonism*, III, 239–78; and Stobaeus 2.67 translated in A. A. Long and D. N. Sedley, *The Hellenistic Philosophers*, 2 vols, Cambridge: Cambridge University Press, 1987, pp. 379–80.

30. Plato, *Hippias Major*, trans. P. Woodruff, Oxford: Basil Blackwell, 1982.

31. I discuss this term in more detail in Chapter 3, pp. 67–8.

32. Jean-Pierre Vernant, *L'individu, la mort, l'amour; soi-même et l'autre en Grèce ancienne*, Paris: Gallimard, 1989, p. 20. Of course this principle is not infallible: Socrates was notoriously 'ugly'.

33. Seneca, *Letters to Lucilius*, Letter 92.

34. Epictetus, *Discourses* III, ii, 40.

35. Plotinus, *Enneads*, 1, 6, 9. This passage is cited by Foucault and discussed by Pierre Hadot, *Exercices spirituels et la philosophie antique*, Paris: Etudes Augustiniennes, 1981, p. 46.

36. Nietzsche, *The Gay Science*, Section 290.

37. Arnold Hauser, *The Social History of Art*, Volume I, London: Routledge, 1989 (first published 1951), pp. 90, 89.

38. Annas, *The Morality of Happiness*, pp. 72–3.

39. See, for example, Jean Lacoste (*L'idée de beau*, Paris: Bordas, 1986, pp. 11ff),

who speaks of Plato's *Hippias Major* as a debate on the meaning of 'le beau' and not 'the fine' as Woodruff has it. And see Hadot, *Exercices spirituels*, p. 41, where he discusses *Republic* 604b. Hadot renders the passage 'the law of reason says that there is nothing more beautiful than to ... 'The English translation has 'custom and principle say that it is best to ...' (trans. D. Lee, revised 1974, Harmondsworth: Penguin Books, 1983).

40. It is also interesting to note that the English term 'fine arts' is *'les beaux arts'* (beautiful arts) in French.

41. The term 'aesthetics' in its modern sense was first used by Baumgarten in 1750 in his *Aesthetica*. For the ancient Greeks, the term *aesthesis* (sensation) had no particular association with art or its effects.

Chapter 3

1. Friedrich Nietzsche, *The Will To Power*, trans. W. Kaufmann and R. J. Hollingdale, New York: Vintage Books, 1968: Section 882.

2. See the epigraph to Chapter 4.

3. Martha Nussbaum's review of *The Use of Pleasure*, 'Affections of the Greeks', *New York Times Book Review*, 10 November 1985, pp. 13–14.

4. David Halperin, 'Two views of Greek love: Harold Patzer and Michel Foucault', in *One Hundred Years of Homosexuality*, New York: Routledge, 1990, p. 63.

5. Flynn, 'Truth and Subjectivation ...', p. 532.

6. Jon Simons, *Foucault and the Political*, London: Routledge, 1995, p. 104.

7. Peter Dews, 'The Return of the Subject in Late Foucault', *Radical Philosophy* 51, Spring 1989, pp. 37–41. See p. 38.

8. For example, 'the master of the self and the master of others are trained at the same time' (*UP*, 77[90]).

9. Jean-Pierre Vernant, *L'individu* ... , p. 229.

10. Walter Donlan, *The Aristocratic Ideal in Ancient Greece*, Lawrence, KS: Coronado, 1980.

11. Ibid., p. 179.

12. Emphasis added.

13. See, for instance, the title of Foucault's last two courses at the Collège de France, *'Le gouvernement de soi et des autres'*.

14. Simon Goldhill, *Foucault's Virginity: Ancient erotic fiction and the history of sexuality*, Cambridge: Cambridge University Press, 1995, p. 30.

15. Halperin, 'Two views of Greek love ...', p. 69.

16. The (im)plausibility of this claim goes beyond the scope of the present discussion.

17. An English translation of the relevant sections of Artemidoros appears as an Appendix to John Winkler, *The Constraints of Desire: The anthropology of sex and gender in ancient Greece*, New York: Routledge, 1990.

18. Ibid., p. 212.

19. Ibid., p. 211.

20. Kenneth Dover, *Greek Homosexuality*, London: Duckworth, 1978.

21. Ibid., p. 105.

22. Winkler, *Constraints of Desire*, p. 66.
23. *UP*, 239–41[217–19]; Winkler, *Constraints of Desire*, pp. 56ff; Dover's entire study (*Greek Homosexuality*) is framed around a reading of this speech.
24. Cited by Winkler, *Constraints of Desire*, p. 54.
25. A neologism of Foucault's which combines 'autocratic' with the Greek for 'self' – *heautos*.
26. For additional accounts of the competitive nature of Classical public life, see especially the works already cited by Vernant, '*L'individu* ...', and Winkler, *Constraints of Desire*, and also Jean-Pierre Vernant, 'Façons grecques d'être soi', in Roger-Pol Droit (ed.), *Les Grecs, les Romains et nous: l'antiquité estelle moderne?*, Paris: Le Monde Editions, 1991, esp. pp. 105–6.
27. Nietzsche, *Genealogy of Morals*, Essay I, 7.
28. Donlan, *The Aristocratic Ideal*, p. 129; see also his 'The Origin of *Kalos Kagathos*', *The American Journal of Philology*, no. 94, 1973, pp. 365–74.
29. We should note here that one important way that Foucault's genealogy of ethics differs from that of Nietzsche, is that Foucault sees the 'ascetic ideal' developing *within* Classical culture itself; it is not, for him, an ideal that was imposed on the 'masters' by the Judaeo-Christian 'slaves'. See Foucault's discussion of this point in OGE, 366. But for Nietzsche's acknowledgement of the Greek role in the 'preparation of the soil for Christianity' see: *The Will to Power*, Section 427.
30. See the first epigraph to this chapter.

Chapter 4

1. Pierre Hadot, 'Réflexions sur la notion de culture de soi', in *Michel Foucault, Philosophe*, Paris: Editions du Seuil, 1989, p. 267.
2. A. A. Long, 'Representation and the Self in Stoicism', in S. Everson (ed.), *Companions to Ancient Thought*, volume 2, *Psychology*, Cambridge: Cambridge University Press, 1991, p. 118.
3. Stoicism prided itself, in antiquity, on its systematic completeness. For some sources of this claim in Stoic authors and commentators, see A. A. Long, *Hellenistic Philosophy*, 2nd edn, London: Duckworth, 1986, p. 119.
4. Not only is this preference perfectly clear from *CS*, we also have the anecdotal evidence of Paul Veyne, who reports Foucault's view of Stoic logic and physics as opposed to ethics, as '*ce sont d'énormes excroissances*' (these are enormous excrescences). See Veyne's 'Façons grecques d'être soi', pp. 57–8.
5. David Halperin, 'Two Views of Greek Love ...', and his *Saint Foucault* ..., John Winkler, *The Constraints of Desire*. See also the collection, David Halperin, John Winkler and Froma Zeitlin (eds), *Before Sexuality: The construction of erotic experience in the ancient Greek world*, Princeton: Princeton University Press, 1990.
6. Paul Veyne, 'La médication interminable', the introductory essay to Seneca, *De la tranquilité de l'âme*, Paris: Petite Bibliothèque Rivages, 1988; and Veyne's contribution to Paul Veyne (ed.), *Histoire de la vie privée, 1. De l'Empire romain à l'an mil*, Paris: Editions du Seuil, 1985 (*A History of*

Private Life, 1. From Pagan Rome to Byzantium, trans. A. Goldhammer, Cambridge: Harvard University Press, 1992).

7. Hadot, 'Réflexions sur la notion ...'.
8. Ibid., p. 262.
9. Ibid.
10. Ibid., p. 263.
11. Davidson, 'Ethics as Ascetics', n. 23 and p. 133.
12. Halperin, *Saint Foucault*, pp. 73ff. I discuss this book in detail in Chapter 5.
13. David Cohen and Richard Saller, 'Foucault on Sexuality in Greco-Roman Antiquity', in Jan Goldstein (ed.), *Foucault and the Writing of History*, Oxford: Blackwell, 1994. David Cohen, *Law, Sexuality and Society*, Cambridge: Cambridge University Press, 1991. Simon Goldhill, *Foucault's Virginity*.
14. See Chapter 5 below for a more complete discussion of Goldhill's argument.
15. See, for example: Mary Lefkowitz, 'Sex and Civilisation', *Partisan Review*, 52, 4, 1985, pp. 460–66; Henri Joly, 'Retour aux Grecs', *Le Débat*, 41, Sept–Nov 1986, pp. 100–20; G. E. R. Lloyd, 'The Mind on Sex', *New York Review of Books*, 13 March 1986, pp. 24–8; Elizabeth A. Clark, 'Foucault, The Fathers, and Sex', *Journal of the American Academy of Religion*, 56, 4, 1988, pp. 619–41; Bruce Thornton, 'Idolon Theatri: Foucault and the Classicists', *Classical and Modern Literature*, 12, 1, 1991, pp. 81–100; Pierre J. Payer, 'Foucault on Penance and the Shaping of Sexuality', *Studies in Religion*, 14, 3, 1985, pp. 313–20; Averil Cameron, 'Redrawing the Map: Early Christian territory after Foucault', *Journal of Roman Studies*, no. 76, 1986, pp. 266–71.
16. See *CS*, 84–5[67–8] and, for another version, 269–74[235–40].
17. This change, in turn, Foucault attributes to the new political structures which were instituted by the Roman Empire, see *CS*, 101–17[81–95].
18. Thus Epictetus, although he was a freed slave, taught the sons of the political elite of the empire, while Seneca was tutor and advisor to Nero and Marcus Aurelius was Emperor from 161–180 AD.
19. See Foucault's discussion of this point, *CS*, 45–50(59–65].
20. What we could call the medical model of philosophy dominated the philsophical thought of late antiquity. See Foucault's discussion, *CS*, 54–58(69–74]. For more recent accounts, see Veyne, 'La médication interminable'; and Martha Nussbaum, *The Therapy of Desire: Theory and practice in Hellenistic ethics*, Princeton: Princeton University Press, 1994, especially Chapter 1.
21. Nussbaum, *The Therapy of Desire*, Chapter 9, 'Stoic Tonics'.
22. The English translator, inexplicably, renders '*le souci de soi*' here as 'self-preoccupation'.
23. For example, Foucault cites Epicurus's dictum that, 'it is never too early or too late to care for the health of one's soul' (*CS*, 60[46]).
24. See Aristotle, *Ethics*, for example, 1101a14–16; and 1153b14–25.
25. Zeno, 335–263 BC, founder of the Stoa.
26. Both versions are reported by the fourth-century compiler John Stobaeus. A useful source for this and other accounts of early Stoicism is Long and Sedley, *The Hellenistic Philosophers*. The first volume contains English translations of the principal sources, with commentary; the second contains the original texts. On this topic, see vol. 1, p. 394.

27. For example, Stobaeus reports that for the Stoics, '[happiness] consists in living in accordance with virtue, in living in agreement, or, what is the same, in living in accordance with nature', ibid., vol. 1, p. 394.

28. Annas, *The Morality of Happiness*. This emphasis is, of course, largely motivated by Annas's wish to write a history of ancient ethics which is relevant to contemporary moral theory – especially, to contemporary 'virtue ethics'.

29. Gisela Striker, 'Following Nature: A study in Stoic ethics', *Oxford Studies in Ancient Philosophy*, vol. IX, 1991, pp. 1–73. Reprinted in her *Essays on Hellenistic Epistemology and Ethics*, Cambridge: Cambridge University Press, 1996.

30. Annas, *The Morality of Happiness*, pp. 175–6.

31. A. A. Long, *Hellenistic Philosophy*, 2nd edition, London: Duckworth, 1986, p. 129. See also A. A. Long, 'The Logical Basis of Stoic Ethics', *Proceedings of the Aristotelian Society*, 71, 1970–71, pp. 85–104.

32. Nicholas White, 'The Role of Physics in Stoic Ethics', *The Southern Journal of Philosophy*, supplement to vol. 23, 1985, pp. 57–74.

33. Ibid., pp. 66–7.

34. 'Roman' despite the fact that Epictetus was, of course, Greek.

35. Seneca, *Letters to Lucilius*, Letter 41.

36. Marcus Aurelius, *Meditations*, IV, 40. I have used the translation by A. S. L. Farquharson, Oxford: Oxford University Press, 1989.

37. See *DP*, 31[35].

38. Hadot, 'Réflexions sur la notion ...', p. 267.

39. Ibid., p. 268.

40. See *UP*, 26–28(33–35] and cf. pp. 40–4.

41. It is curious that Foucault's re-worked French version of this English language interview gives 'Tout cela n'est pas très attrayant' ('All that isn't very attractive'), *DE* IV, 614. Is Foucault catering for a more 'hellenophile' French audience here, or has his disgust lessened?

42. Giuseppe Cambiano, *Le retour des Anciens*, trans. from Italian by S. Milanezi, Paris: Editions Belin, 1994, pp. 154, 155.

43. Patton, 'Taylor and Foucault ...', p. 276.

44. Translation modified, *CS*, 185[215].

45. See, for example, the discussion in ECS, 125[723].

46. Deleuze suggests that Foucault's four aspects of ethics can be read against Aristotle's account of the fourfold nature of causation – comprising the material, formal, efficient and final causes. See Gilles Deleuze, *Foucault*, trans. S. Hand, University of Minnesota Press, Minneapolis, 1988, p. 104.

Chapter 5

1. Friedrich Nietzsche, 'On Truth and Lies in a Nonmoral Sense', in Daniel Breazeale (ed. and trans.), *Philosophy and Truth: Selections from Nietzsche's notebooks of the early 1870s*, Atlantic Highlands, NJ: Humanities Press, 1995, p. 84.

2. Halperin, *Saint Foucault*, p. 68.

3. See PST, 145(427]; and also the discussion between Foucault and Deleuze, in which Foucault agrees with Deleuze that theory should be viewed as a 'box of tools' (IP, 208[309]).

4. See the discussion in CT.
5. See *VS*, 13[22] and EMF, 37[45].
6. EMF, 39[45].
7. Goldhill, *Foucault's Virginity*.
8. Halperin, *Saint Foucault*.
9. Goldhill, *Foucault's Virginity*, p. 102.
10. Halperin, *Saint Foucault*, pp. 6, 121.
11. *CS*, 230[198], cited by Goldhill, *Foucault's Virginity*, pp. 146, 160. It is worth noting that it is the English translator, and not Foucault, who makes the allusion to the 'order of things'. The French simply reads '*ce régime*'.
12. Goldhill, *Foucault's Virginity*, pp. xiii, 44.
13. In *CS* he discusses at length Plutarch's *Amatorius*, Achilles Tatius's *Leucippe and Cleitophon* and Pseudo-Lucian's *Erotes*.
14. Goldhill, *Foucault's Virginity*, pp. xii, 44.
15. Halperin, *Saint Foucault*, p. 6.
16. The book's sub-title is *Towards a gay hagiography*.
17. Cited in Halperin, *Saint Foucault*, p. 5. For Halperin's 1986 review of *UP* see David Halperin, 'Sexual Ethics and Technologies of the Self in Classical Greece', *American Journal of Philology*, no. 107, 1986, pp. 274-86.
18. The current use of the term 'queer' is itself an example of this tactic: the transformation from homophobic term of abuse to rallying cry for an oppositional politics. For Halperin, the term defines '(homo)sexual identity oppositionally and relationally but not necessarily substantively, not as a positivity but as a positionality, not as a thing but as a resistance to the norm' (*Saint Foucault*, p. 66).
19. Halperin, *Saint Foucault*, p. 162.
20. See my discussion of Hadot's argument in Chapter 3 above. Halperin mentions Hadot's influence on Foucault, but does not explicitly note his criticisms of Foucault's conception of the Greek self.
21. Gay is in parentheses here because many of Foucault's critics leave this connection below the surface; it remains implicit rather than explicit.
22. In aligning Foucault's interpretation with that of Hadot's *Exercices sprituels*, Halperin is perhaps unaware that Hadot himself is critical of Foucault's construction of the ancient self.
23. It is worth noting that Foucault is discussing 'le sujet' here, not 'the self'.
24. Halperin, *Saint Foucault*, p. 75.
25. Foucault makes the Gide comment in OGE, 349. Halperin cites it, and betters it, with the Seneca comment in *Saint Foucault*, p. 103.
26. Halperin, *Saint Foucault*, p. 74 (my emphasis).
27. Ibid., p. 76. This point is rich in possibilities which Halperin does not pursue, but which I will return in Chapter 6.
28. Halperin, *Saint Foucault*, p. 111.
29. Ibid., p. 73.
30. Halperin admits that this is a 'construction': 'if Michel Foucault had never existed, queer politics would have had to invent him – and perhaps it has indeed invented him, or at least partly reinvented him', ibid., p. 120.
31. Ibid., p. 72, my emphasis.
32. Ibid., p. 122.

33. Ibid., pp. 122–3.
34. Halperin criticizes James Miller's biography of Foucault for keeping 'both the author's ass and ours ... firmly, safely out of sight', ibid., p. 184. See J. Miller, *The Passion of Michel Foucault*, New York: Simon and Schuster, 1993.
35. Michel de Certeau, *Heterologies*, Ch. 13, p. 192. Hayden White, however, speaks of the 'combination of extravagance and obscurity' in Foucault's style: 'Foucault's Discourse: The historiography of anti-humanism', in *The Content of the Form*, Baltimore: Johns Hopkins University Press, 1997, p. 106.
36. For a useful overview of Foucault's reception by 'disciplinary history' see: Allan Megill, 'The Reception of Foucault by Historians', *Journal of the History of Ideas*, 48, 1, 1987, pp. 117–41.
37. A comment by Jacques Léonard, cited in PN [10]. Léonard, in a review of *Discipline and Punish*, compares Foucault to a 'barbarian horseman who crosses three centuries with open reins'.
38. Léonard claims to oppose the '*poussière des faits*' to Foucault's 'head in the clouds' hypothesizing. Hence the title of Foucault's response: '*La poussière et le nuage*' (PN).
39. See *DP*, 135ff.
40. One of Foucault's reasons for studying the prison was to reactivate 'the project of a "genealogy of morals", one which worked by racing the lines of transformation of what one might call "moral technologies"' (QM, 4[21]).
41. Despite the fact that the subtitle of *Discipline and Punish* is 'The Birth of the Prison'.
42. See Nietzsche epigraph to this chapter.
43. Nietzsche, 'On Truth and Lies ...', p. 87.
44. Ibid., p. 88.
45. Foucault insists that 'knowledge is not made for understanding; it is made for cutting' (NGH, 154[148]).

Chapter 6

1. Nietzsche, *The Gay Science*, Section 335, emphasis in original.
2. Nietzsche, *Genealogy of Morals*, Essay I, 13.
3. Ibid.
4. See RM, 253(705–6].
5. Cf. 'one would see it [the soul] as the present correlative of a certain technology of power over the body' (*DP*, 29[34]).
6. Paul Veyne, 'Foucault Revolutionizes History', in Arnold Davidson (ed.), *Foucault and His Interlocuters*, Chicago: University of Chicago Press, 1997, pp. 160–1.
7. Although this term could consistently be translated as 'subjectivation', it is sometimes useful to underline its semantic possibilities by giving 'subjection'.
8. See Louis Althusser, 'Ideology and Ideological State Apparatuses', in *Lenin and Philosophy and Other Essays*, trans. B. Brewster, London: New Left Books, 1971, p. 169.

9. As regards Foucault, however, we will see that in his later work he begins to emphasize our freedom as opposed to our subjection – he begins to argue that we are *more* free than we imagine.

10. The discussion of his intellectual development occurs in SPS. The phrase 'to get out from the philosophy of the subject' occurs in the opening passages of HL.

11. See SPS, SS and HL for Foucault's presentation of this verdict on phenomenology.

12. The case of Herculine Barbin is not discussed in *The History of Sexuality*, volume I, but it comes from the same period in Foucault's research and deals with the same general problem.

13. See, for example, the more 'positive' characterization of power in *VS*, 94–6[123–7]. The Nietzschean echo can be found, for example, in the suggestion in Essay III of *On the Genealogy of Morals* that even the ascetic ideal has had some value for humanity – since, through it, '*the will itself was saved*' (Nietzsche's emphasis, Essay III, 28).

14. With government understood here in the widest possible sense.

15. See Thomas Flynn's discussion, 'Foucault's Mapping of History', in Gary Gutting (ed.), *The Cambridge Companion to Foucault*, Cambridge: Cambridge University Press, 1994.

16. See QM, 6[23]. The English translator has, without explanation, added the phrase 'and pluralization' – which does not appear in the French original.

17. In the title, and text, of the interview PPP Foucault uses the term 'problemization' – but most commentators and re-editions modify both the title and the text, preferring to follow the later 'problematization'.

18. See Foucault's modified French version of OGE, in *DE* IV, 612.

19. According to William Connolly, the point is 'to ward off the demand to confirm transcendentally what you are contingently': see 'Beyond Good and Evil: The ethical sensibility of Michel Foucault', *Political Theory*, 21, 3, 1993, pp. 365–89.

20. French version of OGE, ibid.

21. Althusser, 'Ideology and ...', p. 164.

22. The most influential of these readings have been: Peter Dews, 'The Return of the Subject ...', and Thomas McCarthy, 'The Critique of Impure Reason: Foucault and the Frankfurt School', *Political Theory*, no. 18, 1990, pp. 437–69.

23. Deleuze, *Foucault*, see especially the section 'Foldings, or the Inside of Thought (Subjectivation)'. For other key defences of Foucault which follow analogous arguments, see: Paul Patton, 'Foucault's Subject of Power', *Political Theory Newsletter*, no. 6, 1994, pp. 60–71; Connolly, 'Beyond Good and Evil ...'; Chris Falzon, 'Foucault's Human Being', *Thesis Eleven*, no. 34, 1993, pp. 1–16; and C. Colwell, 'The Retreat of the Subject in the Late Foucault', *Philosophy Today*, no. 38, Spring 1994, pp. 56–69. For an account of the importance of Nietzsche in Foucault's approach to power and subjectivity (and for the importance of Foucault in 'producing' this Nietzsche), see Keith Ansell-Pearson, 'The Significance of Michel Foucault's Reading of Nietzsche: Power, the subject, and political theory', *Nietzsche-Studien*, 20, 1991, pp. 267–83.

24. See Deleuze, *Foucault*, p. 106 and n. 30.
25. Ibid., pp. 113–14.
26. Ibid., p. 104.
27. See *VS*, 155[205], and my discussion in Section 1.1.

Chapter 7

1. Friedrich Nietzsche, *Beyond Good and Evil*, trans. W. Kaufmann, New York: Vintage Books, 1989: Section 225.
2. See, for example, André Breton, *Manifestes du Surréalisme*, Paris: Pauvert, 1962: 'Qu'on se donne seulement la peine de *pratiquer* la poésie', pp. 31–2.
3. This forms part of Jurgen Habermas's account of the tradition of thought from Schiller, through Baudelaire, to the avant-garde which attempts to 'level art and life'. See Jurgen Habermas, 'Modernity – an Incomplete Project', in H. Foster (ed.), *Postmodern Culture*, London: Pluto Press, 1985, pp. 11–12. At the end of the article thinkers such as Foucault and Derrida are included in this tradition.
4. Richard Wolin, 'Foucault's Aesthetic Decisionism', *Telos*, no. 67, Spring 1986, pp. 71–86: see p. 85. I have already responded to these charges in my 'Foucault, Politics and the Autonomy of the Aesthetic', *The International Journal of Philosophical Studies*, 4, 2, 1996, pp. 273–91. Cf. Jane Bennett, '"How is it, then, that we are still barbarians?" Foucault, Schiller, and the Aestheticization of Ethics', *Political Theory*, 24, 4, 1996, pp. 653–72.
5. Walter Benjamin, 'The Work of Art in the Age of Mechanical Reproduction', in Hannah Arendt (ed.), *Illuminations*, London: Fontana, 1973. Page numbers henceforth given in the text.
6. I owe this formulation to Howard Caygill, 'Benjamin, Heidegger and the Destruction of Tradition', in A. Benjamin and P. Osborne (eds), *Walter Benjamin's Philosophy*, London: Routledge, 1994, p. 25.
7. For one of the best discussions of this aspect of Benjamin's essay see Susan Buck-Morss, 'Aesthetics and Anaesthetics: Benjamin's artwork essay reconsidered', *October*, no. 62, Fall 1992, pp. 3–42.
8. Walter Benjamin, 'On Some Motifs in Baudelaire', in Benjamin, *Illuminations*.
9. Caygill, 'Benjamin, Heidegger . . .', p. 28.
10. Andrew Hewitt, 'Fascist Modernism, Futurism, and Post-modernity', in R. Golsan (ed.), *Fascism, Aesthetics and Culture*, Hanover: University Press of New England, 1992, p. 39. See also Hewitt's *Fascist Modernism: Aesthetics, politics and the avant-garde*, Stanford: Stanford University Press, 1993.
11. For a partial translation, see R. W. Flint (ed.), *Marinetti: Selected writings*, New York: Farrar, Straus and Giroux, 1971. Page numbers henceforth given in text.
12. Jacques Lacan, 'The Mirror Stage as formative of the function of the I', in Jacques Lacan, *Ecrits, a selection*, trans. A. Sheridan, London: Tavistock, 1977.
13. Ibid., p. 7.
14. Cited in Russell Berman, *Modern Culture and Critical Theory*, Madison: University of Wisconsin Press, 1989, p. 78.

15. Walter Benjamin, 'Theories of German Fascism', *New German Critique*, no. 17, Spring 1979, pp. 120–8. See p. 128.
16. Hitler's speech inaugurating the 'Great Exhibition of German Art 1937' in Munich, in H. B. Chipp (ed.), *Theories of Modern Art*, Berkeley: University of California Press, 1968, p. 478.
17. Benito Mussolini, 'The Doctrine of Fascism', excerpts in H. Kohn (ed.), *Nationalism: Its meaning and history*, New York: D. Van Norstrand, 1965, p. 172.
18. Flint, *Marinetti*, p. 91.
19. Lacan, *Ecrits*, p. 4.
20. Nietzsche, *The Gay Science*, Section 290; Foucault refers to this passage in OGE, 351.
21. Paul Veyne, 'Le dernier Foucault et sa morale', *Critique*, no. 471–2, Aug–Sept 1986, pp. 933–41.
22. Andrew Thacker, 'Foucault's Aesthetics of Existence', *Radical Philosophy*, no. 63, Spring 1993, pp. 13–21: see p. 14.
23. Wolin, 'Foucault's Aesthetic Decisionism', p. 84, emphasis added.
24. See Habermas. 'Modernity ...', pp. 13–14.
25. Ibid., p. 10.
26. Veyne, 'Le dernier Foucault ...', p. 939.
27. Benjamin, 'On Some Motifs ...', p. 220.
28. Bertolt Brecht, *Poems: Part Two 1929–1938*, London: Eyre Methuen, 1976, pp. 308–9.
29. Friedrich Nietzsche, *Ecce Homo*, trans. R. J. Hollingdale, Harmondsworth: Penguin Books, 1979. References to this edition given henceforth in the text.
30. Walter Kaufmann traces the phrase, variations of which recur throughout Nietzsche's work, to Pindar's *'genoi hoios essi'*. See Kaufmann's translation of *The Gay Science*, p. 219, n. 69; and his *Nietzsche: Philosopher, psychologist, antichrist*, 4th edn, Princeton: Princeton University Press, 1974, p. 159, n. 1.
31. 'I celebrate myself, and sing myself'; Walt Whitman, 'Song of Myself', in *Leaves of Grass*, New York: Modern Library, 1921.
32. Alexander Nehamas, *Nietzsche: Life as Literature*, Cambridge: Harvard University Press, 1985.
33. Ibid., pp. 174–5.
34. Ibid., p. 188.
35. Friedrich Nietzsche, *Twilight of the Idols*, trans. R. J. Hollingdale, Harmondsworth: Penguin Books, 1977, see Section 49 of 'Expeditions of an Untimely Man'.
36. Ibid., Section 38.
37. Nehamas, *Nietzsche*, p. 191.
38. I have left all the questions about the justifiability of Nehamas's interpretation to one side here. The most important of these would be whether Nietzsche really thinks that 'one style' can only be achieved through writing. Does Goethe's exemplarity, for example, depend exclusively on his writings? And what of Nietzsche's other heroes – Julius Caesar, Napoleon?
39. One could, for example, usefully compare Foucault's discussion (in Introduction to *UP*) of the personal and intellectual crisis that changed the *History of Sexuality* project, with Nietzsche's description of *Human, All Too*

Human as 'the memorial of a crisis' (*Ecce Homo*, op. cit., 'Human, All Too Human', 1).

40. However, it cannot be ignored that for some readers the appeal to Nietzsche here would only strengthen the concern.

41. See Heidegger's discussion of this aspect of Nietzsche's thought in Martin Heidegger, *Nietzsche, Volumes I and II*, trans. D. Farrell Krell, San Francisco: Harper Collins, 1991: volume I, p. 69.

Chapter 8

1. Friedrich Nietzsche, *Beyond Good and Evil*, Section 205.

2. It should be noted that the published English translation of this passage bears little resemblance to the French original – on which I have based my translation here.

3. James Bernauer, *Michel Foucault's ...*', p. 19; Paul Rabinow, 'Introduction', in *The Essential Works of Michel Foucault*, volume I, *Ethics: Subjectivity and truth*, London: Allen Lane, 1997, pp. xxxiii–xxxvi.

4. I address Foucault's discussion of S/M in Chapter 9.

5. Michel de Montaigne, *Montaigne: Selections from his writings*, selected and introduced by André Gide, New York: MacGraw-Hill, 1964 (based on the translation by John Florio, 1604), p. 30 ['The Author to the Reader'].

6. This phrase, as applied to the ancient practice of philosophy, was introduced by Pierre Hadot in his series of studies *Exercices spirituels*.

7. Plato, *Apology*, in Plato, *The Last Days of Socrates*, trans. H. Tredennick, Harmondsworth: Penguin Books, 1969, 38a.

8. For Diogenes Laertius's account of the story, see his *Lives of Eminent Philosophers*, trans. R. D. Hicks, London: Loeb Classical Library, 1945: Book VI, 20. For contemporary interpretations of this founding principle of the Cynics, see for example: Michel Onfray, *Cynismes: Portrait du philosophe en chien*, Paris: Grasset, 1990, pp. 108–18; H. D. Rankin, *Sophists, Socratices and Cynics*, London: Croom Helm, 1983, p. 230; A. A. Long, 'The Socratic Tradition: Diogenes, Crates, and Hellenistic Ethics' in R. Bracht Branham and M. Goulet-Cazé (eds), *The Cynics: The Cynic movement in antiquity and its legacy*, Berkeley: University of California Press, 1996, pp. 33ff.

9. See the epigraph to this chapter. One might try to justify the gender exclusiveness of Nietzsche's phrase by appealing to the gender exclusiveness of ancient philosophy – notwithstanding important exceptions such as Hipparchia, who adopted the Cynic way of life (and married Crates, a leading Cynic). In any case, unfortunately we cannot change Nietzsche's terminology.

10. See the discussion of this feature of Socrates's method in Gregory Vlastos, *Socrates: Ironist and moral philosopher*, Cambridge: Cambridge University Press, 1991, pp. 113ff.

11. The Stoic Apollodorus of Seleucia, cited in the 'Introduction' to Branham and Goulet-Cazé (eds), *The Cynics*, p. 22.

12. CCF, 82; 6/1/1982.

13. However, Foucault *also* recognizes a critical tradition in the modern

philosophy that leads from some aspects of Kant, through Hegel and Marx, on to Nietzsche and the Frankfurt School.

14. Kimon Lycos, *Plato on Justice and Power*, London: Macmillan, 1987, p. 7.
15. Ibid., p. 12.
16. Ibid., p. 169.
17. Pierre Hadot, 'Conversion' in *Exercices spirituels*, pp. 173–82.
18. Ibid., pp. 175–6.
19. If there is a sense in which Foucault does imply a notion of conversion it would of course be of the 'mutation/rupture' variety, rather than the 'return/ fidelity' variety: that is, it would be an anti-Platonist form of conversion. However, whether it is possible to leave out this Platonic aspect, while hoping to preserve the notion itself, is a question that is worth asking. In this regard we should remember Hadot's comment that the aim of 'every spiritual exercise' was to 'return to our true self' ('*pour revenir à notre véritable moi*'), *Exercices spirituels*, p. 49.
20. See Plato, *Laches*, trans. I. Lane, in Plato, *Early Socratic Dialogues*, T. J. Saunders (ed.) Harmondsworth: Penguin Books, 1987, 188c–189a, and Foucault's discussion in DT, 62–5.
21. Conventions are *nomoi* – closely related to *nomisma*, coinage. They are that which is accepted, or passes as common currency.
22. Diogenes Laertius, *Lives*, VI, 29.
23. See Foucault's discussion of Dio Chrysostom's account in DT, 81–8.
24. See the 'unofficial' transcript DT; and, for an account of the last Collège de France course, Flynn, 'Foucault as Parrhesiast', pp. 213–29. See also Gary Alan Scott, 'Games of Truth: Foucault's analysis of the transformation from political to ethical parrhesia', *The Southern Journal of Philosophy*, 34, 1996, pp. 97–114.
25. The story is cited in Branham and Goulet-Cazé (eds), *The Cynics*, Appendix A, p. 406.
26. A footnote to DT (p. 2) notes that Foucault justified his use of the masculine pronoun by pointing out that women (along with non-citizens, slaves and children) were deprived of the right to *parrhesia* (although he does go on to discuss Creusa's use of *parrhesia* – in *Ion* – to denounce the god who had raped her). Another example, perhaps, of the 'gender-blindness' I discussed in the Introduction.
27. Plato's *Alcibiades 1*, in which Socrates engages in a 'parrhesiastic game' with his friend Alcibiades is a good example.
28. For an account of this shift that focuses on *aletheia* rather than *parrhesia*, see Marcel Détienne, *The Masters of Truth in Archaic Greece*, trans. J. Lloyd, New York: Zone Books, 1996. See, in particular, Chapter 5 'The Process of Secularization'.
29. Foucault focuses in particular on the late plays, *Ion* and *Orestes*.
30. See Foucault's discussion, DT, 15.
31. The play is *The Phoenician Women;* see Foucault's discussion, DT, 12–14.
32. See Plato, *Republic*, 557a and Foucault's discussion (DT, 54).
33. Foucault singles out Plato's early dialogue *Laches* as presenting Socrates in these terms (DT, 60).
34. 'The true champion of justice, if he intends to survive even for a short time,

must necessarily confine himself to private life and leave politics alone' (Plato, *Apology*, 32a).

35. Foucault makes this and the following comments in the question and answer session after his lecture – they are not included in the English translation.

Chapter 9

1. W. B. Yeats, *Autobiographies*, London: Macmillan, 1955, p. 509.
2. Bernauer, *Michel Foucault's* ..., p. 20. Closer still to my formulation is Bernauer's: 'Genealogy is permanent critique in the interest of an endless practice of freedom', ibid., p. 19.
3. This is Rabinow's preferred translation of the phrase *se déprendre de soimême*. Rabinow, 'Introduction', p. xxxvii.
4. See, for example, Habermas, *The Philosophical Discourse* ..., Chapters 9 and 10. This approach to Foucault's work is, however, more elegantly presented in two articles by Nancy Fraser: 'Foucault on Modern Power ...' and 'Foucault's Body Language ...'.
5. Fraser, 'Foucault's Body Language ...' p. 68.
6. Michael Walzer, 'The Politics of Michel Foucault', in Hoy (ed.), *Foucault*, p. 67.
7. Fraser, 'Foucault on Modern Power ...', p. 283.
8. The Lacanian psychoanalyst Jacques-Alain Miller makes this remark in spoken comments after a paper by Rainer Rochlitz – reported in the conference proceedings: *Michel Foucault Philosophe*, Paris: Editions du Seuil, 1989, p. 300. These comments are not included in the English translation.
9. Fraser, 'Foucault's Body Language ...', pp. 69–70.
10. Patton, 'Foucault's Subject of Power', p. 69, emphasis added. For an analogous argument, see: T. Carlos Jacques, 'Whence Does the Critic Speak? A study of Foucault's genealogy', *Philosophy and Social Criticism*, 17, 4, 1991, pp. 325–44. For a fuller discussion of the implications of this debate, see the exchange between Patton and Taylor in Taylor, 'Foucault on Freedom and Truth'; Patton, 'Taylor and Foucault on Power and Freedom', and Taylor's 'Reply' to Patton in the same issue.
11. Thomas Flynn, 'Foucault and the Politics of Postmodernity', *Nous*, 23, 1989, pp. 187–98.
12. For references, see the introductory section of Chapter 5.
13. All of these quotations are taken from my own transcription and translation of *DG*.
14. Taylor, 'Foucault on Freedom and Truth', p. 261.
15. While this space can shrink to an infinitesimally small degree, Foucault would deny that it can ever completely disappear. See Falzon's discussion of the impossibility of 'total domination': Chris Falzon, *Foucault and Social Dialogue: Beyond fragmentation*, Routledge, London, 1998, pp. 51–2.
16. The English translation misleadingly renders '*cette tâche*' (this task) as 'this duty' (ECS, 131(729]).
17. See Isaac Kramnick (ed.), *The Portable Enlightenment Reader*, Harmondsworth: Penguin Books, 1995, p. 467.

18. The opening line of Jean-Jacques Rousseau, *The Social Contract*, trans. M. Cranston, Harmondsworth: Penguin Books, 1984.
19. Rajchman, *The Freedom of Philosophy*, pp. 92–3.
20. Ibid., p. 93.
21. See Falzon's development of this 'dialogic' conception of freedom in *Foucault and Social Dialogue*, esp. pp. 52–6. Also cf. Romand Coles, 'Foucault's Dialogical Artistic Ethos', *Theory, Culture and Society*, 8, 1991, pp. 99–120.
22. Rajchman, *The Freedom of Philosophy*, p. 60.
23. Ibid., p. 115.
24. The difference (when transliterated) consists simply of a macron (-) over the 'e'. See Aristotle, *Ethics*, 1103a14.
25. This is Foucault's formulation, not Kant's (WE, 34).
26. Again, this is Foucault's formulation, not Baudelaire's (WE, 42).
27. Foucault's discussion focuses on gay men because this was the group with which he was most familiar. This focus does not imply that no other groups offer such a potential.
28. As I noted in Chapter 2, p. 180, the word 'general' is curiously omitted from the English translation.
29. Foucault insisted on his refusal of anarchism (understood as a rejection of *all* 'government') during the discussion which followed his delivery of 'What is Critique?' (QC). This discussion is not reproduced in the English translation. See QC, [59].
30. The closing pages of WE contain numerous instances of all these terms.
31. Geoffrey Galt Harpham, 'So ... What *Is* Enlightenment? An Inquisition into Modernity', *Critical Inquiry*, no. 20, Spring 1994, pp. 524–56. See p. 524.
32. Immanuel Kant, 'An Answer to the Question: What is Enlightenment?', reprinted in J. Schmidt (ed.), *What is Enlightenment?*, Berkeley: University of California Press, 1996.
33. Jurgen Habermas, 'Taking Aim at the Heart of the Present', in Hoy (ed.), *Foucault*, pp. 103–4.
34. I am referring here to Kant's suggestion that the individual can practise freedom of thought within a strictly defined sphere, and that the monarch can allow this *if* they have a 'well-disciplined army' at their disposal. See Kant, 'An Answer to the Question ...', p. 63.
35. Ian Hacking identifies this point of agreement between Kant and Foucault as the idea that, in the absence of a revealed truth, we must '*construct* our ethical position'. In this way, Foucault preserves the 'spirit', rather than the 'letter and the law' of Kant's thought: Ian Hacking, 'Self-Improvement', in Hoy (ed.), *Foucault*, p. 239.
36. These 'dangers' are only very briefly described in this lecture, but they can be taken to include attempts to set up a 'scientific' account of human nature as a normative base and attempts to found a social order on a rigidly defined (and imposed) notion of human essence.
37. Lewis Hinchman, 'Autonomy, Individuality and Self-Determination', in Schmidt (ed.), *What is Enlightenment?*, p. 506.
38. Dreyfus and Rabinow extend this argument to the claim that 'modernity' has happened 'several times in our history' – most notably in fifth-century

Athens and eighteenth-century Europe: Hubert Dreyfus and Paul Rabinow, 'What is Maturity? Habermas and Foucault on "What Is Enlightenment?"', in Hoy (ed.), *Foucault*, p. 117.

39. On reactivating Enlightenment, see WE, 42; on actualizing the care of the self, see ECS, 125[723].
40. Habermas, 'Taking Aim', in Hoy (ed.), *Foucault*, p. 105.
41. Both Habermas and Foucault agree – although in very different ways – that the Enlightenment is an 'unfinished project', cf. Habermas, 'Modernity – An Incomplete Project', in Foster (ed.) *Postmodern Culture*.
42. Foucault, however, came to recognize his closeness to Habermas, at least in terms of his general approach to the present: see QL, 95[688].
43. Emphasis added.
44. Emphasis added.
45. See Patton, 'Taylor and Foucault ...' and 'Foucault's Subject ...' for a full discussion of the way freedom operates as historical constant (my term) in Foucault's middle works.

Conclusion

1. Friedrich Nietzsche, *The Gay Science*, Preface 3.
2. Hélène Cixous discusses her friendship and her intellectual relationship with Foucault, in 'Cela n'a pas de nom, ce qui se passait', *Le Débat* (numéro spéciale sur M. Foucault), no. 41, Sept.–Nov., 1986, pp. 153–8.
3. Pierre Vidal-Nacquet, 'Foreword', in Marcel Détienne, *The Masters of Truth ...*, p. 14.
4. The German Enlightenment thinkers were *Aufklärer*, the French were *lumières* ('lights'/'enlightened ones'). The phrase 'We "Other Victorians"' is of course the title of Part One of *The History of Sexuality*, volume I (*VS*).
5. Immanuel Kant, 'An Answer to the Question ...', p. 58.
6. Friedrich Nietzsche, 'Schopenhauer as Educator', in *Untimely Meditations*, p. 187.

Bibliography

Section A lists all the works of Michel Foucault that have been cited in this thesis; Section B lists all the cited works by other authors.

A: FOUCAULT BIBLIOGRAPHY

This list is arranged chronologically according to date of original publication (whether in French, English, or Italian); I then give publication details for the edition(s) I have cited. It is not intended to be an exhaustive list of varying editions, but simply of those editions I have consulted.

(1966) *The Order of Things: An archaeology of the human sciences*, London: Tavistock Publications, 1982 (*Les mots et les choses: une archéologie des sciences humaines*, Paris: Gallimard, 1966).

(1971a) 'The Order of Discourse', trans. Ian Macleod, in Robert Young (ed.), *Untying the Text: A post-structuralist reader*, Boston: Routledge, 1981 (*L'ordre du discours*, Paris: Gallimard, 1971).

(1971b) 'Nietzsche, Genealogy, History', in D. F. Bouchard (ed.), *Language, Counter-Memory, Practice*, New York: Cornell University Press, 1977. ('Nietzsche, la généalogie, l'histoire', in Michel Foucault, *Dits et écrits 1954–1988: II 1970–1975*, D. Defert and F. Ewald (eds), Paris: Gallimard, 1994).

(1971c) 'Préface à *Enquête dans vingt prisons*' (Champ Libre, Paris, 1971), in Michel Foucault, *Dits et écrits 1954–1988: II 1970–1975*, D. Defert and F. Ewald (eds), Paris: Gallimard, 1994.

(1971d) 'Je perçois l'intolérable', in Michel Foucault, *Dits et écrits 1954–1988: II 1970–1975*, D. Defert and F. Ewald (eds), Paris: Gallimard, 1994).

(1972) 'Intellectuals and Power', in D. F. Bouchard (ed.), *Language, Counter-Memory, Practice*, New York: Cornell University Press, 1977 ('Les intellectuels et le pouvoir', in Michel Foucault, *Dits et écrits 1954–1988: II 1970–1975*, D. Defert and F. Ewald (eds), Paris: Gallimard, 1994).

(1975a) *Discipline and Punish: The birth of the prison*, trans. Alan Sheridan, New York: Vintage Books, 1995 (*Surveiller et punir: Naissance de la prison*, Paris: Gallimard, 1975).

(1975b) 'Prison Talk', in Cohn Gordon (ed.), *Power/Knowledge: Selected interviews and other writings 1972–1977 by Michel Foucault*, Hemel Hempstead:

Harvester Wheatsheaf, 1980 ('Les jeux du pouvoir', in Michel Foucault, *Dits et écrits 1954–1988: II 1970–1975*, D. Defert and F. Ewald (eds), Paris: Gallimard, 1994).

(1976a) *The History of Sexuality*, volume I, *An Introduction*, trans. Robert Hurley, Harmondsworth: Penguin, 1987 (*Histoire de la sexualité*, 1, *La volonté de savoir*, Paris: Gallimard, 1994).

(1976b) 'Two Lectures', trans. Kate Soper, in Colin Gordon (ed.), *Power/Knowledge: Selected interviews and other writings 1972–1977*, Hemel Hempstead: Harvester Wheatsheaf, 1980 (originally published in Italian).

(1977a) 'The Confession of the Flesh', trans. Colin Gordon, in Colin Gordon (ed.), *Power/Knowledge: Selected interviews and other writings 1972–1977*, Hemel Hempstead: Harvester Wheatsheaf, 1980 ('Le jeu de Michel Foucault', in Michel Foucault, *Dits et écrits 1954–1988: III 1976–1979*, D. Defert and F. Ewald (eds), Paris: Gallimard, 1994).

(1977b) 'The History of Sexuality', trans. Colin Gordon, in Colin Gordon (ed.), *Power/Knowledge: Selected interviews and other writings 1972–1977*, Hemel Hempstead: Harvester Wheatsheaf, 1980 ('Les rapports de pouvoir passent à l'intérieur des corps', in Michel Foucault, *Dits et écrits 1954–1988: III 1976–1979*, D. Defert and F. Ewald (eds), Paris: Gallimard, 1994).

(1977c) 'Power and Sex', trans. D. J. Parent, in Lawrence Kritzman (ed.), *Michel Foucault: Politics, Philosophy, Culture; Interviews and other writings 1977–1984*, New York: Routledge, 1990 ('Non au sexe roi', in Michel Foucault, *Dits et écrits 1954–1988: III 1976–1979*, D. Defert and F. Ewald (eds), Paris: Gallimard, 1994).

(1977d) 'Truth and Power', trans. Colin Gordon, in Colin Gordon (ed.), *Power/Knowledge: Selected interviews and other writings 1972–1977*, Hemel Hempstead: Harvester Wheatsheaf, 1980 (originally published in Italian).

(1977e) 'Power and Strategies', in Colin Gordon (ed.), *Power/Knowledge: Selected interviews and other writings 1972–1977*, Hemel Hempstead: Harvester Wheatsheaf, 1980 ('Pouvoirs et stratégies', in Michel Foucault, *Dits et écrits 1954–1988: III 1976–1979*, D. Defert and F. Ewald (eds), Paris: Gallimard, 1994).

(1978) 'Governmentality', trans. Rosi Braidotti, in G. Burchell, C. Gordon and P. Miller (eds), *The Foucault Effect: Studies in governmentality*, Hemel Hempstead: Harvester Wheatsheaf, 1991 (this is a translation into English of an Italian transcription and publication of Foucault's Collège de France lecture of February 1978).

(1979) 'Foucault Examines Reason in Service of State Power', *Campus Report*, no. 6, 24 October 1979 (I have been unable to locate this edition, so I refer to the French translation: 'Foucault étudie la raison d'Etat', in Michel Foucault, *Dits et écrits 1954–1988: III 1976–1979*, D. Defert and F. Ewald (eds), Paris: Gallimard, 1994).

(1980a) 'Questions of Method', trans. Colin Gordon, in *Ideology and Consciousness*, 8, Spring 1981, pp. 3–14 ('Table ronde du 20 mai 1978', in Michel Foucault, *Dits et écrits 1954–1988: IV 1980–1988*, D. Defert and F. Ewald (eds), Paris: Gallimard, 1994).

(1980b) 'Entretien avec Michel Foucault', in Michel Foucault, *Dits et écrits 1954–1988: IV 1980–1988*, D. Defert and F. Ewald (eds), Paris: Gallimard, 1994 (originally published in Italian; the English translation [*Remarks on*

Marx, New York: Semiotext(e), 1991] is so poor that I have not referred to it here).

(1980c) 'Introduction', in *Herculine Barbin, Being the Recently Discovered Memoirs of a Nineteenth-Century French Hermaphrodite*, New York: Pantheon Books, 1980 (the full French text of this 'Introduction' is published in Michel Foucault, *Dits et écrits 1954–1988: IV 1980–1988*, D. Defert and F. Ewald (eds), Paris: Gallimard, 1994).

(1980d) 'The Howison Lectures: Truth and subjectivity', transcript of two lectures delivered at the University of California, Berkeley, 1980.

(1980e) 'La poussière et le nuage', in Michel Foucault, *Dits et écrits 1954–1988: IV 1980–1988*, D. Defert and F. Ewald (eds), Paris: Gallimard, 1994.

(1980f) *Power/Knowledge: Selected interviews and other writings 1972–1977*, Hemel Hempstead: Harvester Wheatsheaf, 1980 (originally published in Italian).

(1981a) 'Friendship as a Way of Life', in S. Lotringer (ed.), *Foucault Live: Interviews 1961–1984*, New York: Autonomedia, 1989 ('De l'amitié comme mode de vie', in Michel Foucault, *Dits et écrits 1954–1988: IV 1980–1988*, D. Defert and F. Ewald (eds), Paris: Gallimard, 1994).

(1981b) 'Sexuality and Solitude' (with Richard Sennett), in David Rieff (ed.), *Humanities in Review*, volume I, New York: Cambridge University Press, 1982 (originally written and published in English).

(1981c) 'Subjectivité et vérité: cours du 06/01/81 au Collège de France', Recording held at Bibliothèque du Saulchoir, Paris.

(1982a) 'Sexual Choice, Sexual Act: Foucault on homosexuality', in Lawrence Kritzman (ed.), *Michel Foucault: Politics, Philosophy, Culture; Interviews and other writings 1977–1984*, New York: Routledge, 1990 (interview originally conducted and published in English).

(1982b) 'The Subject and Power', in Hubert Dreyfus and Paul Rabinow, *Michel Foucault: Beyond structuralism and hermeneutics*, Chicago: University of Chicago Press, 1982 (originally written and published in English).

(1982c) 'The Social Triumph of the Sexual Will', *Christopher Street*, 6, 4, 1982, pp. 36–41 ('Le triomphe social du plaisir sexuel', in Michel Foucault, *Dits et écrits 1954–1988: IV 1980–1988*, D. Defert and F. Ewald (eds), Paris: Gallimard, 1994). I have only been able to consult the French translation of this interview.

(1982d) 'Foucault: non aux compromis', in Michel Foucault, *Dits et dcrits 1954–1988: IV 1980–1988*, D. Defert and F. Ewald (eds), Paris: Gallimard, 1994.

(1982e) 'L'herméneutique du sujet: cours du 06/01/82 au Collège de France', Recording held at Bibliothèque du Saulchoir, Paris.

(1983a) 'On the Genealogy of Ethics: An overview of work in progress', in Paul Rabinow (ed.), *The Foucault Reader*, New York: Pantheon Books, 1984 (this interview was originally conducted and published in English, although the French translation was significantly revised by Foucault, see *DE*, IV, 609–31).

(1983b) 'Discourse and Truth: The problematization of *parrhesia*', Joseph Pearson (ed.), transcription of six lectures delivered at the University of California, Berkeley, 1983.

(1983c) 'The Minimalist Self', in Lawrence Kritzman (ed.), *Michel Foucault: Politics, Philosophy, Culture; Interviews and other writings 1977–1984*, New York: Routledge, 1990 (interview originally conducted and published in English).

(1983d) 'Structuralism and Post-Structuralism: An interview with Michel Foucault' ('Critical Theory/Intellectual History'), in Lawrence Kritzman (ed.), *Michel Foucault: Politics, Philosophy, Culture; Interviews and other writings 1977–1984*, New York: Routledge, 1990 (interview originally published in English).

(1983e) 'Preface', in English trans. of Gilles Deleuze and Felix Guattari, *Anti-Oedipus: Capitalism and Schizophrenia*, Minneapolis: University of Minnesota Press, 1983.

(1984a) *The History of Sexuality*, volume II, *The Use of Pleasure*, trans. Robert Hurley, Harmondsworth: Penguin Books, 1988 (*Histoire de la sexualité*, 2, *L'usage des plaisirs*, Paris: Gallimard, 1984).

(1984b) *The History of Sexuality*, volume III, *The Care of the Self*, trans. Robert Hurley, Harmondsworth: Penguin Books, 1990 (*Histoire de la sexualité*, 3, *Le souci de soi*, Paris: Gallimard, 1984).

(1984c) 'An Aesthetics of Existence', trans. Alan Sheridan, in Lawrence Kritzman (ed.), *Michel Foucault: Politics, Philosophy, Culture; Interviews and other writings 1977–1984*, New York: Routledge, 1990 ('Une esthétique de l'existence', in Michel Foucault, *Dits et écrits 1954–1988: IV 1980–1988*, D. Defert and F. Ewald (eds), Paris: Gallimard, 1994).

(1984d) 'The Concern for Truth', trans. Alan Sheridan, in Lawrence Kritzman (ed.), *Michel Foucault: Politics, Philosophy, Culture; Interviews and other writings 1977–1984*, New York: Routledge, 1990 ('Le souci de la vérité', in Michel Foucault, *Dits et écrits 1954–1988: IV 1980–1988*, D. Defert and F. Ewald (eds), Paris: Gallimard, 1994).

(1984e) 'The Ethic of Care for the Self as a Practice of Freedom', trans. J. D. Gauthier, *Philosophy and Social Criticism*, 2, Summer, 1987, pp. 112–31 ('L'éthique du souci de sol comme pratique de la liberté', in Michel Foucault, *Dits et écrits 1954–1988: IV 1980–1988*, D. Defert and F. Ewald (eds), Paris: Gallimard, 1994).

(1984f) 'Politics and Ethics', in Paul Rabinow (ed.), *The Foucault Reader*, New York: Pantheon Books, 1984 (interview originally published in English).

(1984g) 'Preface to *The History of Sexuality*, Volume II', trans. William Smock, in Paul Rabinow (ed.), *The Foucault Reader*, New York: Pantheon Books, 1984 (this early version was never published in French).

(1984h) 'The Art of Telling the Truth', trans. Alan Sheridan, in Lawrence Kritzman (ed.), *Michel Foucault: Politics, Philosophy, Culture; Interviews and other writings 1977–1984*, New York: Routledge, 1990 ('Qu'est-ce que les lumières?', in Michel Foucault, *Dits et écrits 1954–1988: IV 1980–1988*, D. Defert and F. Ewald (eds), Paris: Gallimard, 1994).

(1984i) 'The Return of Morality', trans. T. Levin and I. Lorenz, in Lawrence Kritzman (ed.), *Michel Foucault: Politics, Philosophy, Culture; Interviews and other writings 1977–1984*, New York: Routledge, 1990 ('Le retour de la morale', in Michel Foucault, *Dits et écrits 1954–1988: IV 1980–1988*, D. Defert and F. Ewald (eds), Paris: Gallimard, 1994).

(1984j) 'Sex, Power and the Politics of Identity', in *Foucault Live: Interviews 1966–1984*, S. Lotringer (ed.), New York: Semiotext(e), 1989 (interview originally conducted and published in English).

(1984k) 'What is Enlightenment?', in Paul Rabinow (ed.), *The Foucault Reader*, New York: Pantheon Books, 1984 (first published in English).

(1984l) 'Polemics, Politics and Problemizations', in Paul Rabinow (ed.), *The Foucault Reader*, New York: Pantheon Books, 1984 (interview conducted and published in English).

(1988a) 'Technologies of the Self', in Luther H. Martin, Huck Gutman, and Patrick H. Hutton (eds), *Technologies of the Self: A seminar with Michel Foucault*, London: Tavistock Publications, 1988 (seminar delivered and published in English).

(1988b) 'Truth, Power, Self: An Interview with Michel Foucault', in Luther H. Martin, Huck Gutman, and Patrick H. Hutton (eds), *Technologies of the Self: A seminar with Michel Foucault*, London: Tavistock Publications, 1988 (interview originally conducted and published in English).

(1989) *De la gouvernementalité: leçons d'introduction aux cours des années 1978 et 1979* (deux cassettes), Paris: Editions du Seuil, 1989.

(1990) 'What is Critique?', trans. K. P. Geiman, in J. Schmidt (ed.), *What is Enlightenment?*, Berkeley: University of California Press, 1996 ('Qu'est-ce que la critique?', *Bulletin de la Société française de Philosophie*, 84, 2, 1990).

(1993) 'About the Beginning of the Hermeneutics of the Self: Two lectures at Dartmouth', *Political Theory*, 21, 2, 1993, pp. 198–227.

(1994a) *Dits et écrits 1954–1988: II 1970–1975*, D. Defert and F. Ewald (eds), Paris: Gallimard, 1994.

(1994b) *Dits et écrits 1954–1988: III 1976–1979*, D. Defert and F. Ewald (eds), Paris: Gallimard, 1994.

(1994c) *Dits et écrits 1954–1988: IV 1980–1988*, D. Defert and F. Ewald (eds), Paris: Gallimard, 1994.

(1997) *The Essential Works of Michel Foucault*, volume I, *Ethics: Subjectivity and truth*, Paul Rabinow (ed.), London: Allen Lane: The Penguin Press, 1997.

B: GENERAL BIBLIOGRAPHY

Althusser, Louis, 'Ideology and Ideological State Apparatuses', in *Lenin and Philosophy and Other Essays*, trans. B. Brewster, London: New Left Books, 1971.

Annas, Julia, *The Morality of Happiness*, Oxford: Oxford University Press, 1994.

Ansell-Pearson, Keith, 'The Significance of Michel Foucault's Reading of Nietzsche: Power, the subject, and political theory,' *Nietzsche-Studien*, 20, 1991, pp. 267–83.

Aristotle, *Ethics*, trans. J. A. K. Thomson, Harmondsworth: Penguin Books, 1976.

Bauman, Zygmunt, *Postmodern Ethics*, Oxford: Blackwell, 1993.

Bauman, Zygmunt, *Life in Fragments: Essays in postmodern morality*, Oxford: Blackwell, 1995.

Benjamin, Walter, 'The Work of Art in the Age of Mechanical Reproduction', in Hannah Arendt (ed.), *Illuminations*, London: Fontana, 1973.

Benjamin, Walter, 'On Some Motifs in Baudelaire', in Hannah Arendt (ed.), *Illuminations*, London: Fontana, 1973.

Benjamin, Walter, 'Theories of German Fascism', *New German Critique*, no. 17, Spring 1979, pp. 120–8.

Berman, Russell, *Modern Culture and Critical Theory*, Madison: University of Wisconsin Press, 1989.

Bennett, Jane, '"How is it, then, that we are still barbarians?" Foucault, Schiller, and the Aestheticization of Ethics', *Political Theory*, 24, 4, 1996, pp. 653–72.

Bernauer, James, *Michel Foucault's Force of Flight*, Atlantic Highlands, NJ: Humanities Press International, 1990.

Blasius, Mark, 'An Ethos of Lesbian and Gay Existence', *Political Theory*, 20, 4, 1992, pp. 642–71.

Bois, Page du, 'The Subject in Antiquity after Foucault', in D. Larmour, P. Miller and C. Platter (eds), *Rethinking Sexuality: Foucault and Classical Antiquity*, Princeton: Princeton University Press, 1998.

Branham, R. Bracht and Goulet-Cazé, Marie-Odile (eds), *The Cynics: The Cynic movement in antiquity and its legacy*, Berkeley: University of California Press, 1996.

Brecht, Bertolt, *Poems: Part Two 1929–1938*, London: Eyre Methuen, 1976.

Breton, André, *Manifestes du Surréalisme*, Paris: Pauvert, 1962.

Buck-Morss, Susan, 'Aesthetics and Anaesthetics: Benjamin's artwork essay reconsidered', *October*, no. 62, Fall 1992, pp. 3–42.

Burchell, Graham, Gordon, Colin and Miller, Peter (eds), *The Foucault Effect: Studies in governmentality*, Hemel Hempstead: Harvester Wheatsheaf, 1991.

Cambiano, Giuseppe, *Le retour des Anciens*, trans. from Italian by S. Milanezi, Paris: Editions Belin, 1994.

Cameron, Averil, 'Redrawing the Map: Early Christian territory after Foucault', *Journal of Roman Studies*, no. 76, 1986, pp. 266–71.

Caygill, Howard, 'Benjamin, Heidegger and the Destruction of Tradition', in Andrew Benjamin and Peter Osborne (eds), *Walter Benjamin's Philosophy*, London: Routledge, 1994.

Certeau, Michel de, *Heterologies: Disourse on the other*, trans. B. Massumi, Manchester: Manchester University Press, 1986.

Cixous, Hélène, 'Cela n'a pas de nom, ce qui se passait', *Le Débat* (numéro spéciale sur M. Foucault), no. 41, Sept–Nov 1986, pp. 153–8.

Clark, Elizabeth A., 'Foucault, The Fathers, and Sex', *Journal of the American Academy of Religion*, 56, 4, 1988, pp. 619–41.

Cohen, David, *Law, Sexuality and Society*, Cambridge: Cambridge University Press, 1991.

Cohen, David and Saller, Richard, 'Foucault on sexuality in Greco-Roman Antiquity', in Jan Goldstein (ed.), *Foucault and the Writing of History*, Oxford: Blackwell, 1994.

Coles, Romand, 'Foucault's Dialogical Artistic Ethos', *Theory, Culture and Society*, 8, 1991, pp. 99–120.

Colwell, C., 'The Retreat of the Subject in the Late Foucault', *Philosophy Today*, no. 38, Spring 1994, pp. 56–69.

Connolly, William, 'Beyond Good and Evil: The ethical sensibility of Michel Foucault', *Political Theory*, 21, 3, 1993, pp. 365–89.

Daraki, Maria, 'Michel Foucault's Journey to Greece', *Telos* 67, Spring 1986, pp. 87–110.

Davidson, Arnold, 'Ethics as Ascetics', in Gary Gutting (ed.), *The Cambridge Companion to Foucault*, Cambridge: Cambridge University Press, 1995.

Davidson, Arnold (ed.), *Foucault and his Interlocuters*, University of Chicago Press, Chicago, 1997.

Deleuze, Gilles, *Foucault*, trans. S. Hand, Minneapolis: University of Minnesota Press, 1988.

Deleuze Gilles and Guattari, Felix, *Anti-Oedipus: Capitalism and Schizophrenia*, Minneapolis: University of Minnesota Press, 1983.

Détienne, Marcel, *The Masters of Truth in Archaic Greece*, trans. J. Lloyd, New York: Zone Books, 1996.

Dews, Peter, 'The Return of the Subject in Late Foucault', *Radical Philosophy*, no. 51, Spring 1989, pp. 37–41.

Diogenes Laertius, *Lives of Eminent Philosophers*, trans. R. D. Hicks, London: Loeb Classical Library, 1945.

Donlan, Walter, 'The Origin of *Kalos Kagathos*', *The American Journal of Philology*, no. 94, 1973, pp. 365–74.

Donlan, Walter, *The Aristocratic Ideal in Ancient Greece*, Lawrence, KS: Coronado, 1980.

Dover, Kenneth, *Greek Homosexuality*, London: Duckworth, 1978.

Dreyfus, Hubert and Rabinow, Paul, *Michel Foucault: Beyond structuralism and hermeneutics*, Brighton: Harvester Press, 1982.

Dreyfus, Hubert and Rabinow, Paul, 'What is Maturity? Habermas and Foucault on "What Is Enlightenment?"', in David Hoy (ed.), *Foucault: A critical reader*, Oxford: Blackwell, 1986.

Droit, Roger–Pol (ed.), *Les Grecs, les Romains et nous: l'antiquité est–elle moderne?*, Paris: Le Monde Editions, 1991.

Ellmann, Richard, *Oscar Wilde*, Harmondsworth: Penguin Books, 1988.

Epictetus, *The Discourses*, trans. W. A. Oldfather, London: Loeb Classical Library, 1925.

Falzon, Christopher, 'Foucault's Human Being', *Thesis Eleven*, no. 34, 1993, pp. 1–16.

Falzon, Christopher, *Foucault and Social Dialogue: Beyond fragmentation*, London: Routledge, 1998.

Flint, R. W. (ed.), *Marinetti: Selected writings*, New York: Farrar, Straus and Giroux, 1971.

Flynn, Thomas, 'Truth and Subjectivation in the Later Foucault', *The Journal of Philosophy*, 82, 10, Oct 1985, pp. 531–40.

Flynn, Thomas, 'Foucault as Parrhesiast: His last course at the Collège de France (1984)', *Philosophy and Social Criticism*, no. 2–3, Summer 1987, pp. 213–29.

Flynn, Thomas, 'Foucault and the Politics of Postmodernity,' *Nous*, 23, 1989, pp. 187–98.

Flynn, Thomas, 'Foucault's Mapping of History', in Gary Gutting (ed.), *The Cambridge Companion to Foucault*, Cambridge: Cambridge University Press, 1994.

Fraser, Nancy, 'Foucault on Modern Power: Empirical insights and normative confusions', *Praxis International*, 1, 3, Oct 1981, pp. 272–87.

Fraser, Nancy, 'Foucault's Body Language: A post-humanist political rhetoric?', *Salmagundi*, no. 61, Fall 1983, pp. 55–70.

Goldhill, Simon, *Foucault's Virginity: Ancient erotic fiction and the history of sexuality*, Cambridge: Cambridge University Press, 1995.

Habermas, Jurgen, 'Modernity – an Incomplete Project', in H. Foster (ed.), *Postmodern Culture*, London: Pluto Press, 1985.

Habermas, Jurgen, 'Taking Aim at the Heart of the Present', in D. Hoy (ed.), *Foucault: A critical reader*, Oxford: Blackwell, 1986.

Habermas, Jurgen, *The Philosophical Discourse of Modernity*, Cambridge: Polity Press, 1992.

Hacking, Ian, 'Self-Improvement', in D. Hoy (ed.), *Foucault: A critical reader*, Oxford: Blackwell, 1986.

Hadot, Pierre, *Exercices spirituels et la philosophie antique*, Paris: Etudes Augustiniennes, 1981.

Hadot, Pierre, 'Réflexions sur la notion de culture de soi', in *Michel Foucault, Philosophe*, Paris: Editions du Seuil, 1989.

Halperin, David, 'Sexual Ethics and Technologies of the Self in Classical Greece', *American Journal of Philology*, no. 107, 1986, pp. 274–86.

Halperin, David 'Two views of Greek love: Harold Patzer and Michel Foucault', in *One Hundred Years of Homosexuality*, New York: Routledge, 1990.

Halperin, David, *Saint Foucault: Towards a gay hagiography*, New York: Oxford University Press, 1995.

Halperin, David, Winkler, John and Zeitlin, Froma (eds), *Before Sexuality: The construction of erotic experience in the ancient Greek world*, Princeton: Princeton University Press, 1990.

Harpham, Geoffrey Galt, 'So ... What *Is* Enlightenment? An Inquisition into Modernity', *Critical Inquiry*, no. 20, Spring 1994, pp. 524–56.

Hauser, Arnold, *The Social History of Art*, volume I, London: Routledge, 1989 (first published 1951).

Hegel, G. W. F., *Lectures on the History of Philosophy*, trans. E. S. Haldane, London: Routledge and Kegan Paul, 1892.

Heidegger, Martin, *An Introduction to Metaphysics*, trans. R. Mannheim, New York: Doubleday, 1961.

Heidegger, Martin, *Nietzsche, Volumes I and II*, trans. D. Farrell Krell, San Francisco: Harper Collins, 1991.

Hewitt, Andrew, 'Fascist Modernism, Futurism, and Post-modernity', in R. Golsan (ed.), *Fascism, Aesthetics and Culture*, Hanover: University Press of New England, 1992.

Hewitt, Andrew, *Fascist Modernism: Aesthetics, politics and the avant-garde*, Stanford: Stanford University Press, 1993.

Hinchman, Lewis, 'Autonomy, Individuality and Self-Determination', in J. Schmidt (ed.), *What is Enlightenment?*, Berkeley: University of California Press, 1996.

Hindess, Barry and Dean, Mitchell (eds), *Governing Australia*, Cambridge: Cambridge University Press, 1998.

Hitler, Adolf, 'Speech inaugurating the "Great Exhibition of German Art 1937"', in H. B. Chipp (ed.), *Theories of Modern Art*, Berkeley: University of California Press, 1968.

Hoy, David (ed.), *Foucault: A critical reader*, Oxford: Blackwell, 1986.

Irwin, Terence, *Plato's Moral Theory*, Oxford: Clarendon Press, 1977.

Jacques, T. Carlos, 'Whence Does the Critic Speak? A study of Foucault's genealogy,' *Philosophy and Social Criticism*, 17, 4, 1991, pp. 325–44.

Joly, Henri, 'Retour aux Grecs', *Le Débat*, no. 41, Sept–Nov 1986, pp. 100–20.

Kant, Immanuel, 'An Answer to the Question: What is Enlightenment?', reprinted in J. Schmidt (ed.), *What is Enlightenment?*, Berkeley: University of California Press, 1996.

Kaufmann, Walter, *Nietzsche: Philosopher, psychologist, antichrist*, 4th edn, Princeton: Princeton University Press, 1974.

Kramnick, Isaac (ed.), *The Portable Enlightenment Reader*, Harmondsworth: Penguin Books, 1995.

Lacan, Jacques, 'The Mirror Stage as formative of the function of the I', in Jacques Lacan, *Ecrits: A Selection*, trans. A. Sheridan, London: Tavistock, 1977.

Lacoste, Jean, *L'idée de beau*, Paris: Bordas, 1986.

Larmour, D., Miller, P. and Platter, C. (eds), *Rethinking Sexuality: Foucault and Classical Antiquity*, Princeton: Princeton University Press, 1998.

Lefkowitz, Mary, 'Sex and Civilisation', *Partisan Review*, 52, 4, 1985, pp. 460–66.

Lloyd, G. E. R., 'The Mind on Sex', *New York Review of Books*, 13 March 1986, pp. 24–8.

Long, A. A., 'The Logical Basis of Stoic Ethics', *Proceedings of the Aristotelian Society*, 71, 1970–71, pp. 85–104.

Long, A. A., *Hellenistic Philosophy*, 2nd edn, London: Duckworth, 1986.

Long, A. A., 'Representation and the Self in Stoicism', in S. Everson (ed.), *Companions to Ancient Thought*, volume 2, *Psychology*, Cambridge: Cambridge University Press, 1991.

Long, A. A., 'The Socratic Tradition: Diogenes, Crates, and Hellenistic Ethics', in R. Bracht Branham and M. Goulet-Cazé (eds), *The Cynics: The Cynic movement in antiquity and its legacy*, Berkeley: University of California Press, 1996.

Long, A. A. and Sedley, D. N. (eds), *The Hellenistic Philosophers*, 2 vols, Cambridge: Cambridge University Press, 1987.

Lycos, Kimon, *Plato on Justice and Power*, London: Macmillan, 1987.

McCarthy, Thomas, 'The Critique of Impure Reason: Foucault and the Frankfurt School', *Political Theory*, no. 18, 1990, pp. 437–69.

MacIntyre, Alasdair, *After Virtue*, 2nd edn, London: Duckworth, 1985.

MacKinnon, Catherine, 'Does Sexuality Have a History?', in D. Stanton (ed.), *Discourses of Sexuality*, Ann Arbor: University of Michigan Press, 1992.

McNay, Lois, *Foucault: A critical introduction*, Cambridge: Polity Press, 1994.

McNay, Lois, *Foucault and Feminism: Power, gender and the self*, Cambridge: Polity Press, 1992.

Mann, Thomas, *Last Essays*, New York: Alfred Knopf, 1970.

Mann, Thomas, *Doctor Faustus* (orig. published 1947), in *Thomas Mann*, various translators, New York: Secker and Warburg, 1979.

Marcus Aurelius, *Meditations*, trans. A. S. L. Farquharson, Oxford: Oxford University Press, 1989.

Megill, Allan, 'The Reception of Foucault by Historians', *Journal of the History of Ideas*, 48, 1, 1987, pp. 117–41.

Michel Foucault Philosophe, Paris: Editions du Seuil, 1989.

Miller, James, *The Passion of Michel Foucault*, New York: Simon and Schuster, 1993.

Montaigne, Michel de, *Montaigne: Selections from his writings*, selected and introduced by André Gide, New York: McGraw-Hill, 1964.

Mussolini, Benito, 'The Doctrine of Fascism', in H. Kohn (ed.), *Nationalism: Its meaning and history*, New York: D. Van Norstrand, 1965.

Nehamas, Alexander, *Nietzsche: Life as Literature*, Cambridge, MA: Harvard University Press, 1985.

Nietzsche, Friedrich, *The Will To Power*, trans. W. Kaufmann and R. J. Hollindale, New York: Vintage Books, 1968.

Nietzsche, Friedrich, *On the Genealogy of Morals*, trans. W. Kaufmann, New York: Vintage Books, 1969.

Nietzsche, Friedrich, *The Gay Science*, trans. W. Kaufmann, New York: Vintage Books, 1974.

Nietzsche, Friedrich, *Twilight of the Idols*, trans. R. J. Hollingdale, Harmondsworth: Penguin Books, 1977.

Nietzsche, Friedrich, *Ecce Homo*, trans. R. J. Hollingdale, Harmondsworth: Penguin Books, 1979.

Nietzsche, Friedrich, *Beyond Good and Evil*, trans. W. Kaufmann, New York: Vintage Books, 1989.

Nietzsche, Friedrich, 'On Truth and Lies in a Nonmoral Sense', in Daniel Breazeale (ed. and trans.), *Philosophy and Truth: Selections from Nietzsche's notebooks of the early 1870s*, Atlantic Highlands, NJ: Humanities Press, 1995.

Nietzsche, Friedrich, *Human, All Too Human*, trans. R. J. Hollingdale, Cambridge: Cambridge University Press, 1996.

Nietzsche, Friedrich, 'Schopenhauer as Educator', in *Untimely Meditations*, trans. R. J. Hollingdale, Cambridge: Cambridge University Press, 1997.

Nietzsche, Friedrich, 'On the Uses and Disadvantages of History for Life', in *Untimely Meditations*, trans. R. J. Hollingdale, Cambridge: Cambridge University Press, 1997.

Nussbaum, Martha, 'Affections of the Greeks', *New York Times Book Review*, 10 November 1985, pp. 13–14.

Nussbaum, Martha, *The Therapy of Desire: Theory and practice in Hellenistic ethics*, Princeton: Princeton University Press, 1994.

O'Leary, Timothy, 'Foucault, Politics and the Autonomy of the Aesthetic', *The International Journal of Philosophical Studies*, 4, 2, 1996, pp. 273–91.

Onfray, Michel, *Cynismes: Portrait du philosophe en chien*, Paris: Grasset, 1990.

Onfray, Michel, *La sculpture de soi: la morale esthétique*, Paris: Grasset, 1993.

Parry, Richard, *Plato's Craft of Justice*, Albany: SUNY, 1996.

Patton, Paul, 'Taylor and Foucault on Power and Freedom', *Political Studies*, no. 37, 1989, pp. 260–76.

Patton, Paul, 'Foucault's Subject of Power', *Political Theory Newsletter*, no. 6, 1994, pp. 60–71.

Payer, Pierre J., 'Foucault on Penance and the Shaping of Sexuality', *Studies in Religion*, 14, 3, 1985, pp. 313–20.

Plato, *Alcibiades I*, trans. W. Lamb, Loeb Classical Library, London: William Heinemann, 1927.

Plato, *Apology*, in Plato, *The Last Days of Socrates*, trans. H. Tredennick, Harmondsworth: Penguin Books, 1969.

Plato, *Hippias Major*, trans. P. Woodruff, Oxford: Basil Blackwell, 1982.

Plato, *Republic*, trans. D. Lee, rev. 1974, Harmondsworth: Penguin Books, 1983.

Plato, *Laches*, trans. I. Lane, in Plato, *Early Socratic Dialogues*, T. J. Saunders (ed.), Harmondsworth: Penguin Books, 1987.

Plutarch, *The Rise and Fall of Athens*, trans. I. Scott-Kilvert, London: Penguin Books, 1960.

Rabinow, Paul (ed.), *The Foucault Reader*, New York: Pantheon Books, 1984.

Rabinow, Paul, 'Introduction', in Paul Rabinow (ed.), *The Essential Works of Michel Foucault*, volume I, *Ethics: Subjectivity and truth*, London: Allen Lane, 1997.

Rajchman, John, *Michel Foucault: The freedom of philosophy*, New York: Columbia University Press, 1985.

Rankin, H. D., *Sophists, Socratices and Cynics*, London: Croom Helm, 1983.

Richlin, Amy, 'Foucault's *History of Sexuality:* A useful theory for women?', in D. Larmour, P. Miller, C. Platter (eds), *Rethinking Sexuality: Foucault and Classical Antiquity*, Princeton: Princeton University Press, 1998.

Roochnik, David, 'Socrates' Use of the Techne-Analogy', in H. Benson (ed.), *Essays on the Philosophy of Socrates*, New York: Oxford University Press, 1992.

Rousseau, Jean-Jacques, *The Social Contract*, trans. M. Cranston, Harmondsworth: Penguin Books, 1984.

Schmidt, J. (ed.), *What is Enlightenment?*, Berkeley: University of California Press, 1996.

Scott, Gary Alan, 'Games of Truth: Foucault's analysis of the transformation from political to ethical parrhesia', *The Southern Journal of Philosophy*, 34, 1996, pp. 97–114.

Seneca, *Letters To Lucilius*, in Moses Hadas (ed. and trans.), *The Stoic Philosophy of Seneca*, New York: Anchor Books, 1958.

Simons, Jon, *Foucault and the Political*, London: Routledge, 1995.

Stanton, Donna, *The Aristocrat as Art*, New York: Columbia University Press, 1980.

Striker, Gisela, 'Following Nature: A study in Stoic ethics', *Oxford Studies in Ancient Philosophy*, 9, 1991, pp. 1–73 (reprinted in her *Essays on Hellenistic Epistemology and Ethics*, Cambridge: Cambridge University Press, 1996).

Taylor, Charles, 'Foucault on Freedom and Truth', *Political Theory*, 12, 2, 1984.

Thacker, Andrew, 'Foucault's Aesthetics of Existence', *Radical Philosophy*, no. 63, Spring 1993, pp. 13–21.

Thornton, Bruce, 'Idolon Theatri: Foucault and the Classicists', *Classical and Modern Literature*, 12, 1, 1991, pp. 81–100.

Vernant, Jean-Pierre, *L'individu, la mort, l'amour; soi-même et l'autre en Grèce ancienne*, Paris: Gallimard, 1989.

Vernant, Jean-Pierre, 'Façons grecques d'être soi', in Roger-Pol Droit (ed.), *Les Grecs, les Romains et nous: l'antiquité est-elle moderne?*, Paris: Le Monde Editions, 1991.

Veyne, Paul, 'Le dernier Foucault et sa morale', *Critique*, no. 471–2, Aug–Sept 1986, pp. 933–41.

Veyne, Paul, 'La médication interminable', the introductory essay to Seneca, *De la tranquilité de l'âme*, Paris: Petite Bibliothèque Rivages, 1988.

Veyne, Paul (ed.), *Histoire de la vie privée, 1. De l'Empire romain à l'an mil,*

Editions du Seuil, Paris, 1985 (*A History of Private Life, 1. From Pagan Rome to Byzantium*, trans. A. Goldhammer, Cambridge, MA: Harvard University Press, 1992).

Veyne, Paul, 'Foucault Revolutionizes History', in Arnold Davidson (ed.), *Foucault and His Interlocuters*, Chicago: University of Chicago Press, 1997.

Vidal-Nacquet, Pierre, 'Foreword', in Marcel Détienne, *The Masters of Truth in Archaic Greece*, trans. J. Lloyd, New York: Zone Books, 1996.

Vlastos, Gregory, *Socrates: Ironist and moral philosopher*, Cambridge: Cambridge University Press, 1991.

Walzer, Michael, 'The Politics of Michel Foucault', in D. Hoy (ed.), *Foucault: A critical reader*, Oxford: Basil Blackwell, 1986.

White, Hayden, *The Content of the Form*, Baltimore: Johns Hopkins University Press, 1997.

White, Nicholas, 'The Role of Physics in Stoic Ethics', *The Southern Journal of Philosophy*, supplement to vol. 23, 1985, pp. 57–74.

Whitman, Walt, *Leaves of Grass*, New York: Modern Library, 1921.

Williams, Bernard, *Ethics and the Limits of Philosophy*, London: Fontana Press, 1993.

Winkler, John, *The Constraints of Desire: The anthropology of sex and gender in ancient Greece*, New York: Routledge, 1990.

Wolin, Richard, 'Foucault's Aesthetic Decisionism', *Telos*, no. 67, Spring 1986, pp. 71–86.

Yeats, W.B., *Autobiographies*, London: Macmillan, 1955.

Index

'About the Beginning of
the Hermeneutics of
the Self' (Foucault)
13, 33, 34, 35
ACT UP 22
aesthetic, Foucault's use of
the term 128–9, 131
aesthetic ethics, concept
122–3
aestheticism 93
aestheticization, and
fascism 123, 124, 132
aesthetics, and the ancient
Greeks 4
'aesthetics of existence' 1,
6, 7–8, 11, 13, 14,
51–7, 86, 173
'An Aesthetics of Existence'
(Foucault) 39, 52,
109
Aiskhines 64
Alcibiades 44–5, 48,
49–50, 51, 58–9, 71
Alcibiades I (Plato) 44, 45,
47, 48, 49
Althusser, Louis 109, 117
ancient ethics 36, 40, 44,
51, 62, 72, 82, 172
aims of 86
ancient Greece 4, 14–15,
21, 36–8, 58, 172
aesthetic motivation 51
homosexuality in 64–6
philosophies of ethics 6
sexual austerity 67
sexual ethics 39–40,
41–2, 73
see also Hellenistic ethics
Annas, Julia 55, 79
aphrodisia 41, 42, 43, 63,
64, 66, 73, 85
Aristophanes 64
Aristotle 62, 78
Nichomachean Ethics 52,
160
ars erotica 32

art
and life 122
politicized 124
as *techne* 128
'art of living' 52
art of the self, concept 56
Artemidorus, *Dream
Analysis* 62–3
artists 128
ascesis or technique of
ethics 139
austerity 83
autopoesis 16, 133–8
avant-garde movements
122, 123

The Bacchae (Euripides)
149
Barbin, Herculine
(Alexina) 27–8, 111
Baudelaire 2, 125, 161,
169–70
dandy in works of 39
Baumgarten 3
beauty 43, 51, 86, 122,
126, 128, 131, 173
and moral worth 53–4
Benjamin, Walter 16, 132
'The Work of Art in the
Age of Mechanical
Reproduction' 123–5
Bernauer, James 9, 10, 23,
139,
154–5
bio-power 29, 178 n.19
bios 121, 151, 175 n.14
The Birth of the Clinic
(Foucault) 60
Brecht, Bertolt 124, 133
Brown, Peter 90

Cambiano, Guiseppe 83
care of the self 45, 47, 48,
49, 70, 71, 74
The Care of the Self
(Foucault) 7, 48, 55,

63, 65, 71, 73, 74, 75,
76, 78, 84
Cartesian moment 145
Catholic Counter-
Reformation 32
Caygill, Howard 125
Certeau, Michel 96
Christian ethics, and
Hellenistic ethics 74
Christian morality 83
Christianity 38, 39, 45, 134
and confession 33
sexual ethics 41
Cixous, Hélenè 171
Classical Greece, *see* ancient
Greece
Cleanthes 78
Cohen, David 72
'The Concern for the
Truth' (Foucault) 2,
7, 101
confession 27, 30, 31–5
and Christianity 33
'The Confession of the
Flesh' (Foucault) 27,
103
conversion 153, 192 n.19
in Classical and
Hellenistic Greece
146–7
Course at the Collège de
France (Foucault) 98,
145, 151
craft 52
Greek conception 51
critical thought 9
critique, and spirituality
146–53
crypto-normality 156
culture of the self 70–81
'culture without
constraints' 163
Cynics 144, 145, 147, 148

dandy, in Baudelaire's
work 39

dandyism 72, 82, 93, 94
Davidson, Arnold 72
De la governmentalité
     (Foucault) 88, 157
'De l'amitié comme Mode
     de vie' (Foucault) 163
'The Declaration of the
     Rights of Man'
     (French National
     Assembly) 159
Deleuze, Gilles 117–18
desubjectivation 114, 141
Dews, Peter 59
Dialogue on Love
     (Plutarch) 78
Diogenes Laertius 147
Discipline and Punish
     (Foucault) 35, 60, 88,
     96, 97, 98, 101, 109,
     111, 112, 113, 164, 169
'Discourse and Truth: The
     problematization of
     parrhesia (Foucault)
     144, 148, 149, 150
Discourses (Epictetus) 80
Dits et écrits
     volume III (Foucault)
     101
     volume IV (Foucault) 3,
     10, 28
Doctor Faustus (Mann) 5
domination 65, 67
     and power 157–8
Donlan, Walter 61, 67
Dover, Kenneth, *Greek
     Homosexuality* 63, 64
Dream Analysis
     (Artemidorus) 62–3

Ecce Homo (Nietzsche)
     134–6
education 47, 147
'end of morality' 83
ends of life, Stoic
     conception 81
enjoyment 76–7
Enlightenment 161, 165–8,
     169
'Entretien avec Michel
     Foucault' 102, 111,
     141
Epictetus 52, 54, 75, 78,
     134
     Discourses 80
Epicurus 47
erotic self, normative
     model 90
essay, meanings of term
     143–4
'The Ethic of Care for the
     Self as Practice of
     Freedom' (Foucault)

59, 60, 93, 99, 107,
     121, 144, 154, 157,
     158, 160
ethical practices, model 40
ethical subjectivation 72
ethical subjectivity 107
ethical substance, of ethics
     139
ethics
     aim of 169–70
     ascesis or technique 139
     aspects of 83, 133–4
     ethical substance of 139
     Foucault's definition
     11–13
     in the Hellenistic period
     69–70
     history of 15
     mode of subjection 139
     and morality 11, 40
     Stoicism 77, 80
     substance of 15
Euripides
     The Bacchae 149
     Ion 148, 149
eventualization 115
exagoreusis 34
exomologesis 33–4
experience 36, 61
'experience-book' concept
     141

family 71
fascism 125, 126, 127
     and aestheticization 123,
     124, 132
female sexuality 22
Flynn, Thomas 9, 10, 59,
     156
'Foucault: non au
     compromis' 164
'Foucault Examines Reason
     in Service of State
     Power' 96
Foucault, Michel 1
     The Birth of the Clinic
     60
     The Care of the Self 7,
     48, 55, 63, 65, 71, 73,
     74, 75, 76, 78, 84
     'The Concern for the
     Truth' 2, 7, 101
     'The Confession of the
     Flesh' 27, 103
     Course at the Collège de
     France 98, 145, 151
     De la governmentalité 88,
     157
     'De l'amitié comme
     Mode de vie' 163
     Discipline and Punish 35,
     60, 88, 96, 97, 98, 101,

109, 111, 112, 113,
     164, 169
'Discourse and Truth:
     The problematization
     of *parrhesia* 144, 148,
     149, 150
efficacy of work 88, 96
'Entretien avec Michel
     Foucault' 102, 111,
     141
'The Ethic of Care for
     the Self as Practice of
     Freedom' 59, 60, 93,
     99, 107, 121, 144, 154,
     157, 158, 160
'Foucault: non au
     compromis' 164
'Governmentality' 29,
     113
'The Howison Lectures'
     35, 109
influences on 141
Madness and Civilization
     59, 60, 96, 112
'The Minimalist Self' 3
'Nietzsche, Genealogy,
     History' 88, 97, 100,
     101
on Nietzscheanism 4
notion of freedom 160
'On the Genealogy of
     Ethics' 3, 5, 6, 7, 12,
     25, 43, 44, 56, 59, 60,
     68, 83, 85, 121, 122,
     128
'The Order of
     Discourse' 99, 100
The Order of Things 59,
     110, 111
'Polemics, Politics and
     Problematizations' 116
'Politics and Ethics' 160
'La poussière et le
     nuage' 97
'Power and Sex' 24
'Prison Talk' 92
'Qu'est-ce que la
     critique?' 113, 114,
     151, 152
'Qu'est-ce que les
     lumieres?' 166
'Questions of Method'
     98, 115, 152
'The Return of
     Morality' 4, 7, 45, 47,
     48, 59, 60
'Sex, Power and the
     Politics of Identity'
     162, 163
'Sexual Choice, Sexual
     Act' 162, 163, 164
sexuality 1–2, 91, 95

Foucault, Michel – *continued*
'Sexuality and Solitude'
    110
'The Social Triumph of
    the Sexual Will' 163
'Structuralism and Post-
    Structuralism' 110,
    113, 114, 160
'The Subject and
    Power' 13, 21, 31,
    107, 109
'Technologies of the
    Self' 34, 35, 45, 47
'Truth and Power' 95,
    99, 100
'Two Lectures' 95, 113
The Use of Pleasure 2,
    7, 8, 9, 11, 12, 21, 22,
    36, 37, 40, 41, 42, 43,
    44, 48, 55, 59, 60, 62,
    64, 65, 66, 68, 77, 84,
    85, 98, 138, 141, 143,
    156, 162
'What is Critique' 113,
    151
'What is Enlightenment'
    8, 133, 156, 161, 166,
    167, 168
Foucault's Virginity
    (Goldhill) 89, 90
Fraser, Nancy 10, 155,
    160
freedom 154–65, 173
    Foucault's notion 160
    loss of 84
    and politics 158
    spaces of 155–68
    as the telos of ethics 159
French National Assembly,
    'The Declaration of the
    Rights of Man' 159
French Revolution 3

Gallen 77–8
'games of truth' 8, 59, 60,
    98
gay activism 22, 89,
    90–91, 92, 94, 95
gay culture 163–4
gay men 16–17, 161
The Gay Science
    (Nietzsche) 134
genealogical method 140,
    172
genealogy 60–61, 82, 87,
    97, 98, 110, 183 n.29
The Genealogy of Morals
    (Nietzsche) 67, 68
Goethe, Nietzsche on 136
Goldhill, Simon 62, 72
    Foucault's Virginity 89,
    90

Gordon, Colin 10
'governmentality' 10,
    29–30, 113–14, 151,
    161, 178 n.19
'Governmentality'
    (Foucault) 29, 113
Greece, *see* ancient Greece
Greek Homosexuality
    (Dover) 63, 64

Habermas, Jurgen 10, 130,
    155, 165, 167
Hadot, Pierre 69, 70,
    71–2, 75, 82, 92, 93,
    144, 146–7
Halperin, David 22, 59,
    62, 70, 72, 93
    Saint Foucault 89,
    90–92
happiness 76–7, 78
    Stoic definition 78–9
harmony 79
Harpham, Geoffrey 165
Hauser, Arnold 54
health 74, 75, 78
Hegel, G.W.F. 22, 59
Heidegger, Martin 22
Hellenistic ethics 76
    and Christian ethics 74
    and nature 76–7
    reason in 76–7
hermaphrodites 27–8
hermeneutics of the self
    35, 36, 38
Hewitt, Andrew 125
Hinchman, Lewis 167
Hindess, Barry 10
Hippias Major (Plato) 53,
    55
historical accuracy 58,
    103
history
    as fiction 101–2
    and truth 99–100
The History of Sexuality
    (Foucault) 7, 10, 12,
    88, 112
    Volume I 22–31, 23, 24,
    25, 26, 27, 28, 29, 30,
    31, 32, 33, 34, 35, 39,
    91, 101, 103, 109, 111,
    118, 162, 169, 171
    Volume II 14, 21, 22,
    36, 39, 55, 58, 59, 60,
    85, 86, 112, 142
    preface 36, 37
    Volume III 14, 22, 45,
    55, 58, 59, 60, 62, 70,
    73, 77, 86, 112, 120,
    143
Hitler, Adolf 124, 127
'homosexual ascesis' 163

homosexuality
    in ancient Greece 64–6
    in France 164
'The Howison Lectures'
    (Foucault) 35, 109
Human, All Too Human
    (Nietzsche) 135,
    136–7
human being, concept 118
human body 97
Hurley, Robert 55

individual freedom 7
individuality 13
Ion (Euripides) 148, 149
'isomorphism' 44, 62
Italian Futurism 125

Junger, Ernst 126

kalon 51, 52
kalos 53, 55
    multiple meanings 56
    translation of word 55
kaloskagathos 53, 54, 67
Kant, Immanuel 122, 128,
    161, 165–7, 172
King Oedipus (Sophocles)
    148–9
knowledge 36, 145

Lacan, Jacques 126, 127
Lateran Council (1215) 31,
    32
Laws (Plato) 55, 61
Leuret, François 35
life
    and art 122
    as a work of art 121
literature, and the self
    134–8
Long, A.A. 70, 79
Lucilius 51, 53
Lycos, Kimon 146

Madness and Civilization
    (Foucault) 59, 60, 96,
    112
Man 108, 110–11, 159
Mann, Thomas 1
    Doctor Faustus 5
Marcus Aurelius,
    Meditations 81
Marinetti, *War, the World's
    only Hygiene* 125–7
marriage 71, 72, 73, 78
masculinity 63–4
mastery of the self 43–4,
    50, 61, 62, 67, 73,
    85–6, 171
Meditations (Marcus
    Aurelius) 81

'The Minimalist Self'
(Foucault) 3
mode of subjection, in
ethics 139
model of ethical practices
40
modern sexuality 22–31
Montaigne, Michel de 143
moral codes 41, 74
moral problematization of
sexual practice, in
Stoicism 78
moral training 61
moral worth, and beauty
53–4
morality 1, 6, 11, 39, 68
end of 83, 174, 175 n.2
and ethics 11, 40
mysticism 151–2

nature 80
in Hellenistic ethics
76–7
role in ethics 79
Seneca on 80–81
in Stoicism 76, 79
Nehemas, Alexander,
Nietzsche: Life as
Literature 135–6, 137
'neutral substratum' 108
New Conservatives 130
Nichomachean Ethics
(Aristotle) 52, 160
Nietzsche: Life as Literature
(Nehemas) 135–6, 137
Nietzsche, Friedrich 1, 2,
4, 8, 21, 58, 59, 87, 96,
97, 100, 107, 108, 121,
139, 173, 174
on Goethe 136
on self–creation 135
Ecce Homo 134–6
The Gay Science 134
The Genealogy of Morals
67, 68
Human, All Too Human
135, 136–7
'On the Uses and
Disadvantages of
History for Life' 134
Revaluation of all Values
135
Songs of Zarathustra 135
Twilight of the Idols 135
'Nietzsche, Genealogy,
History' (Foucault)
88, 97, 100, 101
normative model of the
erotic self 90
Nussbaum, Martha 59, 75

'On the Genealogy of

Ethics' (Foucault) 3,
5, 6, 7, 12, 25, 43, 44,
56, 59, 60, 68, 83, 85,
121, 122, 128
'On the Uses and
Disadvantages of
History for Life'
(Nietzsche) 134
'The Order of Discourse'
(Foucault) 99, 100
The Order of Things
(Foucault) 59, 110,
111

Paetus, Thrasea 55
parrhesia (freedom of
speech) 140, 147–50,
192 n.26
Patton, Paul 10, 118, 156
pedagogy 47
penetration 62–3
personal choice 7, 12
philia 163
philosophy 8–9, 110, 139,
173
as a way of life 140–6,
144
Plato 9, 45, 52, 54–5, 62
Alcibiades I 44, 45, 47,
48, 49
Hippias Major 53, 55
Laws 55, 61
Republic 54, 62, 146–7
Symposium 49
Timaeus 53
on virtue 52
pleasure 71, 83
Pliny 72
Plotinus 54, 134
Plutarch
on Alcibiades 49
Dialogue on Love 78
poesis 2, 3, 56
'Polemics, Politics and
Problematizations'
(Foucault) 116
polis 40
political activism 89
politicized art 124
politics 101–2
and freedom 158
'Politics and Ethics'
(Foucault) 160
'La poussière et le nuage'
(Foucault) 97
power 23–4, 25, 26, 27,
29, 36, 62, 103, 111,
113
absence of 58–61
and domination 157–8
'Power and Sex'
(Foucault) 24

prison 115
'Prison Talk' (Foucault)
92
problematization, concept
of 37, 115–16
psychoanalysis 32

queer activism 22, 89,
90–91, 92, 94, 95
'Qu'est-ce que la critique?'
(Foucault) 113, 114,
151, 152
'Qu'est-ce que les
lumieres?' (Foucault)
166
'Questions of Method'
(Foucault) 98, 115,
152

Rabinow, Paul 139, 154
Rajchman, John 9, 10, 160
reason
in Hellenistic ethics
76–7
in Stoicism 76, 79
reason and nature, Seneca
on 80–1
relations to the self 5, 37,
60, 77, 121
religion 6
repression 24, 26, 84–5
Republic (Plato) 54, 62,
146–7
resistance 156, 157
Résumé des cours
(Foucault) 45, 47, 48
'The Return of Morality'
(Foucault) 4, 7, 59, 60
Revaluation of all Values
(Nietzsche) 135
rhetor (speaker) 64
Richlin, Amy 11

sado-masochism 140, 162,
163
Saint Foucault (Halperin)
89, 90–2
Saller, Richard 72
scienti sexualis 30, 32, 38,
112
self 2–4, 13–14
in antiquity 93, 94
care of 45, 47, 48, 49,
70, 71, 74
concept of the art of 56
confessing the 31–5
culture of 70–81
enjoyment of 76
hermeneutics of 35, 36,
38
language problem
119–20

self – *continued*
    mastery of 43–4, 50, 61,
        62, 67, 73, 85–6, 171
    relations to 5, 37, 77, 121
    as a work of art 54, 121,
        122–33
    work on 16
self-constitution 36–7, 38,
    61
self-creation, Nietzsche on
    135
self-mastery 61, 67, 73,
    85–6, 171
    and mastery of the other
        62
self-transformation 7, 140,
    154, 173
Seneca 33, 51, 53, 54, 71,
    75, 94, 134
    Letters 81
    on reason and nature
        80–1
sex 118
    subjugation of 26
'Sex, Power and the
    Politics of Identity'
    (Foucault) 162, 163
'Sexual Choice, Sexual Act'
    (Foucault) 162, 163, 164
sexual ethics, of classical
    Greece 12
sexual identity 171
sexual liberation
    movements 7, 25, 26
sexuality
    modern 22–31
    and truth 28–9
'Sexuality and Solitude'
    (Foucault) 110
Simons, Jon 59
singularities 115
skill 3, 52
slave morality 109
slavery 62
'The Social Triumph of the
    Sexual Will'
    (Foucault) 163
Socrates 6, 7, 9, 45–7,
    49–50, 53, 74, 144
    Apology 150
Socratic tradition 145–6,
    151
'Song of Myself'
    (Whitman) 135
Songs of Zarathustra
    (Nietzsche) 135
Sophocles, *King Oedipus*
    148–9
soul 98
speech 25–6, 27, 35
spirituality 144
    and critique 146–53

Stoicism 54, 71, 74, 75,
    92, 93, 134
    conception of ends of
        life 81
    definition of happiness
        78–9
    ethics 77, 80
    moral problematization of
        sexual practice 78
    nature in 76, 79
    philosophy of 70
    reason in 76, 79
Striker, Gisela 79
'Structuralism and Post-
    Structuralism'
    (Foucault) 110, 113,
    114, 160
style 2–3, 4
subject
    concept of 159
    form of 108–10, 117
    and truth 145
'The Subject and Power'
    (Foucault) 13, 21, 31,
    107, 109
subject-formation 112–13,
    118
subjection 27, 42, 49, 75,
    109, 172
subjectivation 30–31, 85,
    112, 114, 118–19
subjectivity 9, 13, 107–8,
    111, 119
    disciplinary aspect 97
    and truth 35, 59, 151
subjugation of sex 26
substance of ethics 107–8
suspicion 6
Synge, J.M. 154, 155

taste 4, 5
Taylor, Charles 157
techne 3, 4, 14, 51, 52, 55,
    56, 147
    art as 128
techne tou biou 56
'techniques of life' 7
techniques of the self 36
'Technologies of the Self'
    (Foucault) 34, 35, 45,
    47
telos 13, 15, 41, 85
temperance 65
    and women 62
Thacker, Andrew 128
Timaeus (Plato) 53
transcendental substratum
    113
truth 87, 100, 113
    and history 98–9, 99–100
    in scholarship 97
    and sexuality 28–9

and subject 145
and subjectivity 35, 59,
    151
'Truth and Power'
    (Foucault) 95, 99, 100
Twilight of the Idols
    (Nietzsche) 135
'Two Lectures' (Foucault)
    95, 113

The Use of Pleasure
    (Foucault) 2, 7, 8, 9,
    11, 12, 21, 22, 36, 37,
    40, 41, 42, 43, 44, 48,
    55, 59, 60, 62, 64, 65,
    66, 68, 77, 84, 85, 98,
    138, 141, 143, 156, 162

Vernant, Jean-Pierre 54, 61
Veyne, Paul 70, 71, 109,
    128, 130
Vidal-Nacquet, Pierre 171
virility 65
virtue 79
    Plato on 52
    as a skill in living 53

Wagner 136
Walzer, Michael 155
*War, the World's only
    Hygiene* (Marinetti)
    125–7
Western philosophy 22
'What is Critique'
    (Foucault) 113, 151
'What is Enlightenment'
    (Foucault) 8, 133,
    156, 161, 166, 167, 168
White, Nicholas 79
Whitman, Walt, 'Song of
    Myself' 135
Wilde, Oscar 1, 2, 39, 51,
    56
Williams, Bernard 8
Winkler, John 63, 64, 70,
    90
Wolin, Richard 123, 129
women 22
    in *The History of
        Sexuality* 10–11
    and temperance 62
work of art, concept 127
'The Work of Art in the
    Age of Mechanical
    Reproduction'
    (Benjamin) 123–5

Xenophon 72

Yeats, W.B. 154

Zeno 78